FOLDED LIES

All I have is a voice
To undo the folded lie
The romantic lie in the brain
Of the sensual man-in-the-street
And the lie of Authority
Whose buildings grope the sky.

— W. H. Auden

FOLDED LIES

Bribery, Crusades, and Reforms

W. MICHAEL REISMAN

THE FREE PRESS
A Division of Macmillan Publishing Co., Inc.
NEW YORK

Collier Macmillan Publishers
LONDON

THE FREE PRESS
A Division of Macmillan Publishing Co., Inc.
866 Third Avenue, New York, N.Y. 10022

Collier Macmillan Canada, Ltd.

Library of Congress Catalog Card Number: 78-3207

Printed in the United States of America

printing number

1 2 3 4 5 6 7 8 9 10

Library of Congress Cataloging in Publication Data

Reisman, William Michael
    Folded lies.

    Includes bibliographical references and index.
    1. Bribery.   2. Corporations—Corrupt practices.
3. International business enterprises—Law and legislation.   I. Title.
K5216.R4   345'.02'32   78-3207
ISBN 0-02-926280-1

Thanks are due to the publishers of the following works for permission to quote copyrighted material:

    W.H. Auden, "September 1, 1939," in *The English Auden: Poems, Essays and Dramatic Writings, 1927–1939,* edited by Edward Mendelson (New York: Random House, 1977). Copyright © 1977 by Edward Mendelson, William Meredith, and Monroe K. Spears, executors of the estate of W.H. Auden.

    Anne C. Flannery, "Multinational 'Payoffs' Abroad: International Repercussions and Domestic Liabilities," *Brooklyn Journal of International Law* 2 (1975), pp. 111–13. Copyright © 1975 Brooklyn Law School.

    Lorenz, Cartoon caption, *New Yorker,* July 5, 1976, p. 29. Copyright © 1976 The New Yorker Magazine, Inc.

    Martin Tolchin and Susan Tolchin, *To the Victor: Political Patronage from the Clubhouse to the White House* (New York: Random House, 1971). Copyright © 1971 by Martin Tolchin and Susan Tolchin.

    Gilbert P. Verbit, *International Monetary Reform and the Developing Countries: The Rule of Law Problem* (New York: Columbia University Press, 1975).

To
Harold D. Lasswell
1902–1978

Contents

Acknowledgments

THIS book is the better for the aid of others. Stanton Wheeler's Faculty Seminar on White-Collar Crime provided many ideas as well as opportunities to expose my own thinking to critical appraisal. Andrew Willard, my research assistant in this project, provided indispensable help at all stages, and Kristen C. Umstattd assisted in the final stages. My colleagues Marvin Chirelstein, Robert Clark, Abraham Goldstein, Jack Katz, Arthur Leff, and Christopher Stone read and commented on different versions of the work. Professors Eisuke Suzuki and Michael Libonati, Dr. Mahnoush Arsanjani, and Russell Caplan, Esq., made many useful suggestions. Professor John Gardiner's criticisms of the manuscript were most useful. As usual, my colleague Myres S. McDougal was an unfailing source of ideas, criticism, and encouragement.

An early version of parts of chapter 1 was published in *Yale Studies in World Public Order* 3 (1977). The bulk of the study was completed in September 1977.

I am extremely grateful to the Yale Law School for the considerable support it has given throughout the project. Two consecutive summer research grants from the White-Collar Crime Program at Yale also helped to make research and writing possible. That program was funded under grant 75N1-99-0127 from the National Institute of Law Enforcement and Criminal Justice, Law Enforcement Assistance Administration, U.S. Department of Justice. Points of view or opinions stated in this book are, however, my own and do not necessarily represent the official position or policies of the U.S. Department of Justice.

Prologue

Studying Bribery

The taboo on research on corruption. . . .
    — Gunnar Myrdal, *Asian Drama*

IN all social systems, prohibitions vary according to the intensity with which they are demanded, the probability of their being sanctioned, and the severity with which they are policed. All these factors may themselves be influenced by the identity and the social location of the violator of specific prohibitions. Most people learn early that there are things they can get away with; from the perspective of an observer, some social "wrongs" are selectively permitted. An observer may distinguish, in any social process, a *myth system* that clearly expresses all the rules and prohibitions (the "rights" and "wrongs" of behavior expressed without nuances and shadings), and an *operational code* that tells "operators" when, by whom, and how certain "wrong" things may be done.[1] An operator is someone who knows the code in his own social setting—certain lawyers, some police officers, some businessmen, an agent, a kid at school.

In one way or another, people come to terms with the many ambiguities and contradictions of life, but for most people some uncertainties, by their nature, continue to be unpleasant. In particular, the difficult distinctions between myth system and operational code will always be disagreeable, for they constantly require people, acting alone and often secretively, not only to determine what is right in a case in which the right thing to do is wrong, but to risk the

1

loss of an opportunity or the incidence of social sanctions. These risks and continuing tensions may contribute to dependencies on operators and to the development of certain deep ambivalences about the law and its practitioners.

Much of what we call white-collar crime—violations of norms characterized, for whatever reason, as criminal, usually nonviolent in their execution if not in their effect, and perpetrated by members of "higher" social strata—falls between myth system and operational code.[2] Bribery—tendering and accepting a private reward for defection from a manifest duty—involves not only the violation of law[3] but also the conscious and premeditated corruption of the processors of the law or, more generally, the custodians of some relevant normative system. Hence it may excite a rather special terror in those within and outside the state organization who are committed to the integrity and continued operation of that organization. The point was made with special zeal by E.A. Ross in his reform classic *Sin and Society: An Analysis of Latter Day Iniquity* (1907):

> All failure to enforce law is bad, but in certain classes of law slackness is not so mischievous as it is in others. There is a group of laws aiming to restrain men from preying on the vices of their fellows and thereby weakening the physical and the moral fibre of the population. If saloon, dive, gambling den, betting ring, or poolroom bribe themselves free of these laws, they not only continue their work of ruin, but incidentally the police is corrupted and, in a measure, all law is weakened.[4]

Bribery is thus different from other species of crime— "worse," if you like—but there is no reason to assume that bribery does not have its operational code. What politician can forget the words of George Washington Plunkitt, the guru of American machine politics: "Nobody thinks of drawin' the distinction between honest graft and dishonest graft. There's all the difference in the world between the two."[5] As for lesser mortals, we can all imagine hypothetical cases in which we would endorse bribery or think it perverse of officials to penalize it. But because bribery operates directly *on* the law, the ambivalences I have mentioned are likely to be more sharply focused where bribery is concerned than they would be with other manifestations of white-collar crime. Popular outbursts of rage and frustration over the anxieties and uncertainties of myth and operational code discrepancies may thus be especially violent.

The reason for these outbursts lies in the very positive attitudes increasingly held with regard to governments. In Sholem Aleichem's now world-famous village of "Anatevka," the rabbi instructed one of his parishioners that the pious prayer for the czar was "May God bless and keep the czar . . . far away from us." Until the comparatively recent rise of popular government and even thereafter, a government was likely to be viewed in many strata of the population as one of the dangers of life every reasonable person diligently tried to evade. Where the government has emerged in the popular mind as the major actor in determining physical security, economic well-being, education, health, and, in general, life opportunities, bribery and governmental corruption—indeed, the concealed operational code—will become obvious targets, especially when things are going wrong and nothing can be done to dispel the sense of despair and crisis. Not targets for everyone, however, only for those who believe in and support "their" government and assume it is working for them. During the Italian phase of the great international bribery scandal, a graffito scrawled on the Via Condotti, an elegant Roman thoroughfare, proclaimed, "I nostri governanti sono venduti" (Our rulers are sold). Would such a lament have warranted public inscription in a Roman slum?[6]

Article II, Section 4 of the U.S. Constitution calls for the impeachment of the president, the vice-president, and all civil officers for "Treason, Bribery, or other high Crimes and Misdemeanors." It should be no surprise that the first modern experiment in popular government fixed so sharply on bribery as a fundamental violation of the trust the people were putting in an elected leader. In this constellation of expectations, bribery is a form of treason. Treason is a capital offense during wartime; bribery is prosecuted vigorously during popular perceptions of crisis.

In Defense of Our Times

We are exhorted and often inclined to think that we are living through a particularly evil time and that businessmen (not to speak of judges, politicians, policemen, and others) are more nefarious now than ever in the past. In fact, the actual practices of merchants may have changed very little over time. In a speech delivered at Yale University, Roderick Hills, then chairman of the Securities and Exchange Commission, commented on the apparent abundance of twentieth-century white-collar crime:

> Taken as a whole, these incidents have not revealed some new low of corporate morality. Kickbacks, embezzlement and large gratuities have been some part of the commercial scene for centuries. Indeed, a thoughtful analysis may well indicate that there has been, since the turn of the century, an improvement in the quality and morality of corporate management.[7]

What certainly appears to have changed is the degree of regulation of business: to a greater extent than in the past, a myth system of socially appropriate practices has been built over a set of traditional practices that make sense to relevant strata in the social organization we call commerce.

Deviance is a function of prescription of norms and their accompanying sanctions. The more prescriptions there are, the more deviance there can be. Thus, part of the reason for the increase in white-collar crime is not that practices are becoming more corrupt but that the state increasingly appears as a direct business party, an indirect party such as insurer or credit guarantor, or the regulator of an exchange system with both commercial and moral justifications. Practices formerly considered acceptable even if "sharp" when enacted between two private parties at arm's length quickly become characterized as criminal when the victim is the state, its constituency, or its legal artifacts.

There are, of course, many ways of characterizing behavior as "deviant"; every society has a graduated scale of symbols and practices to indicate the degree of social disapproval of certain acts. Criminalization is assumed to indicate high disapproval. One ordinarily expects it to be reserved for behavior that really threatens the fabric of social order or an entrenched elite position or that contravenes taboos still venerated but no longer serving a manifest social function.

The broad criminalization of white-collar deviance is thus rather baffling, especially when one discovers that the establishment, funding, and operation of enforcement processes is at best sporadic. Part of the explanation may derive from the excessive readiness of bureaucrats to use what appears to be (but is not) an economic sanction. Part, as Thurmond Arnold and Vilhelm Aubert have suggested, may involve a purposive use of ineffective law to mediate between different social classes, for criminalization also means that enforcement or nonenforcement is henceforth removed from private hands.[8] If the government is not interested in enforcing, criminalization is tantamount to termination. At a deeper level, part may derive from an assumption that the individual owes the community (that is, the apparatus of the state) certain obligations not necessarily owed to private persons. This latter notion is, of course, completely at variance with conceptions of philosophical radicalism and liberalism and may indicate by the very frequency of its invocation the erosion of those principles in our civilization: a shift from the doctrines of coarchicalism that hold it natural and appropriate for people to relate as equals to others in official and private roles to a doctrine of hierarchy with loyalty "owed" to the state rather than to the individual conscience.

Objectives, Problems and Methods

Lest readers be misled by my professional provenance, I emphasize that this is not a conventional "legal" study with meticulous analysis of legal definitions, review of statutes and rules, dissection of past precedents, and the development of some legal "theory" that might then aid enforcers in prosecuting and convicting bribers. The content of the book itself will, I hope, make clear why a study in that genre, without a fundamental inquiry into causes and policy alternatives, would be of very limited value. Instead, this book is a modest attempt at exploration into the interrelations of the myth system and operational code as they pertain to bribery. It is a study of the processes and techniques of social stabilization rather than of social change.

As someone in the academic world who reads and writes books, it is obvious that I believe that ideas can transform reality; that intellectual endeavors have policy relevance. Policy implies implementation. Hence the necessity for an efficient government and "money-honest" decision makers seems inescapable. Bribery is, in this respect, a decision pathology. My personal inclination, argued at different points in the book, is that bribery is probably bad for the sort of body politic I would like to live in. But other social goals are also relevant, and some, such as the maintenance of a richly pluralistic society with many opportunities for the development and maintenance of private realities, may themselves generate the contexts for bribery. Hence legislative interventions may be called for, but legislative overkill may itself cause great social harm. Today's deviance—in art, in business, in politics—may be tomorrow's style; too strict a policing of the mores of the moment may stifle a society's creativity.

Any normative system must be selective in application, deploying limited resources and choosing those instances for sanctioning that promise the greatest return in deterring deviance and reinforcing community values. I am not especially concerned here with the important problem of prosecutorial discretion, the broad discretion of those in the control apparatus to characterize only some behavior as deviant and to select an even smaller number of cases for sanctions. Once one concedes that a prosecutor does, indeed must, exercise discretion, the question becomes how discretion should be applied. Many considerations must be brought to bear. One that has not been explored is the myth system-operational code dimension of the indictable practice. The fact that discretion is applied to withhold prosecution in many cases that violate the formal law does not necessarily mean that an operational code has now prescribed that they are legitimate. But consistencies in certain patterns of nonprosecution may indeed indicate an operational code and a curious public reaction I call *crusade* and will treat in detail.

Virtuous people rarely feel obliged to proclaim their own virtue. The very fact that a discipline feels compelled to announce again and again its "relentless pursuit" of "the truth, the whole truth, and nothing but the truth" arouses the suspicion that something quite different is being done. In fact, a respectable part of the traditional jurisprudential literature has been fascinated with the half-truths of the law. Jhering, Savigny, Maine, Pound, Morris R. Cohen, Fuller, and others[9] have explored in detail the institution of the "legal fiction"; the doctrinal literature of evidence, with its many "presumptions," "weightings," and "burdens of proof," offers compelling proof that in law things are not always what they seem. I think it fair to say that virtually all of these studies treat the legal fiction as an amending or terminating device, an instrument for bypassing obsolete law. In this respect, I am not concerned with "legal fictions," for the myth system is not obsolete. It is as important as the operational code and, without an account of both, the phenomenon of the crusade cannot be understood. Nor am I interested in that category of instances in which a formal legal system *authorizes* actors to deviate from a norm or, in the

Kadishes' phrase, to "interpose" themselves.[10] The fact that
authorized deviations or discretions are accomplished *openly*
usually suggests that the actors are not violating the myth
system. A number of contemporary jurisprudential writers,
such as Hart,[11] the Kadishes, Kenneth Culp Davis,[12] and
Dworkin,[13] have devised complex reasoning systems to
demonstrate that what appear to be deviations from the rules
are in fact part of a larger, coherent legal system, properly
understood. I have not found these theories to be particularly
useful for the operational code matters I address here.

It is, in fact, the consistency of certain deviations from the
myth system and the informal sanctions that *support* the
deviations that warrant the characterization operational code
and impel this inquiry. Chapter 1 is a theoretical inquiry into
the relations between myth systems and operational codes,
developing ideas I began to investigate in some earlier
work.[14] Chapter 2 explores the toleration of bribery in three
of the major and interlocking myth systems of contemporary
life. Chapter 3 examines the types of bribery we encounter in
their social setting and probes the distinctions that an operational code itself may draw. Chapter 4 discusses the forms
and causes of campaigns against bribery and the impacts they
may have on myth system and operational code. Chapter 5
looks at how officials as well as nonofficials decide when offi-
cially prohibited bribery is nonetheless appropriate. In a brief
epilogue, I review the current antibribery campaign and try
to assess the likelihood of its effectiveness. There is no dearth
of bibliographies on white-collar crime in general. For the
reader who wishes to pursue some of the problems explored
here, I have appended a bibliographic note and a selected
bibliography primarily on bribery, especially the transnational variety.

This study has presented certain methodological problems.
The term *bribery* is normatively ambiguous,[15] for it is both
designative and evaluative, that is, it refers simultaneously to
events and to legal conclusions about those events. A more

precise and scientifically acceptable approach would distinguish exceptional or extraordinary payments (the underlying factual event) from authorized conclusions drawn by community decision makers about the lawfulness of those payments. An exceptional payment authoritatively deemed to be unlawful is a bribe. Because not all exceptional payments will be characterized by authorized decision makers as bribes, there is a conclusory aspect to labeling all such events bribery. Nonetheless, I have decided to retain the term as a general reference for two reasons: First, the term *extraordinary payments* has been adopted by segments of United States industry (quite properly, one might add) but has come, in the public mind, to be viewed as a Madison Avenue euphemism, a gimmick or evasion. Second, the thesis developed here is that, under the complex of codes with which we operate, bribes, understood as *improper* payments, may sometimes be deemed lawful.

Another methodological problem arises from the fact that although bribery is prevalent, it is conducted in an atmosphere of understandable secrecy. Part of the reason for this secrecy stems from fear of prosecution and sanctions, *not* for violation of the laws against bribery but rather for violation of the operational code that some types of bribery are acceptable but are not to be talked about. Bear in mind that the term *code* is applied to the operational norms because relevant members of a group not only demand conformity to it but will deploy the power available to them to try to sanction deviation from it. Bribers, like others who are damned if they do and damned if they don't, are reluctant to volunteer information about their activities.[16]

For these reasons, an extraordinary amount of data may be available, but truth-content and reliability vary widely. Reliance on the media as a major source of data on bribery and on white-collar crime in general presents some special sampling problems.[17] In many cases, particularly those smacking of crime, the media are outside observers and hence

are as prey to the creative camouflage of the perpetrators as
the public they seek to inform. Calvin Trillin remarks that "it
was customary in the South for outside observers to interpret
events in terms of ideology (usually racial ideology) and for
local observers to interpret the same events in terms of
money (usually graft)."[18] Where the media are more on the
inside, they may be pressed to behave "responsibly." Thus
the responsible press even in liberal democracies may frequently undertake as one of its public duties the reinforcement of the myth system, even to the point of assuring
Virginia that there is a Santa Claus. Media leaders may be
part of the elite, identify with it, or be dependent on it for
favors.[19] There are other pragmatic reasons for the media's
behavior. As the Tolchins observe:

> The ideological approach to government also receives sustenance
> from the mass media, which find it easier, less costly, and infinitely
> safer to report campaign speeches or depict members of Congress
> standing toe-to-toe in angry debate on the floor of the House than to
> learn, for example, why a congressman changed his vote during a
> closed meeting of a congressional committee. . . . The accent is on
> oratory—flowery, stentorian, and acerbic. Gone almost unnoticed—
> and frequently denied—is the crucial role of the patronage system, of
> debts incurred and IOU's held, accompanied by the overriding theme
> of political ambition.[20]

In contrast, during periods of anticorruption crusades the
media swing to the other extreme. Then they seem to thrive
on social pathologies much as vultures thrive on carrion.
They will generally report deviations rather than confor-
mities. Indeed, the fact that people are complying with the
law would be newsworthy only if it occurred in a context of
widespread and expected lawless behavior. In both extremes,
what is routinely reported in the press is not necessarily
socially routine. The fact that bribery issues currently dominate the media does not necessarily mean that the entire
world is bribe-ridden;[21] nor does the fact that bribery was
not prominently reported at certain times in the past mean

that these were periods when society was bribeless. I have been unable to avoid the use of press reports; for many purposes, they are the only readily available source. In what follows, the *volume* of press reports is not being cited as proof per se of the prevalence of bribery but rather as evidence to support the hypothesis that, under certain conditions, bribery is selectively tolerated, despite the fact that it violates the myth system.

Another methodological problem is that much of the information is anecdotal, some of it coming from the early stages of criminal process, with informants having an interest in minimizing the magnitude of their acts and/or their responsibility. Official investigations may produce harder data; until then scholars with public policy perspectives will perforce speculate. Information used for this phase of research has been drawn from accounts available in documents of public record, social science literature on corruption, political memoirs, trade journals as indexed in the *Index of Business Journals* and general periodicals as indexed in the *Reader's Guide* and newspapers. My original plans called for a large number of interviews. This proved impractical and far fewer than planned were conducted. But a number of individuals with considerable experience in international trade gave extensive and candid interviews.

The interviews I conducted, as well as those conducted and published by others, were sometimes complicated by what I came to call the braggadocio factor or B-factor. Businessmen and others who do not pay bribes are quite willing to say so, and sometimes to assert that bribery is unnecessary and to excoriate those who practice it. Some people who pay bribes or know a great deal about operational procedures will not speak about them at all. Others, for reasons of their own, will. Precisely because bribery is wrong, those informants willing to speak were, I sometimes felt, prone to exaggerate as a way of demonstrating their courage or independence. For a respondent like this, an interview situation can present

extraordinary opportunities for fantasizing about unconsum-
mated evil.

Field researchers are, of course, always sensitive to these
tendencies in informants, especially when the informant is, in
the nature of things, a pariah. A fundamental control technique practiced by science in matters such as these is cross-
checking. But the B-factor is compounded by the difficulty,
sometimes impossibility, of cross-checking as a way of confirming accuracy. It is hard enough to find reliable informants and virtually impossible to find confirming witnesses,
particularly when the investigator seeks to protect the ano-
nymity of the original informant. In such circumstances, the
student does the best he can, acknowledging the problem and
inviting his readers to exercise their own judgment in
appraising the reports he has gathered and his assessment of
their degree of reliability.

In the future, I intend to write on the institution, familiar
to international lawyers, of *jurisprudence confidentielle*: a
confidential or secret theory and practice of law, known to a
few key lawyers who sometimes perform legal functions in
accord with it. *Jurisprudence confidentielle* is never expressed openly. High government lawyers and private practitioners who may advise the elite will be privy to secret
agreements that they interpret; pleadings and arbitrations,
sometimes rendered by judges of public courts acting in their
private capacity, will be suppressed by agreement of the
parties; opinions rendered for corporations will be kept confidential; and vast amounts of legal material in the public
sector will be classified. None of this *jurisprudence confidentielle* will be expressed by these same practitioners in the
jurisprudence publique, that jurisprudence presented to the
public and studied assiduously by students. The *jurisprudence publique* is not a sham, for it may apply to some
events and to certain groups; given the curious and almost
sacramental role of generative logic in legal scholarship, *jurisprudence publique* can always be presented as a complete

system of thought. But since it represents only a part of what is going on, it is inadequate as an explanatory or predictive tool. The study of the legal treatment of bribery is, in large part, a study of the *jurisprudence confidentielle*, the jurisprudence in the shadows. It has required looking at readily available material differently and, often, working with incomplete data. I have used the available data as best I could, but this is less an empirical study than an attempt to make sense of the fact of and reasons for a public record in *chiaroscuro*.

Chapter 1

Myth System and Operational Code

This theory is designed only for the special case of a nearly just society. — John Rawls

FROM the standpoint of the disengaged observer, the most overwhelming feature of social systems is the integrality and the seamless symbiosis of controller and controlled. But for certain problems, inquiry about legal control must distinguish the flow of behavior that makes up group life from those specialized institutions that purport to control, in diverse ways, what that flow of behavior *ought* to be. The specialized institutions—and they are not limited to the apparatus of the state—convey, both for themselves and for their targets, a very complete picture of how the group in question ought to be acting: a picture of the group as its members would like to, and to some extent do, imagine it. Membership in the group involves for most[1] acculturation, a profound shaping of the personality, in processes that impart that preferred picture and make it an integral part of the identity and cognitive structure of the individual. That picture includes the official code of the group and much of its distinctive ritual.[2]

The picture produced by control institutions does not correspond, point for point, with the actual flow of behavior of those institutions in the performance of their public function: indeed, there may be very great discrepancies between

15

it and the actual way of doing things. The persistent discrepancies do not necessarily mean that there is no "law," that in
those sectors "anything goes," for some of those discrepancies may conform to a different code. They may indicate
an additional set of expectations and demands that are effectively, though often informally, sanctioned and that guide
actors when they deal with "the real world." Hence we
encounter two "relevant" normative systems:[3] one that is
supposed to apply, which continues to enjoy lip service
among elites, and one that is actually applied. Neither should
be confused with actual behavior, which may be discrepant
from both.

A disengaged observer might call the norm system of the
official picture the myth system of the group. Parts of it
provide the appropriate code of conduct for most group
members; for some, most of it is their normative guide. But
there are enough discrepancies between this myth system and
the way things are done by key official or effective
actors to force the observer to apply another name for the
unofficial but nonetheless effective guidelines for behavior in
those discrepant sectors: the operational code. Bear in mind
that the terms *myth system* and *operational code* are functional creations of the observer for describing the actual flow
of official behavior or the official picture. The cynic who
delights in nihilistic exercises would say there is no law. But
from the perspective of an observer, as we shall see, parts of
the myth system and the operational code make up the law
of the community. From the perspective of many actors
within a given social process, however, only myth system is
law; hence operational code activities are perceived as "illegal" and profoundly wrong.[4]

The myth system is not legal fiction writ large. Legal
fictions are authoritative statements whose patent falseness
is, by convention, never exposed.[5] They abound in legal
systems in which veneration for existing prescriptions is great
and formal amendment procedures cumbersome and expen-

sive.[6] The device of the fiction permits those charged with making decisions to make existing law obsolete without changing it. From his historical perspective, Jhering called fictions "white lies."[7] Bentham was much less affectionate, calling them "lies" and "swindling."[8] Actually, a fiction is not a lie, for it does not, as Fuller remarks, intend to deceive;[9] it is *consciously* false and, though the degree of explicit consciousness of its falsity may vary, virtually all who use the fiction know it for what it is: a device for circumventing a norm that is obsolete. In contrast, the myth system is not widely appreciated as consciously false. It does not express values that are obsolete, but rather affirms values that continue to be important socially and personally. Though not applied in the jurisdiction of the operational code, the myth system may yet influence decision.

The *locus classicus* of myth systems and operational codes is probably the Code of Hammurabi, a massive casuistic code ostensibly designed to guide decision makers of the ancient Babylonian Empire in a wide range of their official activities. There is substantial reason to believe that Hammurabi's code was never applied; those charged with making decisions and those seeking decisions from officials operated on the basis of an entirely different code of norms.[10] However, the Code of Hammurabi should not be dismissed as irrelevant, for insofar as it expressed key values of the elite and the society of the time, it may have influenced behavior and even the formulation and application of the operational code.

In other studies, my colleagues and I have urged scholars to reserve the term *law* for those processes of decision that are both authoritative and controlling.[11] The fact that people operating within social systems do not speak with such precision is one of the reasons there are discrepancies between myth system and operational code. The point here is that much formal law, which community members continue to view as law and which they are not willing to dismiss as survival, in W.H.R. Rivers's sense of the word,[12] will not only *not* be effectively enforced, but its violation will be accepted by those charged with operating it as the way things are done. Dissension can erupt when those not privy to the operational code become aware of its practices and begin to test them against the standards of the myth system. New strata may be gaining political power, or a counterelite may be in the process of accomplishing a takeover. One might say that these new groups simply do not "know the rules" (or that cynical politicians assume that their constituents don't know the rules). One would predict that in the course of time they too will learn an operational code discrepant in varying ways from their own myth system.[13]

Private Systems of Public Law

Certainly there is nothing startling in the hypothesis of multiple legal systems, in the proposition that within larger, conglomerate groups all small groups have and, indeed, are characterized by their own normative codes. The very role proliferation in life in the modern metropolis, each role with its own distinctive "vocabulary of motive," may accelerate this process.[14] Groups as such—kin, racial, religious, language and dialect, specialist, and others—must have their own legal systems.[15] What is distinctive about the operational code is that it is a *private* public law in systems in which public law is supposed to be public; those authorized to play control functions and those who deal directly with them come to accept procedures that deviate from the myth system as licit. George Washington Plunkitt, the doyen of machine politicians, once submitted a flagrantly unconstitutional bill in the New York legislature. When an opponent branded it unconstitutional, Plunkitt is reputed to have replied, "What's a constitution between friends?"

Elites in a power process are those who have more power and influence than others. Their assumption—a varying mixture of self-service and community service—that they bear special responsibilities generates the feeling that they may, and sometimes must, take certain liberties. Because their function, as they perceive it, is to maintain group integrity, they will "have the courage" to do what is necessary to achieve that objective, but they will suppress publicization of these means of achievement in the interests of the community and to preserve the very integrity of the myth system that has been violated by their operations. Surely the most venerable formulation of this view is in that handbook for the elite, Plato's *Republic*. In book V, Socrates remarks coolly that "our rulers will find a considerable dose of falsehood and deceit necessary for the good of their subjects."[16] The exclusiveness of this elite prerogative is made patent in book III:

> If any one at all is to have the privilege of lying, the rulers of the State should be the persons; and they, in their dealings either with enemies or with their own citizens, may be allowed to lie for the public good. But nobody else should meddle with anything of the kind; and although the rulers have this privilege, for a private man to lie to them in return is to be deemed a more heinous fault than for the patient or the pupil of a gymnasium not to speak the truth about his own bodily illnesses to the physician or to the trainer, or for a sailor not to tell the captain what is happening about the ship and the rest of the crew. . . .[17]

Of course, the elite rationalization of its operational code presents extraordinary opportunities for abuse. In constitutional democracies it short-circuits the very controls on officeholders that are at the heart of popular constitutional government. Since the notion of such controls is itself a key part of the myth, the deceit that elites practice must be further compounded so that responsibility for actions under the operational code can never be attributed to the leader. President Eisenhower took responsibility for the U2 flights over the USSR[18] and somehow the Republic survived. But after President Kennedy had authorized the 1961 invasion of

Cuba, one of his advisors, Arthur Schlesinger, wrote a confidential memo to the president, advising:

> The character and repute of President Kennedy constitutes one of our greatest national resources. Nothing should be done to jeopardize this invaluable asset. When lies must be told, they should be told by subordinate officials. At no point should the President be asked to lend himself to the cover operation. For this reason, there seems to me merit in Secretary Rusk's suggestion that someone other than the President make the final decision and do so in his absence—someone whose head can later be placed on the block if things go terribly wrong.[19]

Almost two decades later, testimony before the Senate Select Committee on Intelligence revealed an extraordinary apparatus of circumlocution to protect the chief executive's plausible deniability.[20]

Practices such as these obviously change the system of public order they are supposed to protect. Elites who are involved in these sorts of defections develop new, though often secret, justifications derived from historicism, mythical communions with the "will of the people," charismatic authority, or confirming vibrations from the Silent Majority.[21] The convenient rule of interpretation for the Silent Majority is, of course, that silence is assent: hence Homer's dead host never fail to validate the politician who invokes them. The style of justification may vary; the persistent generation of the operational code does not. My hypothesis is that the code is a by-product of social complexity, generated by the increase of social divisions and specializations. All foci of loyalty have, by definition, at least the rudiments of a normative code. Those who specialize in the manipulation of power have their operational code. In the power context, the operational code is a private system of public law.

Popular Responses

In systems in which government is generally unpopular in certain sectors or is viewed as a benefice that can be purchased and then used as a business, the privacy of the operational code is not at all startling. Nor, for that matter, would the privacy of the elite's operating procedures in a privately held corporation be deemed startling. It is only when the decision process holds itself as being public and popularly based that accounting for decisions by public procedures becomes a characteristic feature. With this development, tensions increase between the myth system of the group and the operational code of those charged with making decisions or those directly concerned with them. The effectiveness of the operational code, as well as group cohesion, will then depend on the comparative secrecy with which the code is practiced and, in particular, the insulation of those strata of individuals insufficiently "sophisticated" to appreciate its necessity or inevitability.

"Legality" may be taken to refer to conclusions drawn by members of the community as to the propriety of practices determined by some method of logical derivation from the myth system. Virtually all of the operational code discrepant from the myth system is thus "illegal." "Lawfulness," in contrast, may be taken to refer to conclusions drawn by members of the community as to the propriety of practices in terms of their contribution (or lack thereof) to group integrity and continuity, of which the myth system is part. Conclusions of lawfulness are teleological rather than logical and will vary according to time, context, and group need. Many parts of an operational code may be deemed lawful at certain times, though *the conclusion of lawfulness does not thereby integrate them into the myth system.* A director of intelligence who asserts he lied to Congress for "the good of the country" may, in some contexts, find considerable support for his deed. Though virtually no one will say it was or should be "legal," many may say it was "right." Whether an appropriate social goal is to secure conformity of myth system and operational code—that is, to police that for which there is no intention to police—is a question I shall address later.[22]

Precisely because of the discrepancies between myth system and operational code, maintenance of the myth system is a dynamic process requiring ongoing contributions from many. Some obscuring of the operational code is consciously designed. "Not surprisingly, the ideological approach to politics and government is encouraged by the politicians themselves, who would much rather portray themselves as motivated by principle than by power or personal profit."[23] For some who may be gaining few benefits from the operational code, commitment to social order is held at levels of consciousness so deep they are unaware of it. The social philosopher who elaborates a theory, as John Rawls puts it, "designed only for the special case of a nearly just society" substitutes a rosy dream world for the violence and often savagery of political struggles. Intellectual efforts of this sort basically reinforce the myth system and obscure the operational code.[24] Similarly, the economist, equipped with the inimitable proviso of *ceteris paribus*, neatly insulates himself from the operational code and many other aspects of reality. The contribution of law professors, with the brief interlude of the legal realists, needs no comment.[25]

Every belief system has a coercive component, but the apparatus for imposing "evils" or deprivations for deviations from orthodox belief may not be obvious. For example, the potential characterization of eccentricity may be enough to deter the more timid but nonetheless reflective members of a group from verbalizing their perceptions or deductions of the mythic quality of the formal normative code. More serious violators may be solemnly declared insane by the custodians of group sanity.[26] Such characterizations neutralize the deviants and at the same time reinforce the accepted version of reality for the rest of the group. Public and prominent supporters of the myth system, in contrast, may often expect material rewards as well as the warm sunshine of approbation from those who believe the myth system and find public confirmations reassuring.

Where there are discrepancies between myth system and operational code, elites, as I have remarked, have a strong incentive to conceal those activities, acceptable under the code, and to maintain the integrity of the myth system. For a member of the larger public, not privy to the rules and practices of the operational code, the result is a picture of reality that at certain disturbing moments is seen not to be reality but rather a vast production. In book VII of the *Republic*, Plato's extraordinary myth of the prisoners in the cave is evocative of parishioners of the myth system. Socrates, speaking to Glaucon, begins:

> And now, I said, let me show in a figure how far our nature is enlightened or unenlightened:—Behold! human beings living in an underground den, which has a mouth open towards the light and reaching all along the den; here they have been from their childhood, and have their legs and necks chained so that they cannot move, and can only see before them, being prevented by the chains from turning round their heads. Above and behind them a fire is blazing at a distance, and between the fire and the prisoners there is a raised way; and you will see, if you look, a low wall built along the way, like the screen which marionette players have in front of them, over which they show the puppets.
>
> I see.
>
> And do you see, I said, men passing along the wall carrying all sorts of vessels, and statues and figures of animals made of wood and stone and various materials, which appear over the wall? Some of them are talking, others silent.
>
> You have shown me a strange image, and they are strange prisoners.
>
> Like ourselves, I replied. . . .[27]

Few things in life are authentically unilateral, and deception is often a shared process. While elites have an obvious interest in maintaining the integrity of the myth system, key personalities and entire strata in the public may abet the deception, avoiding the truth like someone pulling blankets over his head to avoid the cold reality of dawn.

But support for the myth system is not exclusively benign,

voluntary, verbal, or symbolic. Coercive efforts may be regularly mounted by those who make up the official apparatus to police belief in, and behavior in accord with, the myth system by sanctioning, according to some rationale, defections from it. Efforts directed toward policing beliefs may be even more urgent when there are *widely perceived* discrepancies between myth and operation.[28] Policing is not exclusively hierarchical, a specialist function, or elite-initiated. Many group members who believe the myth may contribute to policing it, gaining in addition a certain gratification in the simple skill of "knowing the rules."[29] Thus, in addition to the more patently coercive elements of the elite, teachers, clergymen, parents, even a stranger on the street may patiently explain to a youngster why a certain act should not be done.[30]

Despite such efforts, there may be a point where perception of discrepancy between myth and operational code becomes so great that part of the content of the myth system changes, belief in it wanes, or crusades for reassertion of the myth burst forth.[31] In group life as in personal life, erosion of the myth system is most serious and underlines the vital though intangible function that myth system performs. Belief in the myth system is a critical part of group organization, the basis for mobilizing many necessary collective activities. Because it has been transmitted, through acculturation, to the core organization of the individual personality, a waning of belief in it, without a replacement, may lead to anomie and personal disintegration. It may also lead to struggles between groups—classes, castes, religions, language and dialect groups—for one aspect of war, as McLuhan and Fiore observe, is the mobilization of the self to protect images of reality challenged by others:

> All social changes are the effect of new technologies (self-amputations of our own being) on the order of our sensory lives. It is the shift in this order, altering the images that we make of ourselves and our world, that guarantees that every major technical

innovation will so disturb our inner lives that wars necessarily result as misbegotten efforts to recover the old images.[32]

Whether the common technique of diabolization of an opponent is a product of intergroup tensions or a cause of them, it underlines a struggle of contending myth systems in which opponents protect, among other things, their own idols.

Anomie here does not mean that an individual no longer knows how to behave in specific settings, but that he has lost the more general guidelines for his orientation and the valuation of his environment. It is this coordinate personal mooring function of the myth system that drives individuals who may behave according to an operational code discrepant from the myth system nonetheless to defend with extraordinary passion the myth system itself.

Perception of a routinized code discrepant from the myth system is not restricted to the elite. Groups, particularly large conglomerations, are composed of many smaller groups. The culture of some of these smaller groups may have unique perspectives on the more general myth system and operational code, for to an extent members of these subgroups may find it easier to apprehend the myths of the larger group as "facts." Perhaps because of this, some members have become specialists in the performance of certain operations for the larger group. But operators are not necessarily outsiders. Phrases such as "you've got to be practical," "watch the bottom line," "take a more realistic view," or "live in the real world" are usually the signals of operators who identify with the myth but perform group functions according to a discrepant operational code. Obvious domestic examples in official behavior might include the activities of intelligence agencies and certain police functions, for example, dealing with informers by paying money or reducing sentences, breaking and entering, planting bugs, unauthorized wiretaps, and the like. More compelling examples might include running undesirables out of town, or police execution of miscreants in vigilante actions. To characterize these activities as "unlawful" would not be illogical, yet it becomes imprecise and incongruous when the activities are carried out by the representatives of the law and routinely supported by judges charged with the supervision of criminal justice processes.[33] The activities do indeed deviate from the myth system, and those who perform them defer to this fact by performing them in a covert or discreet fashion.[34] Of significance here is the fact that those who perform them view them as lawful under the operational code.

In a story about police vigilantism in an American city, novelist Philip Rosenberg describes some of the frustrations of the honest cop who realizes, after years on the force, that he can expend most of his energy collaring small fry, but that he has only limited effectiveness against the criminal elite, for whom police activities will be little more than overhead or a business expense. When a young police officer is invited to join the vigilantes, he sweats out the implications:

> The next three days were a period of intense confusion for him during which he worked his way around all the things he had ever heard about right and wrong, about taking the law into your own hands, about whether anyone could ever be above the law, and about whether any ends could justify a handful of men in killing at their own discretion. And he decided that, yes, people could be above the law, that in fact one had a duty to oneself to put one's own sense of right and wrong above the law. This was, in a sense, sort of a policeman's conscientious objection, a recognition that there was a sort of higher law to which one could appeal, and that this higher law said it was possible that a man who was willing to bear the responsibility could in good conscience take steps he knew to be illegal if those steps would accomplish an end which he knew to be good.[35]

Whether certain types of police vigilantism are parts of an operational code or are themselves unlawful is a question that, obviously, can be answered only in specific contexts.

Even when they are part of the operational code, there are

special dangers in following these informal practices. It is always possible for reformers, some political opponents, or counterelites to prosecute belatedly these defections from the myth system either in response to popular outcry about deviations or in order to provoke such an outcry and then to demonstrate their courage and skill in protecting the myth system. The defense of the operational code will not prevail against these deferred prosecutions.[36] When, as we shall see, there are myth system purges of operational code practices, the practitioners will often stand together and try to thwart the effort. Even if sanctions are imposed and new prescriptions are made to prevent the practices, it is likely that these practices will nonetheless continue if those who control them conclude that they are necessary for group life.

Operators, if pressed, will defend the operational code as self-evidently necessary for organizational efficiency, even survival. Enough of those concerned with appraising or policing lawfulness will accept such justifications to make behavior according to the operational code feasible. A legislature may pass a very open-textured statute to give increased discretion to those charged with applying it, after being told in executive session that some things just "have to be done" and it would be better for all if nothing were said about it. Legislators may avoid investigating certain sectors or during investigations carefully refrain from asking sensitive key questions. Prosecutors, using their broad discretion, will decide not to press investigations and prosecutions against some types of official behavior: mail openings, gift exchanges, or worse. Judges will accept suggestions from secret agencies that the national interest would be best served if a particular case were quashed. Journalists will not report certain things.[37]

What is characteristic of the operational code is that it is shared by key members of the control apparatus, that its deviations from the myth system are selectively tolerated and depend on the contingency, the identities of agents and objects, the purposes of the act and the probable effects on the larger organization. There is no attempt to revise the myth. On the contrary, efforts are made to maintain the integrity of the myth and to suppress all knowledge of the operational code. The justification of the discrepancies expressed in the operational code is that organizational efficiency and survival require it. Hence, in a type of casuistic reasoning, adherence to the operational code is not a violation of an oath to serve an organization, but rather the ultimate affirmation of that loyalty.

Politicians with heterogeneous constituencies sometimes feel obliged to lie or, put more delicately, to dissimulate, to conceal their objectives and, in some cases, the irrevocable steps they are taking to accomplish them. Euphemistically speaking, they may talk among themselves of "preparing" or "educating" the public, but it is often the force of events—for example, a war of which they were covert but critical architects—that ultimately arouses and mobilizes a public whose response is reinforced by feelings of indignation against a cunning enemy. Some operators may secretly delight in the opportunity to exercise and enhance their power this way, but for other, more reluctant, operators an element of pathos tones their predicament. They may crave candor and be revolted by what they are doing, yet they feel themselves trapped by "the facts of life," the unyielding realities from which many are sheltered but which their elite position now permits, indeed forces, them to confront. Precisely because group security is threatened, secrecy about violations of the myth, whose broadcast could weaken group resolve, becomes all the more urgent. Hence "classification" of crimes of state finds new justification.

Doing the forbidden for a good cause, such as group integrity or survival, would presumably draw operators closer to the entire group. But the violations of group myth also create intense complicities and loyalties among the operators, for they are a type of *Blutkitt,*[38] generating an ancillary code of silence, like the Mafia's *omertà*.[39] One outcome of the discrepancy between myth system and operational code, therefore, is the sharpening disidentification of elite and rank and file and the increasing identification of elites.

The Elite Response

La Rochefoucauld's famous apothegm that "hyprocrisy is the homage vice pays to virtue" should not obscure the point that homage *is* owed, and that something should be paid. How much is to be paid is a question of key political importance. Elites are operators and are certainly acquainted with discrepancies from the myth system; more important, they are well aware of the utility (to themselves and, perhaps in rationalized form, to "the system") of the particular practices of the operational code. When popular disquiet grows, they will respond in ways that reinforce belief in the myth system, but often with a planned inefficiency. Some responses are uncomfortably obvious. For example, after a recent revelation of campaign fund abuses, Congress heroically cleaned house, among other things, by shortening the statute of limitations on the offenses involved from five to three years.[40] Other responses are more beguiling in their complexity. The so-called *lex imperfecta* ("imperfect law," or "law without teeth") is often a conscious operator or elite design for dealing with aggravated myth system and operational code discrepancies. Where prescribed norms are clear but an otherwise effective administrative process has not established adequate enforcement mechanisms, has staffed them with exquisite incompetents, has permitted those enforcement mechanisms to atrophy or, as Key's examples show, has insulated certain activities from the reach of an enforcement mechanism,[41] we are probably encountering a discrepancy between myth system and operational code. The late Alex Rose remarked, "To put people in law enforcement for the purpose of non-enforcement is a very big attraction for politicians."[42]

In some instances, the imperfect law may have been designed for cynical motives; for example, to permit operators to do what rank and file are still prohibited from doing or to discharge, via the legislative exercise, popular dissatisfactions with certain public behavior.[43] In other cases, a subtly crafted imperfect law may be a way of restoring confidence in certain discredited institutions or practices. Consider, for example, the Securities and Exchange Commission, established after the great market crash of 1929. A market in which those with substantial liquid capital can lend to those who wish to use it in productive enterprises is indispensable to a capitalist system. But the market cannot work without reassurances to investors that the economic system is productive and that producers are being candid and accurate in revealing how they will use the money and what returns can be reasonably expected. Both of these expectations were dashed in 1929, but apparently restored after the legislation and subsequent administrative activity in 1934. There are reasons to doubt that the SEC, as time-structured, staffed, and budgeted, can really police the market,[44] but it performs its function if it creates *in the minds of potential investors* the expectation that it can. To carry it off effectively, it is vital that the bulk of the policers in the SEC profoundly believe in their cause, constantly and honestly gripe about the inadequacy of their budget and staff, criticize superiors who are too "political" (that is, see the larger picture), and cause periodic shake-ups.

In some cases, the imperfection is genetic, built into the very structure of the law in question. Sometimes the imperfection is blatant. Consider a 1975 amendment to the Arms Control and Disarmament Act.[45] In order to assist the director of ACDA in the performance of his duties, any government agency preparing legislative or budgetary proposals with regard to the general area of armaments and military facilities "shall, on a continuing basis, provide the Director with full and timely access to detailed information, in accordance with procedures established . . . with respect to the nature, scope, and purpose of such proposal."[46] The information gained may be shared with appropriate congressional committees to aid them in the performance of their function.[47] The final subsection of the amendment adds, almost as an after-thought, "No court shall have any jurisdiction under any law to compel the performance of any requirement of this section or to review the adequacy of the performance of any such requirement on the part of any Government agency (including the Agency and the Director)."[48] When Solon gives with one hand and takes with the other, he uses *lex imperfecta*.

A cognate species of *lex imperfecta*, performing a function similar to the imperfect law, is a legislative exercise that produces a statutory instrument apparently operable, but one that neither prescribers, those charged with its administration, nor the putative target audience ever intend to be applied. We might call this a *lex simulata*. The prototype is the Code of Hammurabi. One way of identifying such laws is by the absence of a meaningful legislative history. If the context is one in which legislative bills adverse to the inter-ests of the target group are ordinarily contested but the particular bill is unchallenged and the difficulties of applying it to hard or to marginal cases are not raised, it is not unreasonable to assume that no one ever intended it to be applied.

Where such laws are "legislated," they are akin, in func-tion, to the flying buttresses of a Gothic cathedral; they seem to support parts of the myth system from which the opera-tional code deviates unambiguously and routinely. That apparent support can be most reassuring to diminutive mor-tals looking up at those massive walls. The function of the legislative exercise is not to affect the pertinent behavior of the manifest target group, but rather to reaffirm on the ideological level that component of the myth, to reassure peripheral constituent groups of the continuing vigor of the myth, and perhaps even to prohibit them from similar practices. As elsewhere, the mere act of legislation functions as catharsis and assures the rank and file that the government is doing what it should, namely, making laws. Legislation here becomes a vehicle for sustaining or reinforcing basic civic tenets, but not for influencing pertinent behavior.

An amendment in 1971 to the Internal Revenue Code[49] (it was changed again in 1977) would appear to be a salient example. Under the code, deductions are not allowed for a domestic illegal bribe "which subjects the payor to a criminal penalty or the loss of license or privilege to engage in a trade or business," but, the code continues, "only if such State law is generally enforced." The enforcement proviso permits a tax authority or federal court to temper application of the law prohibiting deductions for bribe payments by a consideration of the operational code actually prevailing in that commercial sector. But regarding bribery of foreign officials no such proviso exists. Section 162 (c) (1) provides:

> No deduction shall be allowed under subsection (a) for any payment made, directly or indirectly, to an official or employee of any government, or of any agency or instrumentality of any government, if the payment constitutes an illegal bribe or kickback or, if the payment is to an official or employee of a foreign government, the payment would be unlawful under the laws of the United States if such laws were applicable to such payment and to such official or employee. The burden of proof in respect of the issue, for the purposes of this paragraph, as to whether a payment constitutes an illegal bribe or kickback (or would be unlawful under the laws of the United States) shall be upon the Secretary or his delegate to the same extent as he bears the burden of proof under section 7454 (concerning the burden of proof when the issue relates to fraud).

Prohibition of deduction of bribe payments to foreign officials applies (1) even if the foreign law making it illegal is *not* generally enforced and (2) even if it is lawful according to the foreign law.[50] This is a standard so pure that one doubts that it was any more than pious aspiration, without intention to control. From the period of its enactment to the current antibribery campaign, I have been unable to find instances of prosecution.[51]

Another example of *lex simulata* is offered in the amendments to the Export Control Act of 1965.[52] Amid agitation for greater United States resistance to the Arab boycott a bill was submitted prohibiting compliance by United States business.[53] When opposition was mounted, the prohibition was diluted to require only a report to the Department of Commerce that a boycott request had been received.[54] The report would go to the secretary of commerce "for such action as he may deem appropriate."[55] The form that was actually prepared by the Department of Commerce indicated that respondents need not answer whether they actually complied with the Arab boycott request,[56] hence few respondents answered this key question.[57] One student of the legislation remarks, "The official opposition to the Arab boycott was essentially ritualistic, and the supposed deterrent effect of the reporting requirement was negated by the decisions not to require an answer to the critical question and to keep the completed forms confidential."[58] What then was the function of the legislative exercise? To reassure those who felt that United States law was being violated by the Arabs, to affirm opposition to boycotts of other governments, and to create a bureaucratic process that seemed to implement the policy but that allowed business to continue as usual: *lex simulata.*

The Functions of Discrepancy

Lex imperfecta and *lex simulata*, in their very ineffectiveness, express and reinforce the essential distinction between myth system and operational code. There is, to be sure, a measure of cynicism, particularly where the function of the discrepancy is to mediate between social classes. In many cases, however, the discrepancy between myth and code, captured by *lex imperfecta* and *simulata*, is cultivated and created in good faith (as a way of retaining fidelity to fundamental social values) and not, as would first appear, out of sheer hypocritical homage to virtue. Here, as elsewhere, the inquirer must accept the complexity of events, the multiplicity of inconsistent normative codes within a single functional legal system, the demands for behavioral accommodation, and the continuity of contradictions.

In their study of one pattern of deviancy within a factory, Bensman and Gerver noted the importance of the criminal practice to the working of the factory. "Crime," they say, "becomes one of the major operational devices of the organization . . . a permanent unofficial aspect of the organization." The operations themselves are performed discreetly, in deference to the "ceremonial aspects of law enforcement," are not characterized as crime, and are sanctioned as long as they are controlled by and serve those in charge. The discrepancy between myth system and operational code enables

the personnel involved to maintain the public values, while performing those actions necessary to attain the public or private ends appropriate to their evaluations of their positions. Thus a form of institutional schizophrenia is the major result of the conflict of ends and the conflict of means and ends. Individuals act and think on at least two planes, the plane of the public ideology and the plane of action. They shift from plane to plane, as required by their positions, their situations, and their means-ends estimations. In a sense, it is a form of double-think, and double-think is the major result of means-ends conflict.[59]

The fact that individuals, including realistic operators, in some or even all cases breach a certain norm does not mean that they wish to terminate it. On the personal level, the self-initiation of ritual penance for breach of a norm by an individual, even while he knows that in comparable circumstances in the future he will breach the norm again, provides us with a telling example. While we cannot here enter into examination of the guilt dynamics that give rise to such rituals, it is clear that one of their major functions is to restore, on both social and personal levels, commitment to the norms.[60]

This is an important dimension of the discussion and, at the risk of repetition, I emphasize that my thesis is not one of nihilism or the hypocrisy that so delights the cynic. On the contrary. The concept of operational code does not mean that everything is lawful, or that, in Ivan Karamazov's anguished words, "everything is permitted." There will be much that remains unlawful and effectively sanctioned by the appropriate community processes. Operators know that some discrepancies from the myth system are licit and will be tolerated; others will not. In other words, determining the "law" or the socially proper behavior in a particular setting necessitates a much wider social inquiry than the simple consultation of the formal law; it may be myth system.

There is often a symbiotic relationship between myth system and operational code, the latter, as we have seen, providing a degree of suppleness and practicality that the myth system could not achieve without changing much of its content.[61] From the perspective of members of the community who are not privy to the operational code of the specialist group, some operational code activities may well seem unlawful. But often there will be a certain toleration or a desire for ignorance. A number of writers have studied "dirty work" in society and have noted the coordinate generation of ignorance when it must be performed.[62]

In extended periods of social stability the discrepancy between myth and practice will tend to be stable and even institutionalized. Unless one puts a special premium on stability per se, this does not mean that every aspect of the operational code contributes to group weal, that some invisible hand directs a complex but nonetheless euphonious social symphony. From the perspective of community goals expressed in the myth system or deduced by a disengaged observer, much of the operational code may be profoundly dysfunctional during these and other periods. Indeed, parts of the operational code may be designed to accord special benefits to elite members while other parts may take on a *Blutkitt* character, making elite membership permanent and irrevocable by participation in a taboo act.[63] Many other practices that deviate from the myth system serve to protect the entrenched position of subgroups, for example, rewards granted on the basis of old-boyism or caste or ethnic ties rather than merit.

During periods of rapid social change, discrepancies between myth and practice will be more unstable. Accommodations and rationalizations ordinarily provided by culture and general past practice will be less available, obliging each individual to make choices for himself. The same sense of comparative rulelessness and anomie often experienced in periods of relative stability by individuals or groups who are suddenly changing social position now becomes a more general experience, imposed on many who never sought change and who were willing to forswear its potential rewards in return for a routinized "peaceful" environment in which the ambit of choice was narrow. For very independent persons, these can be times of great opportunity; but for those who seek guidance and validation from their environment, these are times of heightened anxiety and often desperate searching for new leaders and meaningful rectitude systems.

Chapter 2
Myth Systems and Bribery

. . . only we who guard the mystery will be unhappy.
— Dostoevski, "The Grand Inquisitor"

THE fundamental social precondition for bribery is a degree of effective and normative regulation by a controlling actor (CA) over a transaction whose outcome is valued by an external actor (EA).[1] EA seeks to secure his preferred outcome in violation of the appropriate norm by tendering a private reward to CA. Where the process is consonant with some relevant code, the controlling actor's *quid* is patronage; where it is not, the external actor's *quo* is a bribe. Only the premises of evaluation distinguish the two.

Neither CA nor EA has a major interest in changing the larger system, a point that makes the bribal transaction a very distinctive event. The system, as it exists, is perceived on the whole as beneficial to both actors. EA expects to secure his preferred outcome often enough to maintain his support; for reasons having to do with social proximity (discussed below) the bribal arrangement, even with its periodic losses, may still afford him a competitive advantage against others. The control actor supports the system because it in part generates and accounts for the external actor's incentive to bribe; in short, it is CA's stock in trade. If neither actor holds these views, they no longer seek to bribe, but rather to change the system as such. It is for this reason that bribery is always an essentially hypocritical or, as I have suggested, a discreet event,[2] with both parties contentedly violating the formal

37

norms of a system they must appear to—and, in fact, may—support. This curious duality also explains why bribery is a particularly sensitive and telling indicator of the tensions between myth system and operational code.

The inclination to view bribery as essentially a privately initiated operation against a passive, if not inert, public administration is as understandable as it is unfounded. It is based on a focus that has internalized the values of public administration and the criminalization of bribery. From a more disengaged perspective, it becomes clear that persistent patterns of bribery are part of a larger process in which the bribe recipient, though appearing passive, is, over time, an active participant. If not the active stimulator of a specific bribe transaction, he is the creator or sustainer of an effective political structure that maintains needs and incentives for bribe payments.

Bribery is a term that describes the process from the perspective of the private individual, or EA. "Whitemail" might be used to capture the coordinate perspective of the official, or CA. The bribe initiator—whether he is the private party or the official—is trying to change what is nominally a political situation with its special code into a market situation with its code. Each bribal transaction in which the recipient (and those associated with him who are aware of it and related transactions) participates is, thus, an economic transaction as well as a reinforcement of the constitutive structure of the larger process.

At a certain point on a continuum bounded by coercion and persuasion, the degree of official initiation of a bribe exchange transforms the character of the transaction to extortion. The term *extortion* may be reserved for those situations in which the capacity of the official to withhold a service or benefit otherwise required by law exceeds the capacity of the private party to sustain the loss of that service or benefit. The costs to the private party of not paying the bribe escalate.

Ascriptions of responsibility for the bribery, which in

other cases may have tilted toward the briber or have been divided between the parties, shift here toward the governmental actor. Imputations of responsibility must, of course, be made with great care. Bribers, like most delictors, seek to shift the blame; allegations of extortion—"they made me do it"—are a rather routine defense. Indeed, the farsighted briber may take pains to give the transaction an odor of extortion, like the common criminal preparing an alibi. The old Roman saying "coactus sed voluit" (compulsory but voluntary) dryly expresses a worldly skepticism, and the contemporary investigator would be well advised to heed it. There are, to be sure, some clear cases of extortion. I am inclined to think that most alleged cases would betray, on close examination, more complex power situations in which both the briber and the bribed have some room to maneuver.[3]

Analysis of the governmental dimension yields another insight into bribery organization. Bribery is one of the perquisites of power and a common coin of exchange between power and wealth. It will flourish in monopolistic situations, that is, in social situations where one party has exclusive control over a good or service needed by the other. Often that service can be an intangible such as permission or a "go-ahead." As governments extend their control over more and more sectors of social life, official approbation—in some licit form (such as a license) or illicit form (such as a closing or winking of the eyes)—increasingly becomes a requisite for the conduct of business and other affairs by individuals. Such political structures render power an economic commodity held monopolistically. Hence the whitemail dimension of such regulations and, correspondingly, the built-in incentive of those doing business to bribe.

The prerequisite of bribery—with the exception of a special bribe species we may call transaction bribes, "grease," speed money, or the operators' neo-euphemism, "facilitating payments"[4]—is differential social proximity between competitive EAs and CA. Bribing, as operators will explain, is not merely being willing to fix someone, but knowing whom to fix. Someone in the bribe sequence must be proximate to CA. Because there will always be differences in social distance between members of a class and a power center (political, economic), virtually every social system will fulfill this prerequisite for bribery; however, a system will not characterize some or all tendering of private rewards for defections from a duty as delictual unless the practice violates its myth system.

Myth systems—authorized pictures of groups as group members would like to and, in varying degrees, do imagine them—seem to have certain constant elements: Self-images are extraordinarily positive, norms are quite clear, compliance is believed to be substantial, and the myth system is believed to be very important.

The popular ambivalence to official bribery is a function of the unique constellation of personal and group relationships of our political civilization. Part of the ambivalence is reproduced in conflations or "double exposures": two or more groups—for example, moralists and mercantilists—characterize, in their own terms, the same facts. The ambivalence is captured most dramatically in the discrepancy between our preferred image of ourselves or our myth system and the operational code of elites.

Groups are collections of individuals who share certain distinctive and decisive experiences. While the proliferation of groups attests to the varieties of human experience, the observer may categorize certain group experiences shaped by similar economic and social circumstances and having certain common images of the world. For purposes of studying bribery, I think it useful to study three such interrelated myths: merchants or economic groups, modern representative government, and the contemporary nation-state system. Together they probably make up the key sectors of contemporary social life in large parts of the industrial world. In each, as we will see, the myth system prohibits bribery, but the operational code is more complex and holds bribery in certain instances to be licit.

Merchants: Myths and Operations

Competition, from which quality emerges, is the basic postulate of our commercial myth system. In an amalgam of Smith, Spencer, and social Darwinism, the best of power, wealth, health, and the like will be produced and distributed in appropriate quantities and at the lowest possible price by competition and struggle; and competition will provide quality control. Hence a great deal of legislation takes as its manifest purpose not the determination of quantity and price or the regulation of quality but the maintenance of competitive conditions. In a deeper sense, this maintenance is not viewed as a tampering with nature in favor of one class or another but as a type of conservation, a fidelity to an essentially necessary state of nature. In this fashion, all commercial behavior designed to circumvent or undermine the competitive condition is prohibited by the commercial myth.

Hard statistics on the extent of the deviations, circumventions, and violations are obviously not available, but inferences can be drawn from some parts of the recent public record. Consider five examples from the private and public-institutional sectors:

1. In February 1976, then Deputy Assistant Attorney General Joe Sims said the Justice Department had pending ninety grand jury investigations into possible criminal antitrust violations. "As far as we can tell, a record number. And as we put more resources into the field, we continue to find that price-fixing is a common business practice."[5]

2. Though a federal grand jury investigating soybean trading at the Chicago Board of Trade and Chicago Mercantile Exchange "found evidence of fictitious, prearranged trading . . . the prevalence of such practices is a matter of

some dispute. But even staunch defenders of the Board of Trade concede that some rigged trading has gone on for years on the Board of Trade and other U.S. futures exchanges, though it clearly violates federal laws and the rules of all commodity exchanges."[6] The *Los Angeles Times* adds "that the alleged fraud could have multimillion dollar ramifications in the price of commodities."[7]

3. The Justice Department's continuing investigation of the uranium industry began in the summer of 1975 and turned into a wide-ranging hunt for an international price-fixing conspiracy. Not unlike OPEC, the international oil cartel, this alleged cartel may have tried to manipulate uranium prices between 1972 and 1974. The members of the alleged cartel—Australia; Canada; France; South Africa; and one multinational corporation, Rio Tinto Zinc of Great Britain—"would meet as often as necessary to carve up world demand among its members. Bids would be rigged to distribute business evenly."[8] Given the basic role of energy in industrial civilizations, the radiating impact of such price-fixing would be enormous.

4. The extent of government-supported business (for example, the defense industry) and government-supported special benefits to business provides further examples of routine and at times institutionalized commercial practices that are quite discrepant from the myths of "open competition" and "no government interference." The defense industry, perhaps more than other industries, depends heavily on government patronage. "American Government now accounts for 62% of *Lockheed's* sales (contracts include the Trident and Poseidon missiles), 54% of *McDonnell Douglas'* (this will rise if the Navy is allowed to spend $6.5 billion on 600 or more of the F-18 twin engined lightweight fighters made with *Northrop*) and 40% of *Boeing's*. Lockheed is the largest defense contractor in the United States"[9] (emphasis added).

5. The special benefits accorded to business through tax

statutes and loopholes are well known and too extensive for comment here. However, less well known and almost coun- terintuitive are the advantages available to business through government regulation. R.T. McNamar, the executive director of the Federal Trade Commission, comments that "the con- fusion surrounding the imprecise—and not terribly useful— terms 'deregulation' or 'regulatory reform' provides an um- brella under which a great many companies seek both to eliminate their government-imposed operating cost increases and to shield themselves from the cold rain of increased competition. . . . Clearly, disagreement on the objectives of regulatory reform, coupled with the government's tradi- tionally fragmented, non-systematic legalistic approach en- ables almost any corporation rationally to maintain a schizo- phrenic position. To wit, support for reform or repeal of some regulations, namely the 'burdensome ones,' while seek- ing the retention of those laws or regulations that protect them from competition in markets where they believe they may be weak vis-à-vis competitors."[10]

The myth system of the market should not be confused with capitalism. Capitalism, according to its postulates, encourages the accumulation and use of capital and has a deeply held notion of the relativism of all values and the commonality and ethical acceptability of money. There is nothing inherent in capitalism that would prohibit trusts, price-fixing, kickbacks, or bribes. The critical question in a capitalist calculus is whether such actions are efficient in terms of production and profit. Hence the capitalist—a func- tional term that may include merchants or officials—will characterize a social situation as amendable to these practices if they promise efficiency.

The myth system of the market is an evolved and trans- formed capitalism in which developments now deemed to distort the aggregate of socially desirable consequences of capitalism are controlled and sanctioned by a political system. These distortions are now characterized as "excessive" concentrations of wealth, price-fixing, bribery, and the like. This is no minor change: the mere conception of political processes as autonomous, together with their introduction in a supervisory capacity over "market forces," is a profound revision of capitalism in its organizational as well as in its psychopersonal sense. Competition is an element of the market myth, not of capitalism. Bribery is a neutral instrument to the capitalist, while it is anathema to the "marketeer."

Ironically, commercial bribery is, in many cases, accepted by parts of our civilization as standard business operating procedure. In 1918 the commissioners of the Federal Trade Commission wrote to Congress in shocked terms that "the commission has found that commercial bribery of employees is a prevalent and common practice in many industries. These bribes take the form of commissions for alleged services, of money and gratuities and entertainments of various sorts, and of loans—all intended to influence such employees in the choice of materials."[11] The practice had become institutionalized to the point where employees sometimes claimed their "rights" to bribery:

> How thoroughly insidious this practice has become may be illustrated by two experiences of representatives of the commission. In one case an employee frankly stated that he was "entitled to 10 per cent and anyone who demands more is a grafter." Another was so fully imbued with the justice of his claim that he desired the representative of the commission to assist him in enforcing the collection of an unpaid so-called commission.[12]

The FTC notwithstanding, it seems that not only do commercial operators accept many of these practices as routine but the general civic culture also assumes that many of these bribal practices (that is, introducing factors unrelated to the quality of the product into the process of determining the outcome of the transaction) are integral to the working of the commercial system.

Almost from its inception, the Federal Trade Commission

sought to end such practices.[13] Curiously, it was the federal courts, to which appeals were sometimes taken, that often took a more tolerant view. Thus, when the FTC charged a company with "lavishly giving gratuities, such as liquor, cigars, meals, theater tickets, and entertainment, to employes of customers as an inducement to influence their employers to purchase or to contract to purchase . . .",[14] the Court of Appeals disagreed with the commission, holding that there was no public interest involved and that it did not consider the practices unlawful:

> We take judicial notice of the fact that the method of entertainment found to be unfair has been an incident of business from time immemorial. . . .
>
> The payment of money or the giving of valuable presents to an employee to induce him to influence his employer to make a contract of purchase is a fraud justifying the discharge of the employee within his contract of service and perhaps the recovery by the purchaser of the amount or value of such inducement from the seller upon the theory that it must have been included in the price. But even in such a case we think it would be a matter between individuals and not one so affecting the public as to be within the jurisdiction of the Commission. . . . However, it stretches theory to the breaking point to suppose that the entertainment expenses found unfair in this case constitute fraud practiced by the respondent and by the employees on the purchasers of the respondent's goods.[15]

Courts have sometimes ruled otherwise,[16] but the fact is that a fundamental technique in the repertory of the American salesman (a genus that includes the politician, the lobbyist, the advertiser, and others) is the use of symbols and resources to create a tie of affection and its corollary of loyalty as a way of influencing the potential purchaser. The candor with which this is discussed is striking. A former sales executive for a major United States brewery comments, "The name of the game was sales, pure and simple. You did what you had to do to get the business. A lot of it was small stuff,

like an occasional free keg of beer or a case of glasses for a
guy who had a bar, but it got a lot bigger, too. If what you
were doing was wrong, well, at least you knew you had a lot
of company."[17]

The gift of friendship, of a ready ear, of more tangible
things—women, alcohol, drugs, money, vacations—creates a
coordinate obligation that can be discharged only by purchasing the product. From 1968 to 1973 Herbert Grueter
sold airplanes for Boeing. In an interview with the *Wall Street
Journal* [18] he, along with J. E. Prince, a senior vice-president
for Boeing, discussed the use of "gifts" in the selling of
airplanes. "People-to-people contact is the way Boeing
'bribes' customers," said Mr. Grueter. "I don't mean to say
'bribery'—I mean winning people over." Mr. Grueter went on
to describe the caprice of the head of a major European
airline: he wanted to shoot a grizzly bear. Boeing set up the
trip and the airline executive got his bear. Mr. Grueter added,
"We would have tied up a bear for him if that was necessary
to get a grizzly." Boeing officials confirm that fishing and
yachting expeditions for airline customers are common. John
Wayne's yacht, *Wild Goose,* was once hired for such entertaining, but Mr. Grueter says the "100-foot boat wasn't
adequate for Boeing's purpose." Mr. Prince concurred with
many of Mr. Grueter's comments and added, "I don't think
we've done any more (entertaining) than the average American business."[19]

In some cases, such gifts, rather than being used as purchase inducements, become the currency of the actual business transaction.[20] Bribe-giver and bribe-receiver are engaged
in a private business in which values that each will keep
(subject to deductions for "overhead") are exchanged. The
formal business is no more than a cover and, perhaps, in a
deeper sense, an excuse to engage in the *real* transaction.

Fidelity to the postulates of our myth system should
prohibit these transaction indulgences, for they are usually
beamed at individuals charged with the responsibility of

purchasing the best quality product for some larger group:[21] the function of the transaction indulgence is to introduce something unrelated to the quality of the product as a factor in the procurement decision. The less distinguishable or less distinguished the product (the program, the candidate, whatever) from its competitors, the more decisive the "salesmanship" component. This business style is legitimated and diffused through our culture: pop but nonetheless serious analysis and instruction are devoted to the art of presentation of self ("winning friends and influencing people") in which personal attributes unrelated to the quality of the manifest object of the transaction are supposed to be skillfully used to influence the outcome of the transaction. Training and promoting presentation-of-self skills is a large and respectable American industry increasingly translated and exported to other modernizing countries. Moreover, the costs of granting many business "favors" are viewed as ordinary and routine business expenses that may be deducted from gross income for tax purposes. While there is no public record of outright bribes being allowed, the Supreme Court has permitted kickbacks to be deducted; trade commissions, of course, are as American as apple pie.

There are quantitative limits to this type of licit bribery; the limits are functional and contextual and some extensions can be rationalized. At different levels of the business hierarchy an entertainment allowance will be used to secure food, theater tickets, drugs, sexual pleasures, but the presumed limits of even a lusty appetite provide guidelines for regulators, for example in the Internal Revenue Service. More lavish gifts, such as vacations in posh resorts or corporate hideaways, can be disguised as "seminars." I suspect that even though disguises and euphemisms are used here, there is no sense of law breaking.

Disguises and euphemisms are used to conceal related practices that are probably recognized by their practitioners as unlawful "business necessities." Direct payments to a corporation purchaser, the understanding that a Department of Defense purchasing officer will be hired upon his retirement by the corporation he is ostensibly dealing with at arm's length, or that the son or daughter of a generous contributor will be admitted to the university despite an insufficiently competitive academic record are qualitatively different from the preceding examples. But both involve passing an initial, threshold decision: *transaction indulgences, despite their violation of the myth system, are lawful.* The point of emphasis here is not that the magnitude of the indulgence to a customer or his agent is limited, but rather that our system of law tolerates and facilitates through the device of the licit business expense the practice of transacting business not by exclusive reference to the quality of the product or service but by reference to essentially unrelated personal favors.

The subgroup of merchants has had a culture and cognitive universe all its own with doctrines of secrecy and codes for dealing with different classes that nonmerchant cultures—agrarian or pastoral—viewed and still view as essentially dishonest and exploitative. Even before the full growth of capitalism and the development of the myth of the free market, the Mediterranean merchant revealed many of the traits of the modern businessman:

> The Mediterranean merchant, as he appears in the records, was interested in the acquisition of wealth and cultivation of thrift. He relied upon his own intelligence, but was careful to enlist the support of superior authorities. He was respectful of legal regulations and yet determined to evade them whenever necessary. He was enterprising and adventurous but also cautious and conservative. He invoked the protection of his deity for each of his transactions, but was bent upon pursuing predominantly worldly purposes. He was loyal to his native country but itinerant in his thoughts and actions, always seeking to expand his field of operations. And while he was ever ready to outwit his competitors from abroad, he was yet acutely conscious of the fact that a certain degree of international

cooperation was indispensable for the success of most of his ventures. In other words, the members of the multinational merchant class whom we encounter in this period were not only similarly endowed and oriented but showed themselves to be also similarly ambivalent in their efforts to reconcile their personal predilections with the normative systems prevailing in their respective communities. For since the latter were in their basic premises alike, as we have seen, they presented merchants with the same type of contradiction between freedom and authority, will and law, and autonomy and cooperation. This coincidence explains, in turn, why Mediterranean traders discovered in their several nations similar synthetic formulae for the satisfaction of conflicting motivations. For example, the religious prescriptions against usury were generally circumvented by disguising interest in one way or another, or by not mentioning it at all in writing; and governmental penalties against smuggling and piracy were evaded by dissimulating the nature of the particular transaction and the identity of the persons involved.[22]

With the demise of the theory of the collaborative market and the myth of *justum pretium* (just price) and the slow consolidation of the myth of the general benefits to be derived from competitive self-interest in a free market system, many of the vocational traits of the merchant would appear to have crystallized into something quite distinct from the more general civic culture of the emerging nation-state. In industrial civilizations, where the commercial myth becomes a dominant part of the general myth, and in systems where there is easy interchange between wealth and power elites, these values are transferred to the power arena. As governments increasingly extend their control over more and more sectors of social life, rather than bringing new practices into their commercial operations, they readily adopt many of the existing commercial practices.

Recent revelations concerning government meat inspectors in New York City, federal grain inspectors in fifteen states, and large parts of the Medicaid program show the extent of United States government-related commercial bribery and abuse. In New York, the FBI reported "there was an organized—almost routine—system of payoffs"[23] at many of the meat packing plants in the city and suburbs. In 1976, federal grand juries were nearing a vote on bribery indictments that could implicate more than one-third of the New York area's 200 meat inspectors as well as fourteen area supervisors.[24] In the grain scandal, which spread to fifteen states,[25] the situation became so extreme that one could almost quip that the payments complied with local standards.

Medicaid abuses are apparently also rampant. In 1976, Joseph Ingber told the Senate Special Committee on Aging, "Everybody's cheating and everybody's bragging about it, too."[26] The committee's investigation concluded that " 'rampant fraud and abuse exists' among the doctors, dentists, chiropractors, pharmacists and other health professionals participating in the Medicaid program, matched by an equivalent degree of error and maladministration by (federal and state) government agencies."[27]

In the rash of corporate disclosures by United States-based multinational corporations (MNCs), during the past two years, almost three hundred companies have confessed to making "questionable overseas payments."[28] "Since such payments . . . are made in the hope, if not actually with the promise, of favors in return, they may more bluntly, and more precisely, be called bribes."[29] Most of the reporting corporations do business with foreign governments or with companies and/or agents closely allied with their home government. Even though many MNCs claim with relative, if not absolute, piety that their payments go to agents rather than directly to government personnel, "It is blinking at reality to suppose that sophisticated aerospace managements are not aware that some portion of the fees paid to agents is used to secure favorable decisions on government procurement of aircraft and military hardware."[30]

Former Secretary of State William P. Rogers contends unconvincingly that "Bribery and payoffs abroad, in fact, are basically a problem in dealings with governments, not in company-to-company transactions."[31] The temptation to view these sorts of bribery as exotic foreign phenomena is understandable. But long before the deluge of corporate confessions, *Business Week* magazine was prompted to comment almost prophetically on the Security and Exchange Commission's investigation of questionable overseas corporate payments: "Bribery and kickbacks in international business appear so extensive that the agency could investigate indefinitely."[32] Despite their sensational nature, the highly publicized cases of multinational corporate bribery may be dwarfed by the extent of commercial bribery in the United States. In the Conference Board's *Survey of Unusual Corporate Payments,* one industrial machinery manufacturer, referring to commercial and moral standards abroad, said, "If anyone thinks that these are vastly different in other countries than they are in the United States, then that person must indeed be naïve."[33] Another executive, from a household appliance company said, "We do far less 'entertaining' of potential customers overseas than in our domestic divisions."[34] The *Washington Post* reported in June 1976 that "the amount of money secretly pocketed by American businessmen through commercial bribes and kickbacks may be as high as $15 billion a year."[35] Even the most prolific of self-confessed MNC bribers, such as Exxon, Lockheed, and Gulf, paid out, if their volunteered figures are to be believed, less than $100 million over the last *ten* years. What accounts for the difference? "For every domestic kickback case reported by the news media or taken to court, an 'infinite' number are handled without publicity or prosecution of the companies involved."[36] One source close to the SEC's belated investigation of alleged domestic corporate bribery said, "At first we were told that making payoffs was the price of doing business in some parts of the world. Then came the domestic political payments. But this is the most sinister. It is corruption at the heart of doing business."[37]

Once again we encounter double exposures. Different

specialist groups within a large culture have different values. Practices that the merchant-corporate executive might accept as the very essence of his vocation are occasionally viewed as "sharp" and "shady" practices by more general cultural standards. In periods of political realignment, demands for "regulation" of the merchants can be expected. At the same time, mediators between the merchant and the general culture, such as lawyers, might resolve the ambiguities of their own position by exhorting their clients to undertake self-reform.[38] An outstanding and most fascinating example of this phenomenon is found in Louis Brandeis's *Business: A Profession.*[39] More mundane examples can be found in judicial dicta. In the United States, recruitment to judicial roles is usually preceded by extended professional association with the private sector. Hence judges have internalized in varying degree elements of the commercial operational code while speaking in terms of the myth system. In these circumstances, accomodations between myth system and operational code are quite revealing.

Judicial attitudes toward routine "business"-type bribery are mixed. Commercial bribery may be a criminal offense, and then the judicial role is tightly prescribed. Cases in which bribery is raised as an ancillary matter can be more revealing of judicial attitudes. Often the issue is the permissibility of deducting a payoff or kickback as a business expense in income taxation. Though everyone knows that taxation can be used as a means for policing morality, few judges seem to think it should be. And from the perspective of the Internal Revenue Service, the question is not whether the payment was lawful but whether it was an "ordinary and necessary expense" in conducting business.[40] Nonetheless, tracking the cases does suggest a certain trend toward toleration of illegal practices; if they are widespread or "ordinary and necessary" for business, the tolerance will be evidenced by the courts' willingness to allow deductions for the expenses of these practices. A few selected cases will show patterns and contrasts.

In an early case,[41] the Kelley-Dempsey Company sought to deduct as business expenses bribes to gas company employees who had used harassing tactics and had prevented K-D from performing the contract. There was apparently no question about the honesty and good faith of K-D. The court refused to allow the deduction, concluding that the expenses were not ordinary or necessary.

> Is it an ordinary thing to pay out money to induce the acceptance and approval of work well done, to induce the employees of another to promptly and honestly perform the duties for which they were hired? We believe that it is not. And petitioner's witness, its president, indicated clearly in his testimony that such was his opinion; that he regarded the demands as most unusual and unjust.[42]

According to the court, the burden of proof that certain shady practices are the norm of an industry—that they are "ordinary"—rests on the party seeking to benefit from them, in this case K-D. Exactly how one shifts this burden of proof is not clear, for one is unlikely to find many witnesses, even with some sort of promise of immunity, willing to testify to participation in such practices. One would expect such reluctance to be greatest precisely when the practice was ordinary and necessary and squealers would be jeopardizing their future capacity to do business. The court implied that it would suffice to have notice of the practices or their notoriety, but then intimated a rather high standard:

> Rumors are prevalent concerning extortions, "rackets," "shake-downs," in all lines of business, but veiled hints and "understandings" cannot serve as ground for judicial notice that dishonesty, such as here disclosed, is a normal practice.[43]

Though the court indicated a willingness to entertain evidence that a practice violating the law was an ordinary business practice and hence a deductible expense, it is quite unlikely that it meant what it said. Even if the payment was ordinary, convenient, or cheaper, it was not *necessary*.

> The courts were open to it [K-D], wherein it could have proved the substantial performance of its contracts and demanded payment

therefor. Moreover, the laws of Oklahoma afforded it protection
against extortion. . . .[44]

And, indeed, the court concluded that

> to encourage the accession to demands of this sort, both morally and
> legally wrongful, by straining the common meaning of the words of
> the statute to permit such payments to be deducted as ordinary and
> necessary expenses of operating a business would be poor public
> policy.[45]

Although the principles enunciated in the *Kelley-Dempsey*
case reveal a judicial uneasiness with the possibility that
bribery, though illegal, might be an ordinary way of doing
business, the operation of the principles virtually assures the
triumph of morality. Unless the petitioner can demonstrate
that state and federal courts were in the bribe taker's pocket,
the bribe will never pass the test of necessity. In a more
profound sense, *Kelley-Dempsey* seems to say that one of the
"necessities" for a firm or individual doing business is to
participate in the maintenance and policing of the legal myth
system itself.

Kelley-Dempsey was not appealed. In a later decision, in
which the equities of the briber, if one may make this
juxtaposition, were not as great, the Supreme Court dis-
played more deference for ordinary, though not very nice,
business practices. In *Lilly* v. *Commissioner of Internal Revenue*,[46] a North Carolina optician sought to deduct payments made by opticians to the prescribing physicians who
sent their patients to them. The payments amounted to
one-third of the price charged to customers. This was a
practice forbidden in a number of states and actually prohibited by statute in North Carolina the year the *Lilly* case
was appealed to the Supreme Court.[47] Even without a
statute, the practice seemed rather unsavory if one considered the patients' ignorance and the potential incentive for
physicians to prescribe eyeglasses when they might not be
necessary.

The IRS disallowed the deductions on the ground that they "were void and unenforceable as against public policy and consequently are not deductible as ordinary and necessary expenses."[48] Lilly claimed that "since there is no constitutional or statutory provision, state or Federal, and no canon of ethics of a medical association specifically condemning this 'kickback' practice by opticians to oculists, no public policy exists proscribing such practice and therefore none is violated."[49] The tax court conceded the point but upheld the commissioner on the ground of public policy; a majority of the court reasoned that since a contract for these kickbacks would not have been enforceable in court, they were against public policy and hence not deductible as ordinary and necessary business expenses.[50] One judge dissented on the ground that revenue statutes are designed to raise money and "are none too squeamish about how the income to be taxed was realized." He contended that "the expenses incurred in carrying on of the illegal business have been generally allowed, as the purpose of the tax laws is not to penalize a business because it is one on which the law frowns." Even bribes were not deductible "on the finding that such expenditures could not be characterized as 'ordinary' or 'necessary' in carrying on a trade or business."[51]

The *Lilly* case was ultimately appealed to the Supreme Court, and the commissioner was ordered to allow the deduction unless it violated a declared and "sharply defined" national or state policy.[52] As the Court put it, "Customs and the actions of organized professional organizations have an appropriate place in determining in a factual sense what are ordinary and necessary expenses at a given time and place."[53] The *Lilly* case is in no sense a judicial affirmation of kickbacks. The Court plainly signaled that it expected law and medical ethics to change. But the case does evidence a certain cold realism about business practices and a willingness to accept the practices even when they cut pretty close to the moral and ethical bones of the national character.

Indeed, those practices may be the bones themselves. Consider the remarks of a beer wholesaler in a western city: "I've done just about everything for customers you can think of—tickets to ball games, jobs for their kids, contributions to their favorite charities, free kegs of beer for their family picnics. Individually, it doesn't come to much, but when you add it all up and multiply a couple hundred customers, it comes to plenty. Sometimes the brewery helps me out with a sales allowance, sometimes I carry it myself. . . . But hey, guys in other businesses, they do pretty much the same things. It's the American way, isn't it?"[54]

Modern Representative Government

Rule of law, representative and freely elected government, the equality of all citizens, the equality of opportunity, and public accountability are among the basic myths of our political system. While there is often substantial compliance with these myths in some sectors, the operational code in other sectors and in certain less visible phases of the political process will often diverge quite sharply from the myth.[55] Less striking than the divergence are the indications of often tacit acceptance of the way things are done by many in politically relevant strata.

Substantial sectors of our election system, for example, are still quite corrupt. Operators accept this fact and proceed with only the most perfunctory nod toward the formal law. Consider the following passage attributed to Harry Truman:

> Old Joe Kennedy is as big a crook as we've got anywhere in this country, and I don't like it that he bought his son the nomination for the Presidency. . . . He bought West Virginia. I don't know how much it cost him; he's a tightfisted old son of a bitch, so he didn't pay any more than he had to, but he bought West Virginia, and that's how his boy won the primary over Humphrey. And it wasn't only there. All over the country old man Kennedy spent what he had to buy the nomination. . . . Not the Presidency. The nomination. You can't buy the office itself . . . at least not yet.[56]

Concentration of effective competence to perform key acts is an obvious structural factor increasing bribability; hence a nomination process by a small group is comparatively more bribable than a general election by an undifferentiated mass, though even the latter is susceptible to bribery. Truman's statement is, of course, the sort one inclines to discount for B-factor. We are not, however, concerned here with its truth or degree, if any, of accuracy, but rather with the matter-of-fact distinction the informant draws between myth and practice and the apparent boundaries of the operational code: susceptibility of the nomination process to bribery but resistance of the election process to that technique. Plainly, if payments of this sort are rampant in electoral politics, the doctrine of one man, one vote has only a formalistic significance.

Just as the electoral myth of one man, one vote is challenged in operation, in a related way, myth is challenged by code in the determination of the content of laws. Harry Truman sketches a disturbing landscape:

> It's the same in every branch of Government. There are those who hold out their hand, and there are those who don't.[57] ... It was the same in the senate. There were bribes all over the place ... why, at one time or another I could have picked up a dozen fortunes.[58] ... That sort of thing happens all through politics, the fellow who holds out his hand for a little money, a little bribe. And it always takes two, the briber and the bribee and I don't know who is worse.[59]

The Tolchins' estimate of this behavior on the state level is even more sweeping. "If the Public Officers Law were enforced, and those who accepted or promised a reward in return for a vote were actually incarcerated, few of the state's legislators would remain outside prison bars."[60]

The characterization of a payment to secure a defection from a duty as a bribe rather than as something more ambiguous or even licit depends, of course, upon the relevant normative codes prevailing in the places in which the payment is evaluated. When a multinational corporation pays an agent or

foreign official for favorable legislation or a contract, it's
called a bribe or, at least, questionable payment. But when
the same company lobbies in Washington, factually similar
events will be deemed lawful and perhaps legitimately
deductible business expenses. The myth and operational
codes of different systems give different characterizations to
similar events.

Lobbying, which is usually described rather blandly as a
means of providing information to legislators, is believed by
many students to be a system that invites abuse. The extent
and routine toleration of these practices, which often cause
deviations from the myths of equality of political opportunity and representative government,[61] are attributable to
their social inobtrusiveness. They are probably integral to
the United States political system.

Bribery, understood in its functional sense, is inescapable
in lawmaking in pluralistic communities. Laws, crudely put,
tell an audience to do or refrain from doing something—or
else! It is the "or else" that is one of the distinctive components of the prescriptive process: the communication of
control intention or sanction potential to the appropriate
audience. Without this accompanying communication, the
effort at lawmaking is no more than aspiration. Positivistic
theory has always assumed that the "or else," the sanction
communication, is unitary and rather simple: the threat of
the imposition of an "evil" upon deviation from the will of
the lawmaker.[62] In fact, the sanction communication is
extremely complicated and may be as inflected, multiple, and
modular as the stratification and power allocations of the
audience to which it is directed. Consider Boss Tweed's
description of New York politics: "The fact is New York
politics were always dishonest—long before my time. . . . A
politician coming forward takes things as they are. This
population is too hopelessly split up into races and factions
to govern it under universal suffrage, except by the bribery of
patronage and corruption."[63] Contemporary scholars remark

that "although deals are denounced with regularity, they are an essential tool of the democratic process. The alternatives to 'deals' are legislation by fiat, in which a chief executive employs almost dictatorial powers."[64]

Insofar as the leadership (or part thereof) of the target audience is "persuaded," by either the promise of a new indulgence or the denial of an expected one, to use influence within the group to gain support for the new prescription, it is being bribed. Such bribes are usually accomplished discreetly, while a more conventional sanction, often of the penal variety, is incorporated in the formal prescriptive instrument and is directed to the non-elite components of the audience.

The reward, or "carrot," technique is also used *between* elite levels. Hierarchical loyalty is policed by granting indulgences to mid and low elite members that they in turn must dispense to their respective constituencies in order to retain support and public office. As the Tolchins describe it:

> Punishment for disloyalty, for "not going along" customarily involves withdrawing from the congressman his capacity to perform the services—both large and small—expected by his constituents, who soon angrily conclude: "Old Joe just doesn't seem to know his way around Washington." Conversely, the leadership's ability to help a compliant legislator runs the gamut of favors from the sublime to the minuscule.[65]

This technique of social control would be no more than "business as usual" were it not for a set of ideals about how democratic government is supposed to operate. The incorporation of these ideals in a myth system generates a persistent tension between the ideals and the actual practices of the elite.

The discrepancies between myth system and operational code with regard to representative government are not exhausted in the promotion and prescriptive functions of decisions. The myth of meritocratic recruitment of personnel for elite positions at different levels seems to fare just as badly

when checked against what is actually done and *what oper-*
ators expect to be done. Certain sectors of federal and state
service seem to be rather carefully regulated. But if one
aggregates appointive positions to include official and quasi-
official (for example, party positions on a full- or part-time
basis, which either provide direct recompense or rather obvious means to secure recompense), a substantial number of
remunerative jobs are distributed on the basis of private
loyalty systems or in return for a "service." Indeed, at the
federal level the most important jobs seem to be given out
this way.[66] Even down at the "natural democratic" levels of
our towns and small cities, kinship lines may be a fair
indication of the distribution of political office.[67]

Despite the frenzy of self-reform legislation,[68] the reported behavior of political operators would appear to indicate that their expectations are derived in large part from the
operational code. The Currie case is particularly instructive.
Dr. Currie, the former director of defense research and engi-
neering, was one of the top-ranking officials in the Defense
Department. He was also a former employee of the Hughes
Aircraft Company, the principal subcontractor on the Condor missile, then being built by Rockwell International for the
U.S. Navy. The Condor has been described as "one of those
'nice-to-have weapons,' but only if its cost was low and its
reliability high."[69] Its cost was about $1 million per missile,
and questions were raised concerning its reliability. Neverthe-
less, Dr. Currie lobbied extensively for the Condor program
and may have been the target of lobbying. He visited, against
Defense Department regulations, a fishing lodge maintained
by Rockwell International in the Bahamas.[70] Dr. Currie
admitted his error and was fined one month's pay by Donald
Rumsfeld, then secretary of defense. Despite requests from
Common Cause[71] that he be removed from any role in
decisions regarding Defense Department money and Rockwell, Currie was cleared of any conflict-of-interest violations
by Rumsfeld[72] and continued to work on the project. In the

meantime, the *New York Times* reported in June 1976 that he had "half a dozen job offers," including some from major defense contractors.[73]

Senator Thomas Eagleton called the Rumsfeld investigation of Currie "superficial"[74] and a congressional committee, created to conduct its own investigation, reported in September 1976.[75] Dr. Currie continued to wield his $10-billion-a-year budget until the change of administrations, whereupon he resumed his employment at Hughes Aircraft.[76]

The Nation-State System

Augustine characterized the "city of this world" as "a city which aims at dominion, which holds nations in enslavement, but is itself dominated by the very lust of domination."[77] A reading of the formal documents of international law conveys a different picture, one of an essentially peaceful world, composed of "sovereign and equal" states that respect each other's jurisdiction and do not intervene in one another's affairs, and in which extended periods of peace are disrupted only by exceptional episodes of war. During peaceful periods, states interact through certain institutionalized and rather gentlemanly modalities. The economic structures of the world community are comparable: national economies compete, but through the miraculous mechanism of the free market and "comparative advantage" everyone benefits.

This lovely and, even by its own terms, somewhat improbable picture is, of course, a myth. Unfortunately, the international system is, in substantial part, a war system not unlike, though not entirely similar to, Augustine's version: "a social system conditioned by high expectations of violence, experiencing enough violence, directly or vicariously, to sustain that expectation, and incorporating within its myth and folklore a cosmology of war."[78] It is this rather than the mythic picture that conditions the code of operators. Nation-states are increasingly garrison states, with mass anxiety used to mobilize for defense and for other elite objectives. The basic pattern of relations between elites of the different states is one of calculating short-term interests in cooperation with specific adversaries, with the unstated postulate that the duration of all relationships and policies is determined by "national interest."

Zakaria Mohieddin, former vice-president of the United Arab Republic, expressed the essence of the international system, as seen by the operators:

> The Game of Nations is what happens when all Nations, in their respective self-interest, pursue their national goals by means—any means—short of war. It presupposes the existence of conflicting interests even between the friendliest nations, and it assumes that many of the gains of any one nation will be at some cost to the others. A skillful player will get all he can for his own side, he will form tactical coalitions with other players in the pursuit of mutual advantages, and he will distribute the costs among the losers in such a way that no one of them will be moved to drastic counter action or to drop out of the game altogether—that is, resort to war.[79]

In this "game," it is prudent to keep a wary eye not only on contemporary enemies but even on today's friends, for they can be tomorrow's foes.

There is no need for extensive disquisition on the techniques that national elites in the global war system apply to each other.[80] It is important, however, to point out that operators, both in the covert and in the public portions of the official apparatus, condone such techniques despite their deviation from the myth.[81] Apparently the more one "knows" about the game, the greater the toleration of myth discrepancy. Thus one writer remarks on the seeming complicity of even the Senate in maintaining the code rather than the myth:

> The Government has participated in a number of war-like acts, termed "covert activities," against countries with which the United States is at peace. These activities include the use of military-type

force, bribery, and tampering with the internal politics and domestic tranquility of other countries.

Although our Constitution provides that Congress, not the President, must decide when we go to war, the President continues to assert a right to initiate such action without prior congressional approval.

Instead of removing all doubt and declaring such activities unlawful unless expressly permitted, the Senate is on its way to adopting a resolution containing a watered-down compromise that hardly changes the status quo.[82]

Bribery, which has no place in the myth system, is a routine strategy. Though it is apparently prohibited in customary and conventional international law, there is substantial reason to assume that it is one of the most frequent of covert operations undertaken by the intelligence agencies of nation-states. For there is nothing quite like having someone in the adversary's government secretly working for you. Miles Copeland, a candid, international Machiavellian, counsels, "Buy the man, not his information, it's the regularity and dependability of the pay that matters, not the amount."[83]

Bribery as a means for securing national objectives is used in high theater as well as offstage. In the United Nations, bribery assumes as many guises as it does in the United States Government. In 1976, the *New York Times* reported that Daniel Moynihan, former United States representative to the United Nations, said "he was aware his term last fall that votes on critical General Assembly resolutions were bought and sold by diplomats."[84] Major powers were not party to such transactions because they could gain support through the licit bribal techniques of loans or profitable trade agreements. Moynihan "did not find it shocking that countries engaged in bargaining and saw not much difference in whether votes went for cash or wheat. 'All countries sell their votes in one way or the other,' he commented. 'I don't find it surprising or shocking what countries do to maximize their interests.' "[85]

The vicious competitive character of the war system is not restricted to the political arena. Because all the institutional processes of the nation-state are components of its power, security may require supervision or even control over them "in the national interest." One of the results of these factors has been the use of political power abroad to secure national economic and trade advantages. One political gambit in 1976 may thus be considered a peerless macro-bribe. "Secretary Kissinger has apparently promised leaders of copper-producing nations in Africa (Zambia and Zaire) that he would try to halt the slump in metal prices generally."[86] His plan called for the stockpiling of copper. In return, the African nations reportedly offered to assist in Kissinger's peace efforts in southern Africa. In this case either the African countries used their potential political leverage to extort the economic concessions from Kissinger or Kissinger offered copper stockpiling in exchange for the African nations' cooperation.

International operators routinely and unambiguously deviate from both the tenets of the international myths of the nation-state as well as those tenets of the myth system of world trade and the beauty of competition. The dictum that trade follows the flag is culled from the operational code and not from the myth system.

The clearest example of this phenomenon is offered by the armaments industry. In the United States, the armaments industry is important not only as arms provider and developer but as a basic element in the national economy.[87] The scale of production that it must maintain to be viable and to invigorate the national economy requires the development and retention of markets abroad, markets that counterpart nations with counterpart institutions also covet. It is hardly a giant step from bribery by political agencies of our government in "the national interest" to bribery by our economic agencies for the same objectives.[88] And it can hardly be coincidence that, as J.F. terHorst remarked, "the American companies caught up in the international bribery scandal aren't selling pencils or soap or candy bars. They are marketing expensive items of advanced technology, including weapons of war, for which most of the research and development was done under government contract and with our tax dollars."[89]

A concise and I think essentially sober summary of the extent to which multinational corporations use state bribal techniques "in a customary, if not institutionalized way" is provided by Anne C. Flannery:

> In April of 1973, Harold Geneen, the chairman of the International Telephone and Telegraph Corporation, testified before the Senate Foreign Relations Subcommittee on Multinational Corporations (hereinafter referred to as Multinational Subcommittee). Mr. Geneen admitted that ITT had, on two occasions, offered $1,000,000 to the Central Intelligence Agency "to prevent the election of the late Chilean President, the Marxist Dr. Salvador Allende Gossens." Both offers were refused.[90]

According to Geneen, however, "it would appear from published reports that authorities of the U.S. Government both knew of and encouraged at that time funding of this type, by several corporations, as furthering the U.S. Government's own objectives."[91] Flannery continues:

> On May 16, 1975, an official Honduran investigation commission identified its former Economic Minister, Abraham Bennaton Ramos, as the recipient of a $1,250,000 bribe from United Brands Corporation; the bribe was paid by the huge fruit exporting company to obtain favorable tax treatment on banana shipments. The Honduran government reported that the bribe was given to Bennaton by a United Brands executive in Zurich in September of 1974. The money was traced through the Paris branch of the Chase Manhattan Bank to the Zurich office of the Swiss Credit Union.[92]
> On May 24, 1975, Elio Scotto, the chief state prosecutor of Italy, announced that a judicial inquiry was being conducted concerning charges that United Brands had given Italian government officials $750,000 between 1970 and 1974 to obtain favored treatment for

banana shipments to Italy. On May 22, 1975, the Securities and Exchange Commission announced that it had filed charges against United Brands for attempting to conceal the "true scope and extent" of the payment of bribes to foreign government officials to obtain reduction of banana export taxes. Several shareholders of United Brands have filed suit against the directors and officers of the corporation to recover the corporate funds paid as bribes to the Honduran government.

The Chairman of the Board of Gulf Oil Corporation, Robert R. Dorsey, testified before the Multinational Subcommittee that in 1966 the corporation had provided the late President of Bolivia, Rene Barrientos Ortuna, with a $110,000 helicopter. Payments of $240,000 and $110,000 were made to Ortuna's political party as well. Mr. Dorsey further testified that Gulf may have made political contributions in Italy. He also admitted that some $5,000,000 in illegal political contributions had been made abroad. Of that amount, Gulf had paid $4,000,000 to the South Korean Democratic Republican Party; $3,000,000 of these payments had occurred in 1971 after the Party's finance chief, S.K. Kim, had demanded $10,000,000. Mr. Dorsey explained to the Subcommittee that all of the payments were made through a Gulf subsidiary, Bahamas Exploration, with the knowledge of only four or five Gulf officers. In urging federal prohibition of such payments so that MNE's might resist pressure to contribute, Mr. Dorsey complained that the State Department did not help United States corporations which had such problems abroad. On May 23, 1974, Gulf shareholders filed suit against Gulf directors and officers to recover funds distributed as political payments in foreign nations.[93]

Richard W. Millar, the Chairman of Northrop Corporation, also testified before the Multinational Subcommittee. Mr. Millar disclosed that bribes totaling $450,000 were paid to two Saudi Arabian generals in 1972 and 1973. Mobil Oil Corporation has admitted making political contributions in Italy and Canada.

At an annual stockholders' meeting in May of 1975, J.K. Jamieson, Chairman of the Exxon Corporation, disclosed that its subsidiary, Exxon Italiano, had contributed to political parties in Italy and that its Imperial Oil subsidiary had made contributions to Canadian campaigns. Orin E. Atkins, the Chairman and Chief Executive of Ashland Oil, admitted at Ashland's annual meeting that

almost $500,000 in corporate funds had been paid to foreign govern-
ment officials.

The Exxon disclosure of payments to the Italian political
parties offered a glimpse into a thoroughly international
corporate episode. All the major oil companies operating in
Italy were party to the scheme, including the American
companies Exxon (Esso), Mobil, Gulf, and Chevron; the
French company Total; the British companies British Petroleum (70 percent owned by the British government) and
Royal Dutch-Shell; and the Italian state-owned company
Agip. These companies, operating through the Unione Petro-
lifera, of which they are all members, collected money to be
given to political parties—chiefly the Christian Democrats but
also the Socialists and possibly even the Communists. In
return the companies were to receive specific legislative benefits. "In some cases, the payments were calculated as five
percent of the amount the companies expected to gain from
legislative concessions."[94]

> In testimony before the Senate Banking Committee, Daniel G.
> Haughton, the Chairman of Lockheed Aircraft Corporation,
> admitted the company's long-standing practice of paying what he
> termed "kickbacks" to foreign governments in order to obtain
> contracts. He acknowledged that Lockheed had spent at least
> $22,000,000 in this manner.[95]

Popular reactions were not uniformly condemnatory. Thus
one columnist observed that "United Brands apparently
breached the standards of its industry when it bribed a
Honduran cabinet member to cut a banana tax in half, but
the bribe was morally not much different from the accepted
practice in the arms business of paying multimillion-dollar
fees to highly placed agents—fees in many instances sanctioned and monitored by the Department of Defense."[96]

It would seem unfair to ignore the probabilities of substantially positive signals that may have emanated from many
parts and levels of the federal decision process on these

matters. Some state it with certainty: "The Defense Department authorized legitimate sales commissions as part of overseas military equipment sales,"[97] and "has revealed that it is
a common practice for arms contractors to pay multi-million
dollar 'commissions' to foreign politicians to induce them to
buy U.S. weapons."[98]

The exigencies of the myth system prohibit governmental
agencies from openly supporting bribery.[99] By the same
token, the eruption of scandal requires the government to
join in the clamor of condemnation. But one dare not go too
far. The point was made with an almost eery clarity in one of
the phases of the Lockheed affair. When Japanese reaction to
disclosures of bribes threatened to lead to a cutoff of substantial contracts,[100] the secretary of defense and the
department intervened on the company's behalf.[101]

Chapter 3
Operational Codes and Bribery

"I am not a crook." – Richard Nixon

THE previous chapter documented the divergence, with regard to bribery, of myth system and operational code in three key sectors of contemporary life. There was no intention to suggest that all bribery was lawful or always lawful or that all bribery was the same. That is hardly the case. Bribery appears to flourish in certain social settings and not in others and to be viewed differently depending upon one's location and identities.[1] There are substantially different types of bribery, with different impacts on the larger social system in which they take place and different degrees of lawfulness. The operational code is a *normative* code. Like Plunkitt, it distinguishes between types of bribery, tolerating and even encouraging some while severely sanctioning others. There are three basic bribe varieties:[2] *transaction bribes, variance bribes,* and *outright purchases.* If the fact of the distinction is not edifying, it is sufficiently intriguing to warrant inquiry.

Transaction Bribes

A transaction bribe, or a TB, is a payment routinely and usually impersonally made to a public official to secure or accelerate the performance of his prescribed function. Examples of transaction bribes include the ten-dollar bill that an attorney probating a will in an American city may routinely give to the clerk to accelerate the operation, or the bribe given to a customs official on the Mexican border to move things along more rapidly. There are a number of distinguishing characteristics here. First, the payment is made not to violate a substantive norm but rather to assure the performance of the official act with dispatch. The bribe to the probate clerk is not made to "cure" some critical defect in the will but simply to save the attorney a half hour or fifteen minutes in line.[3] The clerk's "shakedown" is based on his control over the time features of the process. He can move one will from the top to the bottom of the pile, he can putter through bureaucratic "mysteries" for twenty minutes and disappear into an office for another half hour, or, if fixed appropriately, probate you in less than five minutes. Similarly, the customs official's bribe secures speed, not a variance on the law. If the importer fails to get the signal, he may find it takes three days to clear customs. Hence the popular epithets "speed money," "grease money," "vigorish," and the like.

The transaction bribe is described—sometimes euphemistically, sometimes with a tone of resignation, sometimes with an almost bemused affection—as "taking care of" an official. There is a tendency among some informants to appraise the TB as quite innocuous and to assimilate it to the "tip" or gratuity voluntarily paid as a reward *post hoc* for the satisfactory performance of a task. Some TBs are like tips in amount yet some may be quite large, for example, the custom of a 5 percent "finder's fee" to a public official who arranges for a very large contract with his government. It would appear that key distinguishing aspects of the TB are ignored if it is viewed as no more than a *nunc pro tunc* tip in a seller's market. The TB is *collected* by a *public official,* and a sanction, though often mild, is imposed for nonpayment. Hence it affects perspectives about the probity and general task performance of officials and, most important in popular governments, superordinates the official at least in the performance of that task.

Second, the transaction bribe does not "buy" the official who pockets the bribe nor does it purchase a service different from that normatively prescribed. Time is, of course, an economic commodity. The accelerated performance of a task for one member of a class and not for others gives that member an edge and, at a certain point, begins to shade into quality. But this is a subtle point, pertinent only for some TBs and not always appreciated by those involved in the transaction. In this respect, the recipient of the transaction bribe is not corruptible in the broad acceptance of the term: he cannot be "bought" and he will not do "anything—for a price." Try to get the clerk to probate a defective will. Not only will he refuse but he is likely to be quite indignant. As in most conforming behavior, fear will be an element, for the clerk would become involved in acts over which he does not have exclusive control and that are, moreover, susceptible to review. But I believe that a critical element would be the clerk's rectitude; probating a will defective in formal requirements would be wrong. Recipients of transaction bribes don't do that sort of thing. Responses such as these indicate that we are dealing not with a strictly economic event but with an event governed by a code sounding in many values beside wealth. The concrete result of a bribe may be the transformation of a political or "nonmarket" situation into a market one in which time is sold, but the process introduces many other factors.

A transaction bribe can be corrupted into something else. For example, you may give the official four times what both of you know is the going rate for a particular transaction. If the official accepts, you have transformed the operation into a different type of bribe, perhaps a down payment on a variance bribe or an outright purchase, bribe types we will discuss shortly. But if you pay the going rate, you are paying for a service that is fungible—available to any member of the public on about the same terms.

Which brings us to the third characteristic of the transaction bribe: it is a general service available to the public.

Though often effected surreptitiously, it is not secret but is discreet[4] in the sense in which we have used the term. Indeed, those who are rather unfamiliar with the operational code and know they are violating the myth system in tendering a bribe may be the ones insisting that the operation be done in almost exaggerated secrecy. A Latin American attorney remarked to me that he placed the equivalent of ten dollars, which one pays as "grease" in the passport office for passport and exit permits, in an envelope before he gave it to the clerk because, he observed with a certain self-derision, he is "overly refined." That ten dollars is divided up according to an operational tariff among all the functionaries in the office who play some role in processing the required document. There is no need to be surreptitious and, according to my informant, the clerk who takes the bribe, without being ostentatious about it, may distribute the shares quite openly.[5]

Compared to the substantial literature examining the social conditions of the types of bribery,[6] the material explaining where and why transaction bribery flourishes is quite scant. There are, as we have seen, certain features inherent in TBs: they are severable micro-acts, most often with the implicit penalty of delay for nonpayment of the bribe; the rather exclusive and effectively nonreviewable competence to impose the penalty is in the hands of the official soliciting the bribe; because the bribe does not affect the quality of the official service performed, the entire transaction is traceless. TBs tend to occur in routinized situations in which time is of recognized economic value, and the payments tend to be comparatively small.[7]

As far as I can tell, no one has undertaken the lugubrious task of actually detailing the extent of transaction bribery. To say that it is Eastern rather than Western or Latin American rather than North American might satisfy certain parochial demands but would be patently incorrect. In different societies there appear to be sectors in which TBs are acceptable according to an operational code and sectors in which they are not. The discovery of the social boundaries demarking bribal and nonbribal sectors is explored in chapter 5. But the actual extent of TB practices seems to vary according to the informant and, on inquiry, often according to what he views as a transaction bribe.

Some efforts have been made to account for the reasons that TBs flourish, but they are not always persuasive. I find the explanation of simple economics—that officials solicit these bribes to supplement low salaries—unsatisfactory. Many officials with unsatisfactory salaries apparently do not solicit TBs. The cultural explanation—for example, that TBs are solicited and paid in Indonesia for the performance of virtually every act because they are part of the culture—is like much functional anthropology, essentially truistic. Anything done anywhere is part of the culture; the examples we have used thus far should make clear that TBs, like toadstools, can pop up whenever it rains.[8] Factors such as professional esprit, structural features such as the distribution of a task among many individuals and departments rather than its concentration in one person or department, and the acuity of supervisory and control systems would appear to contribute to the low incidence of transaction bribery.

"Controllability," the relative ease and administrative cost of identifying and interdicting certain types of behavior, is probably as important a factor in decisions to criminalize certain conduct as is the degree of social harm of the conduct. We might hypothesize that the ease with which an activity can be deflected from its normative course and the ease of detection of the deflection are inversely proportional to the number of participants involved in it: the fewer people involved, the easier it is to cheat and the harder it is to discover the cheating. Compare fixing a game of jai alai to fixing a game of baseball. For obvious reasons, solo operations are more corruptible and less detectable, and TBs are often solo operations. Hence one reason they may be deemed tolerable is the comparative difficulty in arranging for the administrative control.

De minimis non curat praetor (The ruler does not bother with trifles). Because the threshold of criminalization can have a quantitative component, bureaucrats involved in transaction bribery may also have built-in incentives to keep the price low.[9] On the other hand, administrators who wish to control a pattern of transaction bribery may fractionate the activity among many different individuals and groups in the bureaucratic process, a technique that, Vaitsos reports, seems to have had some success in Latin American experience.[10] This technique will not be effective, we may assume, when the operational code tolerates TBs or when the bribers operate with determination and impunity. "Cornelius Vanderbilt and Daniel Drew each bribed New York's entire Common Council of Aldermen, including the infamous Boss Tweed, in their fight to control New York City's Harlem Railroad; they bribed the New York State legislature as well."[11] These bribes were probably of the variance rather than the transaction variety and the operation was facilitated by the prevailing environment of New York politics, where such exchanges seem to have been part of the operational code.

It is also difficult to assess exactly how deleterious, if at all, these bribes are on general public order.[12] Westerners, particularly of the middle classes, might assume that if the civil service presents itself as utterly incorruptible even though large numbers of officials do take transaction bribes, the practice will demean the image and lead to public cynicism and an erosion of expectations of authority. If, on the other hand, everyone assumes the prevalence of this type of petty corruption, it may have only the most minimal deleterious effect.[13] Where benefices are purchased in order to harvest TBs or are awarded by a monarch to key families and then transmitted intergenerationally, TBs may be said to be the very system itself. It would be incongruous to say that they are harming the system.

Another factor that can affect the level of harm is the price of the service: if it is beyond the means of certain strata, it "chills" rights to that service, that is, it effectively prevents its members from invoking the pertinent norms. It thus becomes an instrument of class reinforcement and discrimination,[14] performing a function roughly akin to the pricing of legal services in liberal democracies. But if its price is reasonable, the TB may actually facilitate invocation of a norm by a comparatively prepolitical stratum and is, thus, democratizing.[15] The economic position of the bureaucracy receiving TBs relative to that of the paying public may also be a factor. If the officials are patently underpaid, in terms of their class position, the bribes may be viewed as reasonable salary supplements and hence fair. If the bureaucratic TB-takers are popularly viewed as overpaid in terms of their class position, transaction bribes will be characterized as blood-sucking and are likely to exacerbate the latent and ever-present tensions between governing and governed, no matter how small the particular bribes may be. Under these circumstances, TBs could be rather deleterious to public order.

Variance Bribes

A second and generally more noxious type of illicit payment may be called the variance bribe. Here the briber pays not to facilitate or accelerate acts substantially in conformity with a norm but rather to secure the suspension or nonapplication of a norm to a case where the application would otherwise be appropriate. The transaction bribe is more difficult to track, for it involves no variance from the law, hence leaves few traces. A variance bribe can be tracked and thus is more dangerous and more expensive. Examples of variance bribes include

(1) payment to a customs officer, not to accelerate his performance of a lawful act but rather to allow the importation of goods that are legally prohibited;

(2) payment to a fire inspector to ignore violations of safety regulations and to certify a building as habitable;

(3) payments to an officer for a draft deferment, an early demobilization, or for a cushy assignment behind the lines.

You pay a variance bribe to make the system work for you. The payment is a bribe because a legal prescription in a particular instance is working against you and you want its operation suspended. This is a power and money-making opportunity for the official you address. In liberal democracies and market economies, politicians try to gain the political advantages of the variance bribe by enlarging their ambit of discretionary competence. For example, incumbents will defend a list of non-civil-service appointments,[16] the right to grant architectural contracts, insurance contracts on government buildings, the placing of public funds in bank accounts, and so on, for all of these decisions are discretionary. Since they are not subject to legal review, they can be used to pay off past debts or as down payments on immediate or future rewards from recipients. The more rigid the normative specification, the greater the tendency for variance bribes.

Variance bribes are often initiated by the briber to evade norms that are to be applied to a class of which he is a member. Hence they may be viewed as a much more serious departure from the law of the community than a transaction bribe. Insofar as law is viewed as a technique for securing an authorized pattern of production and distribution of values in a community, the VB frustrates the technique by and for those endowed with power and wealth. But the VB process may be complicated by other factors and may itself indicate an operational code commitment to special treatment for precisely those so endowed with power and wealth. VBs may be initiated by those in the control apparatus and become a form of extortion, as we will see shortly.

Consider a very white-collar example: a speeding ticket has been given to your son or daughter. Since this is a matter that may involve a police record, escalated insurance costs, and other unpleasantness, you "fix" it by a visit to your local committeeman. Depending on who you are or your relation to the political party represented by the committeeman, you may leave some money to "take care" of someone downtown, make a contribution to the party, or pay nothing, with the understanding that when you are contacted later, you will provide monetary or political support. The code covering this sort of variance can be quite complex and is not available to every violator. You may have to "plead" that your child is a good kid, that it is a first offense, and though some of this may be a skit that you and the committeeman act out to assuage your anxiety and to give a legal tone to what is in fact a fixing operation, part of it may involve registering the' fact that the child is not a rotten apple and that no social purpose would be served by imposing the legal sanctions.[17]

Some variance bribe contexts may take on transaction bribe characteristics. There are circumstances in which part of the legal apparatus initiates regulations you can escape only by payment of a bribe. Though you pay for what appears to be a variance, the process is so routinized that it almost amounts to a levy, which may even be deemed authorized under the operational code. Where the committeeman, for example, is an integral part of the traffic-fine decision process and police officers know that most tickets will be fixed, they will be much less restrained in resorting to that sanction; the sanction becomes a type of special tax or levy. In many commercial sectors, some argue that public regulation becomes a general form of shakedown. The regulatory code is cumbersome, they contend, and it is virtually impossible to comply with its many requirements and web of interlocking bureaucracies without self-bankruptcy. Hence the system requires variance bribes; shakedown and collection become major functions. Examples volunteered include building codes in some cities as well as customs and tax schemes in a number of developing countries.

A variance secured by a bribe need not involve a substantive violation of the law or of the operational code. Norms are often framed in general terms, appliers have a recognized ambit of discretion and it is expected that many factors will be taken into account in determining whether and how to apply them. Sometimes a variance is appropriate and available without a bribe, but bribery is quicker. In other cases the variance, though not available without a bribe, is generally deemed to be right in the circumstances. In cases such as these, the variance bribe takes on many of the characteristics of the transaction bribe.

But the real variance bribe, as its name suggests, involves a deviation from the proper application of the norm, accomplished surreptitiously, by illicit payment or by a money substitute. Two types of variance bribe can be distinguished. First, and more common, are those bribes that effectively suspend the proper application of an already prescribed or existing norm. Second are bribes intended to transform or change in an unlawful way, rather than merely to suspend, existing community norms.[18] Examples of the first type include paying meat inspectors not to inspect meat, or paying[19] grain inspectors to ignore or simply not to examine the discrepancies between the amount billed and the amount of grain actually shipped.[20] Other examples of the first type include bribes to legislators or other effective operators designed to ensure special treatment.[21] These payments, often exchanges of cash for political influence, circumvent or suspend the proper application of an entire range of prescriptions, ranging from the procedures for awarding of contracts[22] to the introduction of special bills[23] to the auditing of a company's tax return.[24]

The second type of variance bribe is characterized by the injection of bribery into the process of creating community norms. This occurs both domestically[25] and internationally.[26] When a multinational corporation bribes an official, whether directly or through a sales agent, in order to win a specific contract,[27] the corporation has suspended the existing commercial norm of fair competition. But when a multinational corporation bribes an official, whether directly or through a sales agent, in order to influence general legislation, the electoral process, or the entire constitutional order, we encounter the second type of variance.[28] Whether this type of payment is criminal will depend upon the local norms for legislation. These types of variance bribe are interrelated and the distinction between the two is sometimes unclear.[29]

In contrast to the transaction bribe, the variance bribe is a special product, not a fungible like a TB. As such it distorts the prescriptive program of the community in serious ways. In the short run, it is used to evade the application of norms to events for which they were designed. In the long run, variance bribes tend to reshape the general system in a process worth close attention.

Variance bribes begin as deviations from the prescribed norms of the community. They are secured by tendering a private favor or payment to the official charged with applying the law. The process of variance bribing may institutionalize itself over time and become a legitimate coordinate or even dominant process of authoritative decision. One example of this particular transformation is encountered in the development of equity jurisdiction alongside the common law courts in the English legal system. Though a review of this genealogy is irreverent, it is very instructive in the context of our discussion.

The Curia Regis, the King's Council, was the source of most of the decisions that developed the key institutions in the English system. One of the earliest institutions was the King's Bench, a network of courts that applied law according to a comparatively coherent and fixed code (derived in part from past judicial decisions). If the litigants were dissatisfied with the decisions of the King's Bench, they might turn to the king himself for a special discretionary justice that would set aside the accomplished (and later the anticipated) decision of the King's Bench. As more and more litigants sought variances from the decisions of the courts, the workload was shifted from the king to another official in the Curia Regis, the chancellor.

Now we may assume that the chancellor's dispensation of discretionary justice was given in return for a payment of some sort to the king's treasury or to the chancellor himself or, most plausibly, to both. In other words, the chancellor's was initially a system of variance bribes; indeed, a basic norm of this system was that certain variances could be purchased from the king himself. Over time, however, the chancellor's workload increased to the point where a bureaucracy for processing variance bribes was generated, ironically taking the form of a complementary system of tribunals alongside those of the common law courts. These chancery courts, whose origin was in a variance bribe system, gradually acquired a legitimacy no less than that of the king's original courts. Legitimization proceeded to the point where the bribe system was totally and openly integrated into the official system.[30] Those who take exception to the seamy origin of equity would do well to recall Freud's mordant observation that "neurotics and many others, too, take exception to the fact that *inter urinas et faeces nascimur.* . . ."

Initially, the chancery system outranked the common law courts. However, over time a system of coexistence and sharing of jurisdictions was established. Expectations crystallized, and both litigants and judges understood a rather complex code according to which some matters lay within the competence of the chancery courts while others lay within the competence of the common law courts. It was no longer accurate to say that one secured relief from common law courts through repairing to the chancery courts. Rather there were two systems of justice that interacted and overlapped to some extent but for the most part lived in accommodation.

The West African republic of Liberia[31] presents a variance bribe system that is authoritative but far less institutionalized and legitimized than common law and equity. For historical reasons that cannot be thoroughly explored here, Liberia's decision structure is made up of many comparatively autonomous components. Along the coast, an area quite influenced by Western European political traditions, one finds the system of courts and executive agencies roughly comparable to those found in the English and American legal system. But inland one encounters a system of tribal councils, often under the domination of a single figure, the chief. In Monrovia during the long administration of President Tubman, a type of equity jurisdiction developed. According to observers, many individuals who had the option of seeking the aid of the authorized courts or the official apparatus of government might nonetheless turn directly to President Tubman for a special type of justice—a discretionary justice rendered directly by the president. This justice was generally deemed to be superior, in terms of effective power, to the courts, though ironically it was a system of justice whose dictates were not deemed to survive the death of the president. Tubman justice may be viewed as a type of variance bribe system in its early stages.

If the Tubman system became institutionalized, we would begin to encounter a phenomenon roughly like that of the chancery- common law jurisdiction in England. There are similar examples in American cities where a certain allocation of jurisdiction is effected between the official apparatus—for example, the mayor's office—and the unofficial, effective apparatus—for example, the boss's machine.[32] An operator there could tell you for which matters you went to the boss and for which to the mayor, much as his ancestor could have told you when to repair to Rome and when to Constantinople.

A similar, although nonjudicial, example of the institutionalization of a variance bribe system is provided by the contemporary macro-political bribe. It is often thought that a bribe of, say, $1.1 million paid by an American aviation company to a foreign official is for the private account of the foreign official. Indeed, this may be the case, though it would seem implausible in most countries in which such bribes have been reported. In some countries a secondary structure of organization based upon party membership, political order, or, in some circumstances, tribal or kin-group membership overlays and interpenetrates the formal government at many points. Frequently the payment of the supplementary salaries from the general treasury of the party, the political order, or similar sources may be a reward for those who are members of these groups, a necessary cost-of-living increment in inflationary situations, or, as a result, a technique of internal control.[33] Funds for these supplemental salaries very often come from supplementary payments made by outsiders who seek special favors or variances from the government.

Consider the following example: an enterprising businessman in a small Latin American country would like to secure the exclusive dealership for an American automobile. He pays the equivalent of $100,000 to an official in the ministry of commerce and in return is granted the dealership for a period of twelve months. There is, of course, a regular license fee payable at a twelve month interval. The businessman must then regularly pay the official license fee as well as the supplementary $100,000 under-the-table bribe to the official on an annual basis.[34] The $100,000 paid to the official, we will often discover, is not for the private account of that official but is in fact transferred to party coffers or to the coffers of a smaller group that is using the government as a base of power. The money is thereupon divided up.

Many reported cases of very large bribes paid to individuals in developing countries would appear to be most plausibly construed as payments to mediators or operators; substantial parts of the funds are then distributed within the country and in some circumstances injected directly into the official apparatus of the government. They may well be reprehensible, but they are not *private* bribes paid to those individuals themselves, though agents can be expected to skim for themselves.[35] Skimming itself may be subject to a normative code that sets limits and indicates sanctions for excessive greed.[36]

In a formal sense the briber's scheme in the receiving country would seem to be wholly illegal. In fact it may be part of a thoroughly internalized operational code and indeed may itself be in the process of legitimization and incorporation into the general myth system. In many developing countries legislation in the early days of independence has been either mimetic of the metropolitan or promiscuously romantic. Even in the so-called developed countries, legislative ardor may exceed enforcement intentions or abilities. As a result, the laws themselves are or become unrealistic and inapplicable and almost demand a tempering and bending. For example, country X may provide salary limitations for high public officials that runaway inflation has made unrealistically low; everyone in the country who is politically aware recognizes that additional sums will be required. Such sums are usually provided by the political party of the high official.

The technique of payment of supplementary salaries gives the party a high degree of effective control over the official, for the power of the purse means that an official who is expelled from the party will find continued participation in government financially impossible. Funds for the payment of these supplementary salaries will regularly be gathered through contributions as well as through a secondary transaction or variance bribe system such as the one just described. Like all components of the operational code, the salary-supplement system is very susceptible to abuse. When all the rationalization is scraped away, it may be exposed as a mean and self-serving scheme: no more than an annuity plan or a get-rich scheme for party regulars or an instrument for maintaining vertical discipline.

Where the technique of variance bribes is integrated into the basic authority structure of the receiving state, it would be as perverse to construe the tendering of bribes there as unlawful as it would be to construe plea bargaining in the United States as unlawful. The practice may, of course, violate policies expressed in the local myth system or in some transcending code of values. The variance bribe can hardly be called socially progressive. If natural law, as Stammler put it, has a "variable content," popular welfare objectives might almost be characterized as a natural law demand of governments in this century. Theoretically, Robin Hoods of bribery may exist, but in relatively few cases will the VB system benefit broad strata of the population.

To say that bribery is lawful under the operational code is not to say that all aspects of bribery transactions are lawful. The secrecy with which bribery is accomplished creates multiple opportunities for ancillary delicts. Any system in which large sums are transferred under a skimpy record-keeping system invites skimming, diversion of a percentage of those funds by the transferring agent for his own account. I believe that the extent of skimming has been exaggerated. But even when it occurs, the mere fact that particular transactions may themselves be infected with illegality under either the operational code or the official myth system does not necessarily invalidate or render unlawful the entire transaction.

I suggest that most people would tend to treat as a lawful bribe one tendered to representatives of an institution who are well advanced in the process of institutionalizing a variance bribe system. The corollary of this criterion holds that bribes tendered at the earlier stages of the deterioration of an institution are likely to be viewed as unlawful insofar as the viewer internalized the values and the authority structures of the system undergoing deterioration; paradoxically, the viewer might even prefer the values of the new system on the horizon.

Harold Lasswell has hypothesized that effective power

tends to make itself more authoritative, and it appears that a variance bribe system that bureaucratizes will recruit, reward, and shape different personalities who may then seek respect and legitimacy even though this erodes the real economic commodity on which the variance bribe trades. Variance bribe systems institutionalize when

(1) They enjoy overt or tacit support at the pinnacle of the power process;
(2) the volume of variance business is large; and, as a result,
(3) a bureaucracy must be developed to process the volume.

In the absence of any of these elements, the variance bribe system will remain ancillary to the official decision-making system, acceptable, perhaps, under the operational code but not under the myth system.[37]

The legitimization of the variance bribery system thus paradoxically invites the development of a new variance bribe system.[38] Insofar as discrepancies in the distribution of authority and of effective power develop, additional variance systems will develop. We can hypothesize that the propensity for the institutionalization of variance bribe systems will increase in rough commensurance with the increasing discrepancy between authority and effective control; we might refer to this, for convenience, as *unauthorized change*. As a corollary, we can assume that the propensity for the institutionalization of VB systems

(1) will increase with the radical or discontinuous character of unauthorized change,
(2) will increase when the changes are initiated by a counterelite,
(3) will decrease when the changes are initiated by authoritative elites in accordance with authorized procedures.

Variance bribes, whatever their degree of institutionaliza-

tion, perform a variety of social functions, some of which
may be positive. V.O. Key suggests that this sort of bribery
may achieve provisional accommodations between groups
with dissimilar and incompatible moral codes:

> The stream of puritanism encounters powerful opposition from
> masses with different standards of behavior and from those who
> profit by catering to their tastes. Sentiment wavers. The newspapers
> and the churches "turn on the heat" occasionally. The community
> as a whole takes a hypocritical attitude. In this state of indecision
> and conflict the system of police graft makes possible prostitution,
> gambling and other practices. It serves in a way to "regulate"
> control, license and keep within bounds practices which are beyond
> the law. They cannot be controlled through the forms of law.[39]

Key also suggests, less persuasively, that such bribery may
have facilitated or accelerated beneficial social changes.[40]
This, however, would appear to be an accidental feature. The
quality of the change depends, of course, on the preferences
of the observer. VBs may also accelerate social dysfunctions
if evaluated from a different set of social goals.

Those who want to believe that VBs are good for the
system are Panglossian or are defining system only in terms
of those elites actually involved in the variance bribery.[41]
VBs are real violations. First, they violate the expectations of
those people who believe in the laws that are being subverted.
They also violate the basic rules of the market, which, in our
civilization, are supposed to police quality and control price
in the interests of consumers. But in circumstances in which
the laws being violated are not related to market mechanisms,
the noxious quality of VBs may be somewhat diminished.

If you are playing a variance bribe game, you ascribe
utility to particular laws, not in terms of whether they
contribute to community weal but whether they permit you
to demand variance payoffs without impeding indispensable
social and political functions. Hence the VBs should flourish
where the salient laws were created for no other purpose than
to generate a market for variances. For example, one informant claims that some safety regulations for elevators in a

particular American city are, for all intents and purposes, unfulfillable. Even if compliance could be secured, scarcely any real increment of safety would result. Every elevator in town is in technical violation; when the inspector comes around he is paid to overlook it. (He will not overlook a real violation that does, in fact, jeopardize elevator riders.) The law in question may not have been created to generate a variance market, but that is its only function now.

In a larger organizational sense, the VB may, indeed, be said to perform a *homeostatic* function, easing social conflicts caused by rigidification of formal structures discrepant from the distribution of effective power. This can be viewed as a *positive* social function only from the most sterile organizational standpoint. The statement that an organization or a person survived tells us very little, for every entity always has some range of options for realizing a certain preference, each with a different cost-benefit constellation. Which options, with their unique costs, are rejected and why are the critical questions, from the standpoint of both organizational and moral theory. In this regard, one should note the very special costs of the variance bribe and why, paradoxically, an authoritative elite itself may encourage resort to it.

At one point in the Watergate affair, Richard Nixon is reported to have sighed, "Where will it all end?" The variance briber buys a service, but pays a larger and more continuing price than he may realize. The briber has done something often traceably unlawful, and at least one person in the official apparatus is privy to the fact; since the variance may have required the cooperation of other officials, the briber's actions may be known to quite a few people. The briber is, in some sense, a captive of the process he has subverted;[42] what he may have envisaged as a single transaction contains the kernel of a continuing association.[43] In general, he is likely to become reluctant to criticize corruption and may, in some circumstances, undergo general political paralysis.

From an elite perspective, anxiety is a preferred form of

social control, for it is economical and quiet. A ruling group may decide that it is in its own interests to encourage a degree of variance bribery, tracking and recording it, but not policing it. In India, for example, an informant reports that businessmen secure variances for private payment, only later to discover that the government knows this has been done; thereafter, the businessmen may be committed to support the government in monetary and other ways. Once this pattern is appreciated by businessmen, they will assume that their variance bribes are known to the government and behave accordingly. If the normative code and the bureaucracy are so complex as to require variance bribes in order to stay solvent, some strata may discover that there is virtually no evading this form of anxiety control.

In Iran I was told by a number of informants that the shah is believed to encourage bribery and corruption; but SAVAK, his secret police, keeps track of the corruption and leaks its activities. This knowledge thus becomes a subtle form of intimidation and police control.[44] A cognate and intriguing example is reported by Rebecca West in a study of treason and espionage. She observes that most non-Soviets who engage in espionage for the cause recruit themselves for "ideological" reasons; they do not seek monetary reward and are insulted when it is offered. Nonetheless the KGB's practice is to press payment, which may be intended as a potential instrument of blackmail if the volunteer should molt his ideology at a later stage.[45] The point is that where the transaction bribe may promote the sharing of power, the variance bribe may be used to paralyze political participation and to increase the concentration of power.[46]

The Outright Purchase

A third distinct type of bribery is the *outright purchase*, not of a service but of a servant. Here the objective is *not* to secure the performance of a particular act, but rather to acquire an employee who remains in place in an organization to which he appears to pay full loyalty while actually favoring the briber's conflicting interests. Every personality is a bundle of selves and no civil servant is without some loyalties to groups and individuals distinct from the official apparatus that employs him. The shift of loyalties is facilitated in modern society by the transitory character of loyalty itself: we are trained to generate intense but temporally limited loyalties to each of the series of "teams" we are members of through life.

OP does not refer to circumstances in which an official leans or tilts toward one faction in his exercise of discretion or perhaps leaks information to the press to aid or defeat a policy. Nor does it refer to the practice common in America and in some European systems according to which a civil servant or, let us say, a judge is appointed as and is known to be a machine or party man whose decisions are expected to reflect this loyalty and dependency. The outright purchase is a distinct concept, though it is blurred by the fact that it may be accomplished in a series of incremental and less visible operations, or through tacit promises of subsequent employment by the party with whom you are supposed to be at arm's length.

The term *conflict of interest* is often a euphemism for outright purchase bribes. In the United States, a public official's manifest loyalty is to the public. Where a public official works secretly for a special interest, whether a corporation, foreign country, or whatever, he has breached the public trust and can theoretically be severely sanctioned.[47] The current focus on conflicts of interest in the regulatory agencies and the legislative and executive branches of the United States government[48] is probably due to the uncertainty as to whether public officials are merely leaning or tilting toward one faction or special interest in a particular case, or whether some public officials may have actually sold themselves or have been purchased by special interests.

Though an outright purchase may be aided by ideological or kin ties, its core, regardless of prior conditions, is the surreptitious shift of service loyalty, for all or some purposes, to someone different from the manifest authority.[49]

The outright purchase is a widespread practice. Popular accounts of espionage have given currency to the official who is "turned," bought, or blackmailed into staying in place and from that position provides information or other services for his hidden principal or purchaser. Perhaps the most graphic account of the method of OP is supplied by Agee:

> Liaison officers [of the CIA] make money available to officers of the local service and it is expected that the local colleague will pocket some of the money even though it is supposed to be strictly for operations. The technique is to get the local police or intelligence officer used to a little extra cash so that not only will he be dependent on the station for equipment and professional guidance but also for personal financing.
>
> Security officers such as police are often among the poorest paid public servants and they are rarely known to refuse a gift. Little by little an officer of a local service is called upon to perform tasks not known to anyone else in his service, particularly his superiors. Gradually he begins to report on his own service and on politics within his own government. Eventually his first loyalty is to the CIA. After all, that is where the money comes from.[50]

Though the OP paradigm assumes distinct competing organizational structures, OP can occur within single organizations, in which organs, departments, even kin groups maintain comparatively discrete identifications. In the United States government, for example, the Joint Chiefs used an ensign assigned to a clerical position in the National Security Council to keep tabs on Henry Kissinger, then assistant for national security affairs. Informants have assured me that similar cases abound in corporations and even at the lower levels of commerce. A jobber, for example, may buy "into" a clerk in the employ of a distributor he uses with the expectation of receiving information, preferred treatment, or collaboration in stockroom thefts. By the same token, the outright purchase may be used by a government or a party to retain the loyalties of civil servants and politically relevant constituents in systems with minimal common identification and loyalty. In this country, machine politics is a control system that basically uses the outright purchase bribe.[51]

The utility of having a man "on the inside" hardly requires amplification,[52] but a word on the varying techniques of recruitment is necessary. In some settings, as Copeland asserts, the civil servant himself goes in search of a client.[53] Evelyn Waugh recounts the amusing case of one Wazir Ali Bey, who sold his information and loyalty, on an exclusive basis, of course, to every correspondent in Addis Ababa.[54] In other cases, as Agee has shown,[55] the client cultivates the official either by direct offer or, as we have seen, by somewhat more subtle techniques of entrapment.[56]

The consideration for services performed by an OP may vary from money and money equivalents[57] to promises of future indulgence, for example, a visa, a secure position in the company upon retirement from the government or the military, and the like.[58] Some OPs are recruited by threat and blackmail, but this involves techniques not considered in this essay.

Some patronage in American machine politics is an institutionalized system of outright purchase bribery, distinguished from some of the other examples only by the comparative openness with which it is conducted by politically relevant strata.[59] Favors are distributed by elites to officials and constituents as a means of creating and sustaining loyalties. Patronage is presumably necessary when (1) symbols alone will not generate sufficient loyalty, (2) spontaneous perceptions of common interest are low, and (3) coercion is deemed uneconomical or impractical. Patronage is the insider's bribe or outright purchase and it may be viewed by its practitioners as prophylactic to potential OPs from outsiders. Hence Boss Hague's apothegm that an honest man stays bought.

Machine politics is not always a nasty phrase in America; many who identify with the strata that benefited view machine practices with a certain nostalgic warmth.[60] In strict organizational terms, this system works, though it probably has an inherent inflationary dynamic.[61] Alas, it is a system with little potential for the authoritative control of power. A frightening current example is found in Idi Amin's regime in Uganda, a machine system in which supporters are created and sustained by pork, not from wealth accumulations of the state, the proverbial pork barrel, but from the living flesh of Leviathan.

Operational Distinctions

The Knapp Commission and the Nadjari operation in New York City distinguished early on between different violations of the myth system. The fact that judgeships were purchased was not corruption if the purchaser was seeking respect or opportunities for community service. But if he was buying a place at the bench to make money, he was corrupt. A cop who was taking the small bribes that many officers seemed to accept was distinguished from the one who was selling significant variances or providing information for the mob.[62] The small fry might be threatened with prosecution in order to make them cooperate in the investigation of the larger malefactors, but the small fry and their activities were not the major targets of the commission.[63] All bribery was, of course, illegal. Though it was not expressed, distinctions between lawful and unlawful bribery were being drawn, indicating that the community agents and the bribers shared some parts of an operational code.

It is interesting and revealing that in both SEC and Senate subcommittee confessionals the major sin corporations are admitting is transaction bribery or succumbing to extortion or whitemail. No one confesses variance bribes and *no one* confesses outright purchases. Perhaps our corporations are, as they claim, only TB bribers. But there are grounds for skepticism. Undoubtedly counsel have advised their clients that VBs and OPs may invite antitrust and criminal prosecutions, whereas TBs can be defended as no more than compliance with local standards and, in any case, are matters of limited materiality to investors. But I believe that the uniformity of self-characterization reveals a distinction drawn in the operational code: some bribery violates even the operational code.

TBs seem to have minimal effects on the working of the system. VBs do in fact change systems by aligning formal law with effective power. They also increase elite control by generating manageable anxiety. OPs undermine a system by penetration and infiltration. Of all the bribe categories, OPs require secrecy rather than discretion. And of all the categories, OPs elicit the most severe sanctions. In all this seamy behavior, they stand out as an ultimate betrayal and are most likely to be deemed unlawful under the operational code. But lawfulness, like beauty, is in the eye of the beholder and the normative content of his moral universe, a matter we have yet to consider.

Chapter 4
Campaigns against Bribery

> *"Warrington Trently, this court has found you guilty of price-fixing, bribing a government official, and conspiring to act in restraint of trade. I sentence you to six months in jail, suspended. You will now step forward for the ceremonial tapping of the wrist."*
>
> — Lorenz, *New Yorker* cartoon

AT first glance, it appears as immobile as stone. In fact, there is an enormous amount of energy in that apparently inert pencil on the desk. To compute the energy consumed in the production of an implement such as a pencil, you must include some fraction of all the energy expended in planting and tending the forest from which the wood came, the energy consumed in designing and fashioning the tools and machinery used to cut and process the wood, to transport it, to find and process the graphite, and to establish and maintain market structures. A comparable computation must be made in measuring the coercion concealed in an apparently consensual and peaceful social relationship. There is a common tendency to assume that what exists is peaceful. It is change that is violent. But what appear to be voluntary and spontaneously regenerating relations may be conditioned by coercion; many of these relations rest upon a variety of institutional practices that use high levels of coercion in order to maintain themselves.

The operational code is one technique for maintaining social order. Those comparatively more skilled in the forceful techniques of influencing have created and are maintaining a given social order because they believe, on a conscious as well as deep unconscious level, that on balance it fulfills their own interests and the interests of those with whom they identify. The conclusion that certain practices no longer serve those interests or a redefinition of those interests, perhaps through the replacement of an elite group by another with different goals, may lead to changes in the operational code.

Dieting, "kicking" smoking, integrating, changing language, lifestyle—human beings can change themselves and others. Some changes are comparatively simple and may muster substantial voluntary support. Others are expensive and violent and some may require the radical transformation or even destruction of the group. Changes of this last type are usually eschewed by those charged with evaluating potential decisions; they can be expected to conclude that the prospective cure is worse than the evil it addresses. The point of emphasis is that change is no more and no less possible than stasis, for despite their nominal polarity, they refer to the use of the same social instruments and the same techniques.

Campaigns to change bribery practices take two forms. One, by far the more common, is the "crusade" against corrupt practices. It is a highly open and often ostentatious elite-initiated or elite-coopted campaign that may publicly humiliate or penalize some elite members but does not change the basic power structure, the composition of the elite, or their fundamental practices. The social significance of its sound and fury lies in the popular catharsis and reinforcement of the myth system that result; its political significance lies in the reinforcement of the elite. Its instruments are *lex simulata* and *lex imperfecta* and its results in reducing bribery or other discrepancies from the myth system are, as its directors intend, minimal. For obvious reasons, the crusading style of politics is especially prevalent in mass industrial systems in which media provide indispensable and insatiable channels. The second type of antibribery campaign is the reform. It is intended to, and does in fact, result in some changes in the operational code.

One prerequisite for an antibribery campaign is, as we have seen, a public, or a segment thereof, that views its government as popular in the derivation of its authority and as obliged to operate in accord with openly prescribed procedures. Bribery is viewed as wrong only if these preconditions obtain. In the Banfields' system of amoral familism,[1] or in any system in which the government operates by naked power against a population that has no choice but to accommodate it, bribery will not arouse disquiet, much less indignation. Within a single country, different groups may thus view bribery through entirely different lenses. In South Africa, for example, a member of the white middle class might be recruited to an antibribery campaign; a Bantu would not.

The propensity for bribery campaigns is compounded when government is not only popular but is widely deemed to be vital for the provision of security and other life opportunities. Dependencies generate anxieties. Every man has his Hobbes, who whispers in one ear that each person is by nature selfish and looks out for himself. At some level of consciousness, every human being is aware of drives for self-aggrandizement and for the ecstasies of power. The ascription of these same drives to others is one cause of anxiety. It can be assuaged by many methods. Horney, for example, suggested affection, submission, power, and withdrawal.[2]

The options of submission, voluntary dependence, and subordination—increasingly mandatory aspects of industrial life—generate latent suspicions of the real motives of the "expert" to whom one has subordinated oneself. If the expert performs, or at least appears to perform, his function, he affirms his own good faith and the trust of the temporary subordinate. If, on the other hand, he does not fulfill his function, he stirs doubts about his skills or his fidelity to his role. If physician X cures my child and I attribute remission to his intervention, my trust in physicians and their art increases. If he does not, my distrust increases.

In comparatively simple social systems, coarchicalism is

one response to the anxieties of social life. In the United States, the availability and, thereafter, the myth of the frontier provided another possibility.[3] But in complex societies and in societies tightly bounded both horizontally and vertically, there is no escape from subordinations. Even in contemporary democracy, the individual finds himself increasingly subject to a technocracy of social scientists, physicians, lawyers, psychiatrists, security specialists, and planners. Each profession jabbers a language incomprehensible to the others. (Indeed, one of its very functions may be its incomprehensibility to the uninitiated.) As long as things go well, the wisdom of the technocrats is affirmed and the very incomprehensibility of their patter is reassuring. When things go awry, popular responses to the skills of the technocrats[4] will include anti-intellectualism and know-nothingism; a key response to putative defections from fidelity to their roles will be antibribery campaigns. The period straddling the sixties and seventies was perceived by many groups as one of crisis, both external and internal, with regard to the erosion of their own social and more general value positions. In this respect, part of the intensity of public reactions to the Watergate saga may have derived from delayed anger about specialist failures. The successful Democratic campaign of 1976 played to this feeling with a very skillful blend of two leitmotifs: the breach of role fidelity and the essential inadequacy of the skills of the Washington-based technocrats. Both themes, of course, were quickly muted upon installation of the new administration.

Crusades: Affirming the Myth System

A key and indispensable figure in popular antibribery crusades is the crusader, or moral entrepreneur. At any moment, there are always some crusaders fulminating against corruption and pursuing power by promising a thoroughgoing social douche. The fact that in most cases the crusader remains peripheral to power, a cranky, somewhat ludicrous figure in folk culture, suggests that some other factor is the key variable accounting for his infrequent political successes. In cases in which the crusader is successful, contemporary or subsequent accounts will suggest that a charismatic personality was responsible. But this is itself an insufficient explanation, for charisma is an interpersonal process, with the charismatic leader requiring "charismanic" followers.[5] The question why a particular leader, at a particular moment, extends his magnetic field from a small, infatuated following to a mass audience directs the inquirer to other factors, many of which concern audience perceptions rather than attributes of the leader.

The assumption that programs against corruption derive their motive force from unorganized and untapped "honest" elements in the population is also an unsatisfactory prime explanation; these elements are as persistently present as bribery itself. In any group there are some individuals whose personal demands for rectitude are extremely high, who "cannot tell a lie," who experience the most intense dysphoria if they or others deviate from the myth system. The fact that crusades against certain violations of the myth system are episodic and that the violations are tolerated during what often prove to be extended intervals tends to dilute the force of the "honest folks" explanation for anti-bribery campaigns. The candidate leadership of moral entrepreneurs and the latent support of those most deeply committed to the myth system do not in themselves explain why more general popular support for crusades suddenly grows and coalesces into an effective political force.

To some extent, official responses that attempt to control bribery by themselves increase the likelihood of bribery by creating the substructure of new bribal institutions.[6] Consider the phenomenon of bureaucratic red tape. Red tape generally refers to complex and onerous systems of record keeping aimed usually at controlling the discretion of the bureaucratic process. Red tape tends to abound in those circumstances in which the general public or superiors in a bureaucratic system have lost confidence in the probity and judgment of the bureaucracy; the response is to attempt to control virtually every transaction either by dividing it among many individuals or by insisting on the most detailed record keeping. In many circumstances, red tape is a response to corruption and an attempt to control it. And yet the very complexities and time-consumption factors introduced by a red-tape control system invite enterprising people to find or bore shortcuts. In some cases, the remedies create new incentives for bribes.[7] Hence it is no surprise that systems in which there is red tape often tend to have a larger degree of transaction and, at times, variance bribery.[8]

Certain social features may support anticorruption crusades and suggest reasons for their frequency or intensity. A civilization may be rational, in Weber's sense, and hence assume that purposive interventions in the social process can succeed. Thus the popular belief that reforms will work. It may assume that the human character is malleable and hence redeemable despite the persistence of certain reprehensible traits. Tocqueville remarked on the Americans' predilection for self-correction and self-improvement, aspects of our national character that predispose many of us to believe that major reforms of ills and corrections of moral transgressions are possible.[9] One of the classics of American reform literature is E.A. Ross's *Sin and Society: An Analysis of Latter Day Iniquity,* which appeared in 1907 with an introductory letter by Theodore Roosevelt. Though Ross used the term *sin* to mean conduct causing social harm, the very choice of words like sin and iniquity evokes a world view and a morality that seem distinctively American and are an indispensable key to the millennial rhetorical styles of Theodore Roosevelt, Wilson, Bryan, Dulles, and even Carter. Yet precisely because these factors are persistent, they cannot explain the episodic character of these crusades.

Many European observers have remarked that the notion of bribery seems to arouse a much more intense anger and anxiety in our society than it does in many others.[10] Part of this reaction may derive from our popular democratic credo and resulting anger at public servants who betray our trust. Daniel Bell has written

> Americans have had an extraordinary talent for compromise in politics and extremism in morality. The most shameless political deals (and "steals") have been rationalized as expedient and realistically necessary. Yet in no other country have there been such spectacular attempts to curb human appetites and brand them as illicit, and nowhere else such glaring failures. . . . In America the enforcement of public morals has been a continuing feature of our history.[11]

But part may also derive from the deeper implications of a bribery system. As we have seen, bribery involves resort to an operational code that is understood by operators and that deviates significantly from the normative code or myth system of the larger group. For a culture that puts tremendous emphasis on social organization, on the rationality of group relationships, and on the security to be gained from knowing the rules, it is most disquieting to think that those rules are no more than myth and that there is a real set of rules one may never really know.

In a sense, recognition of bribery as part of an operational code is akin to some of the horror captured by Kafka. In *The Trial*, for example, the hero knows the formal code, which plainly no one is applying, but never learns the operational code according to which his own fate is determined. For a civilization that puts store in the security to be gained from knowing rules and a significant part of whose civic acculturation involves learning those rules, the realization that those rules are no more than mirage and that an entirely different set of principles and practices must be learned in order to secure preferred outcomes is profoundly, even existentially, frightening. Hence the tremendous unwillingness to accept the notion that there may be a different code.

Judith Shklar has suggested, in a related way, that American law puts little premium on bargaining and negotiation precisely because it involves a set of relationships for which, at least apparently, there are no rules; in contrast "going to law" involves invocation of a very clear set of principles.[12] I have no idea where Prof. Shklar found lawyers with such beliefs, for my own exposure to members of the bar leads me to exactly the opposite conclusion. Yet her observation, if inaccurate with regard to its object, may be quite revealing with regard to its subject. It may express what the uninitiated think "about" American law, the myth system. "Nowhere in the American context are ideals so firmly held and yet so consistently violated as in the legal process. The gulf is not only wider here. Its potential for stimulating outrage and a sense of betrayal when exposed is unequalled."[13] In contrast to our civilization, one may refer to a number of the expectation-sets of the ancient Greeks, which casually assumed that life was essentially disordered and that one could not expect much from faith; ultimate decisions were in the hands of the gods, who could be expected to behave most capriciously.[14] For those equipped with that sort of world view, the notion that there may be a different operational code or that the myth system has only partial, if any, application at all is much less disturbing. Thus the strong response to bribery in our own culture, even where the bribery is practiced and condoned abroad, may indicate a clash of cultures, of values, of world views.[15]

In addition, our culture desperately tries to achieve a formal separation between money and politics. Since the founding of the Republic, this has been a central and continuing tension for which there is no resolution, for it is at the very core of a democratic-capitalist society. Money is the natural form of influence in the marketplace, but it is an illicit form of influence in the democratic forum.

There are latent tensions in any collectivity that can become pronounced during purity purges. Some of these may derive from class and ethnic identification in the traditional political sense, and some may derive from the latent strain between governed and governors everywhere.[16] But these strains are always present and hence do not, in themselves, explain sudden purges.

The media in contemporary mass societies play prominent roles in purity crusades. They are an industry that requires an unending flow of dramatic material, whose appraisal can be made simple enough for the news processor as well as his audience. Bribery is made to order for the media in a democratic and stratified society. It combines affirmation of authority with the delights of attacking it. For journalists and audiences not disposed to reflection, the exposure of bribery provides a continuous morality play in which hostility to authority can be expressed and then resolved in favor of authority. But what is the overall impact?

Plainly the media are substantial influences in opinion formation and are even more important in sustaining and maintaining opinions already formed (or, alternatively, allowing them to die) by providing supporting information and authority. But how fundamental that role or whether the media are the key cause is difficult to say. Without empirical studies, I am inclined to doubt that there are substantial causal dimensions to an obvious correlation. The fact is that there are always reform sheets or tracts on sale; even in organs of more general circulation, there are regular and syndicated crusading, bellyaching, and muckraking columns and features. You can't crusade without the media, but a crusade is much more than a media event.

There are elite-stimulated crusades designed to secure limited political objectives but presented in the guise of anticorruption crusades. These tactical operations can be distinguished from popularly based anticorruption crusades because they do not secure mass popular support and often are not designed to. Rather, they are designed to cover interelite actions in which one component may seek to destroy or sever an opposing group from its constituency or, where the constituency's leadership has already been coopted or bribed, provide for the continuity of myth despite the change of personnel. While the reform may aim at a *bouleversement,* the crusade has a much more precise and limited objective. Moral entrepreneurs may seek and actually succeed in transforming crusades into reform movements, hence crusaders must always mend their fences.

The danger of losing control of a crusade often stimulates distinctive elite responses. Consider Roderick Hills, then chairman of the Securities and Exchange Commission:

> I begin my response with the fervent hope that we will not rush for new laws to require our courts to enforce all the laws of the world or to change the very nature of our corporate structure without first trying to restore the integrity of the system that has served us so well . . . ; this then, must be our primary focus: to restore the efficacy and integrity of the existing system. Until this is accomplished, we cannot ignore the proposals for drastic change of the system.[17]

These reassurances are not likely to suffice once a crusade is well under way. At that point, legislation, a system's manifest response to a problem, must of course issue, as a reassurance of systemic effectiveness and fidelity to its norms; as a catharsis for any popular agitation that may have been stirred; and as a way of preempting erstwhile moral entrepreneurs from transforming a crusade into a real reform.[18] But the legislation must be ineffective! The *lex imperfecta* and the *lex simulata,* as we have seen,[19] have as distinctive and indispensable functions in politics as do the deficit corporation and the sure-fire Broadway flop in business. Hence the legislative response of the elite will have engorged symbolic components but stunted limbs: inadequate enforcement machinery, no procedures for staffing, insufficient budget, the appointment of manifest incompetents (who also have a very special value in political systems), and so on. Programmed ineffectiveness is distinctive of crusades.

The enforcement techniques of the crusade must be symbolic, highly public, and appear to have dramatic results. They must validate the norms in question, yet must not seriously impede those practices of the operational code that are deemed indispensable to the elite. They aim at perspectives and not operations.

The symbolic is, of course, an important component of all social order. In mass societies, in which substantial parts of many people's conceptions of reality are not directly experienced but are derived from key social symbols, the symbolic grows in importance as a political base of power. Not surprisingly, more and more political struggles center on control of the formation, content, and diffusion of these symbols, for the media comprise the nerve network of modern society. The symbols and images of "reality," including enforcement, are delivered in "news reports," and indeed may be modulated as well through fictional representations.

We frequently think of enforcement as direct intervention into the behavior of those who have deviated from social norms. This is an anachronistic conception of enforcement, a vestige from small groups or the face-to-face societies of the past. In mass society, enforcement in crusades is aimed increasingly at the symbolic component. For some strata in society, the police may serve as enforcers if they are viewed on weekly TV serials. Presentation of the police as honest in the media may sometimes be as important for the maintenance of the symbolic integrity of the myth system as the actual behavior of the police. The media become the custodians of the "noble lie."

Crusade enforcement, aimed at the perspectives of the audience rather than the operations of the violators, will take a number of forms, although common to all methods is the protection of the elite and its operational code:

1. *Sound and fury*. Many cases will be initiated with full publicity, but the vast majority of them will be settled or dropped. In settlements, the defendants will be permitted to plead guilty to an often ludicrously innocuous offense. The "sound and fury" technique can generate imposing statistics, which, for all their quantity, may indicate no changes in the operational code. A crusading vice squad in City X, for example, may make innumerable and widely publicized arrests, but few cases will go to trial and fewer still to judgment.

2. *Scapegoating*. It is sometimes possible to deflect attention from real violators or from widespread violations while still affirming the norm in question by designating potential pariahs as the "real" violators. Thus, for example, Jews in the USSR or Chinese in Indonesia or the Philippines may be exposed as the perpetrators of economic crimes, when in fact large numbers of the population also violate the economic laws.

3. *Selecting downward*. A technique related to scapegoating involves focusing public attention on violators who are doing the prohibited activities but are not related to the elite. The norm ultimately affirmed is that certain groups may not deviate from the norm, while others may do so, albeit discreetly. Thus, Elias writes:

> The reluctance to prosecute the men and firms at the top in Wall Street is not confined to regulatory bodies such as the Exchange and the SEC. The most serious and famed crime-busters, those elected by the people or appointed by the federal government, show a marked tendency to avoid running down high-level crime in the Street. The late Tom Dewey, for example, was undoubtedly New York's most successful crime-buster. But Tom Dewey pursued what is euphemistically called "organized crime," members of the Mafia and waterfront murderers. New York's very respected district attorney William Hogan has not made his reputation by digging away at Wall Street, although clearly there has been enough reason to begin an investigation. Nor has New York State's respected attorney general,

Louis Lefkowitz, initiated actions against any Wall Street principals, although he and his staff consistently develop surveys of wrong-doing. At the Stock Exchange, in fact, Lefkowitz is considered a friend.

Even the U.S. Attorney in New York, Whitney North Seymour, Jr., has seen no reason to look into Wall Street at high managerial levels, although his office on Foley Square is only a few short blocks from the Street. Of more interest to him, apparently, is the run-of-the-mill kind of thief. An inquiry in the summer of 1970, a period when Wall Street's insolvencies were at their peak, showed that the typical wrong-doer being pursued by the U.S. Attorney's office was hardly in the big leagues of crime. In a Tom Mix scenario he might have been one of the thugs working for the crooked banker.[20]

4. *Eliminating rivals.* By applying the norms of the myth system to a rival who, while in power, had practiced the operational code, an ambitious new politician can kill several birds with one stone. He can reinforce the norms of the myth system, win a reputation as a righteous politician, and, at the same time, eliminate and succeed rivals. Unless he is then willing and able to reform the code, it is probable that he and his own cronies will shortly be living according to the same operational code. In time they, too, will become likely candidates for a new youngster's crusade. In systemic terms, this type of crusade, though motivated by little more than personal ambition, always works to sustain the myth system.

5. *Human sacrifice.* Selected members of a constituent group may be prosecuted for things that many other members of the group are doing. They are usually selected for sacrifice because of a special vulnerability. They may cooperate in return for a negotiated deal or submit quietly and not take others with them because they know that evidence for even more damning charges has been gathered.

In crusades, the systemic functions of the incompetent, or "boob," in organizations with diverse constituencies cannot be overstated. The incompetent is often a fixture in *lex imperfecta.* A politician or administrator may be pressed by one group of constituents to make good a particular promise or to "prepay" for its support. But the demanded action will not be feasible from the political or administrative standpoint because it will alienate other important groups, challenge a secret program, and create other disturbances. The successful politician rarely says, candidly, "Sorry, but cannot comply." He is more likely to say that he will do it, a promise in the political realm akin to the great lie of the business world that "the check is in the mail." After saying that on several occasions, the politician will ultimately say, "I'm putting one of my best men on it," and give the petitioners the name of the official who is being charged. His agent may also be a rogue, but in some cases the best sort of official from the standpoint of the administrator is an incompetent or boob: the person who sincerely tries, but will surely fail. In order to be effective, the incompetent must be a person of good breeding and education (a respected but basically obsolete political family name is sound) and must occupy a visibly high appointive office just below that of the administrator delegating the task. Thus the compleat minister will have at least one incompetent deputy minister in his retinue; if his constituency is particularly diverse and competitive, the workload may require several boobs.

The cryptocrusade is commonly used as a fig leaf for a coup or putsch in which an elected leader is removed by unauthorized elements allegedly to prevent further corruption and to cleanse the nation. Since few people take seriously the justifications forwarded by power-seizers, the rationalizations can be carried to absurd lengths. Thus Mrs. Gandhi in India and Mr. Marcos of the Philippines conducted "insider coups"[21] against constitutional governments on grounds that they were ridding their respective governments of corruption. In American politics, this is equivalent to running against your own record; we have produced a few national geniuses who have actually succeeded in doing it.

Crusades and Crisis

Antibribery crusades are a species of moral legislation in the sense in which Svend Ranulf used the term.[22] Ranulf believed that moral legislation was initiated by lower-middle-class social formations whose power in the body politic was increasing; it was aimed against upper-middle-class formations and was stimulated by envy. Harold Lasswell has suggested that other data indicate that moral legislation may, in some contexts, also be stimulated by upper-class formations that are declining and seek to suppress the distinct cultural manifestations of the ascending formations in a desperate effort at social control.[23] I do not believe that Ranulf's thesis explains the phenomenon of the antibribery crusade, but it does direct attention at what I suspect is a very basic part of it: the popularly shared perception that something being done by the targets of the crusade is causing what is believed to be the decline of the crusading group.

Antibribery campaigns do not get under way when things are going very well. People who have identified with, and put their faith in, government and have come to assume that government is indispensable to many of the values they demand will be ripe for a crusade when they think, realistically or not, that things are going very badly.[24] I believe that the critical factor that accounts for the increased support necessary for popular crusades is a shared perception of societal crisis. There is a pervading sense that something is going very very wrong, that the value positions of certain groups are diminishing, but that rational responses are apparently exhausted: neither cogent analyses nor meaningful countermeasures have been forwarded or can be agreed upon. Traditional explanations of social problems—the enemy, outside agitators, communists, lower classes, Jews, Chinese, whatever—are not palpable because their cathartic potential has also been expended. Troubled by the vast discrepancy between aspiration and achievement with respect to all values, attention shifts to violations of the myth system; bribery, because of its manifestly corrosive effect on the governmental process, and its seductive simplicity compared to the complexities of other problems, becomes a handy target. The discrepancies between myth system and operational code, formerly ignored, are now brought forward with heightened disquiet and even guilt. Violence is directed at governors and those closest to them, for it is the bribery and corruption and the violation of the myth system that are declared to be the causes of all the trouble.

Crisis is of interest and concern to students of decision because of its effect on cognitive and facultative functions. When the factors precipitating the crisis cannot be effectively analyzed and resolved, repetitive, ritualistic, and, in a sense, virtually autistic responses may be undertaken; though presented as solutions, they are, in a deeper sense, tension and anxiety-release mechanisms. In this respect, perceived but hitherto unacknowledged discrepancies between the myth system and the operational code become very appropriate candidates for crusade targets. One obvious folk explanation of a crisis is that the group's behavior has departed from the myth system, which may take on a sacrosanct quality. The passionate search for those who have acted according to the operational code becomes a ritual purging. Bribery or other practices of operators may have little or nothing to do with actual crisis, and in some circumstances there may be no objective crisis. But catharsis is achieved.

Reforms: Changing the Operational Code

Crusades, as we have seen, are aimed not at changing behavior but at reasserting the values of the myth system and reassuring those committed to it of the continuing validity of the myth without changing the behavior that was the manifest stimulus of the crusade. Crusades invest heavily in symbols and that type of legislation—*lex simulata* and *lex imperfecta*—

designed to have no effect. Reforms, though they are expressed in symbols and legislation, are interventions that
intend to, and do, achieve significant changes in the targeted
behavior. Though crusades have the smell of violence and
may claim some victims, it is the reform that is truly violent.[25]

A reform is an effective change in the operational code of
the elite involving greater approximation to the myth system
and effected not only by interelite agreement but also by the
mobilization of elements of the broader population.[26]
Reforms are directed not necessarily at the composition of
the elite, but at its practices. Reforms seem to have four
characteristics:

1. The operational code is essentially an elite pattern of
behavior. When an elite concludes that the continuity of its
ascendant position will require changes in the operational
code, it will seek to initiate and enforce such changes.[27] One
factor contributing to the success of the reform will be the
degree of consensus among elite members as to the urgency
of the need for reform. If the elite is divided and some
members anticipate net gains by maintenance of the existing
operational code, those members will seek to blunt the reform or to transform it into a crusade, producing simulated
or imperfect laws rather than effective legislation and coordinate changes in attitude and behavior. In these dissensual
circumstances, would-be reformers—whether diplomats,
machine politicians, police, or gangsters—are likely to appeal
to the common interests of the extended elite group: "We
will all lose if we don't make these changes."[28] Rhetoric
notwithstanding, resolution of the differences between elite
members as to changes in the operational code is a political
process in which the full repertory of coercion and indulgence can be expected to be skillfully used.

2. Changes in the operational code may also be initiated
by a newly ascendant elite that decides it can consolidate its

power and prevent a revanche of those recently dispossessed only if it quickly effects certain critical reforms.[29] Notions of loyalty to a patron, which may have been a key postulate of a prerevolutionary operational code, will be systematically suppressed and replaced by notions of loyalty to a monarch, a republic, or a party.

A "loyal opposition" is an elite group that shares with incumbents commitment to existing institutional patterns; a "counterelite" does not share such a commitment.[30] Politics tend to be more "gentlemanly" between elite and loyal opposition, though, as Richard Nixon demonstrated, changes in social goals or paranoid propensities may transform a loyal opposition into a counterelite. The initiation of reforms by "new elites" is more likely when counterelites seize power than when a loyal opposition is installed. But reform is not an inexorable feature of what our century imprecisely calls revolution.[31] The newly installed counterelite may discover that the secret police of the ancien régime is very useful, perhaps even indispensable to the maintenance of power. Hence its operational code will adapt many of the norms of its predecessor. The new myth system may ignore these discrepancies or, if it is sufficiently supple, justify them as transitional or required by a special revolutionary morality. The dialectic, in Lenin's hands, proved to be an extraordinarily useful instrument in this regard.

3. Elite interest and even success in changing components of the operational code do not in themselves amount to a reform. The operational code, like any normative system, is under constant pressure for stabilization or change; tinkering, fine-tuning, or even fundamental changes do not concern us here if they do not significantly involve the myth system. A reform is a distinct species of social change. It is one that must appear to initiate an increasing approximation of elite practices to the myth system and, hence, must recruit the support of those who are viewed as custodians of the myth system: clergymen, journalists, teachers, and the like.[32]

A reform is characterized by an increasing approximation to the community's myth system of the behavior and attitudes about correct behavior of elites or operators. Hence we cannot speak of reform without accounting for the indispensable participation of custodians of the myth system. Whether the reform is initiated by members of this latter group or they join, are recruited or bought at a later stage, their participation is a key element of reform.

Myth system custodians are sought by operators because they can deliver something useful in power processes. They have some skill in the shaping and mediating of symbols that can activate people of potential political significance who are not ordinarily effective in the power arena.[33] This mass mobilization is a key element of reform. Some writers assume that mass mobilization is only likely in periods in which certain strata are changing social position.[34] Implicit in this view is the assumption that the rank and file are *lumpenmenschen*, ordinarily passive until historical forces jolt them into some involuntary spasm. This unflattering assumption also ignores the role of the media in complex mass societies and the capacity of key contemporary social institutions to stir or dissipate popular anger of potential political vector.[35]

4. One characteristic feature of a reform is its result. The fact that a campaign actually succeeded in moving some operator practices closer to the myth system means that the observer can characterize it as a reform and not a crusade. The threshold of success is not high. Reform changes in the operational code need not be complete prohibitions of behavior formerly appropriate for operators. Much of law is of general application only in the myth system; in practical operation, it may be so routinely selective that people in different groups and strata will know whether or not to expect application of particular norms to them, or how to gauge the comparative likelihood of their application.[36] Hence a reform may aim to do no more than prohibit (or, alternatively, authorize) certain individuals or groups to do or refrain from doing something. In general, appraising a reform's comparative success is difficult and complicated.

Assessing Success

Operators, as a group, are the targets of reforms. Their first defense is an attempt to quash the campaign. If the effort fails and popular dissatisfaction mounts, operators seek to transform it into a crusade by deflecting public dissatisfaction into symbolic activity; if legislation must issue, it is simulated or imperfect. Under cover of this noisome but essentially inconclusive activity, elite positions may be maintained and the old practices continued.

Because campaigns such as these are a series of skirmishes rather than a single decisive confrontation, only over time is it possible to conclude whether they were merely brief interruptions or real changes in the operational code. Even if passed, "reform" legislation, that is, legislation actually *intended* to change the operational code, is not equivalent to reform, for it may be blunted by operators at lower levels of the bureaucracy who may prevent or indefinitely postpone the drafting of rules or secondary, implementing legislation. If implementing machinery is actually created, it may be starved to death by an inadequate budget allocation or emasculated by the assignment of incompetents to positions of responsibility. If the implementing machinery actually tries to be effective, it may be overwhelmed by larger and superior legal teams who will mount adjudications protracted even beyond the wildest dreams of the pettifoggers of Bleak House or conclude settlements that are translated into overhead costs and passed on to consumers. Consider commercial reforms. A ten- or twenty-year suit may well permit a business firm to continue business as usual, passing legal expenses on to the consumer in the form of higher prices. A piece of reform legislation of this sort is a windfall to all those who specialize in dispute resolution and, in in-group parlance, is often referred to affectionately as "The Lawyers' and Accountants' Relief Act."[37]

Thus it is not always easy to determine whether a particular campaign is a reform or a crusade. The final judgment can be made only years later, when it is possible to assess whether legislation has led to aggregate changes in targeted behavior. The mere fact that legislation has issued is not a significant indicator, for it may be undercut at many later stages. Congress may pass legislation aimed at prohibiting conflicts of interest in the regulatory agencies. If the agencies have still not enacted implementing legislation a decade later, the legislation is, to all intents and purposes, a dead letter. What had perhaps started as a reform has been transformed into a crusade.

Some reform campaigns have been rather successful. Civil service reforms in the United States,[38] for example, have probably succeeded in depoliticizing many levels of public service, though it would appear that many levels continue with patronage arrangements not dissimilar to those before the reforms; there is, however, a different style of justification. The extent to which some of the major reforms of the American market system have succeeded is more difficult to gauge. Is there, in fact, less concentration of capital and more competition in American industry as a result of the great antitrust acts and the continuing efforts of the antitrust division of the Department of Justice? Or have the concentrations survived and even increased with publicized "trust busting," merely reaffirming a myth of the market? Is advertising cleaner and less misleading? Meaningful empirical tests are virtually impossible, and comparisons through time are difficult because practices change radically.

Consider advertising. In the 1880s, a Dr. Scott advertised electric corsets, urging that his product be tried by women suffering any bodily ailment. There was hardly a disease, Dr. Scott's ad assured its readers, that electricity and magnetism would not benefit and cure.[39] Perhaps this sort of quackery is less likely now and perhaps its decrease is due to the efforts of the Federal Trade Commission. But the bottom line, as traders would put it, may not have changed much. The manifest content of a contemporary ad may not be blatantly outrageous, but it may be craftily ambiguous, snared with weasel words and delivered quickly. Is a result comparable to the one sought by the venerable Dr. Scott now secured by media blitz, saturation ads, and the expert use of psychological data? The point of emphasis here is that it is meaningless to use the word *reform* to characterize modulations in operator technique through which the pre-reform outcome is still (perhaps even more efficiently) achieved. Where the outcome of the new practice is substantially the same as before, the campaign is a crusade. A crusade is not a reform.

Do not minimize the importance of a crusade and certainly don't dismiss it as an empty and cynical maneuver. While it may be deemed a failed reform from the perspective of the erstwhile reformer, it is a successful social operation from the standpoint of the threatened operator and all those who identified positively with those aspects of the operational code under attack. A crusade is successful when it reasserts the values of the myth system. Paradoxically, a failed reform may have few disrupting consequences. In contrast, a failed crusade is quite likely to mean the termination of certain norms within the myth system.

Organizationally and ethically, many types of bribery will be a serious challenge to myth systems that stigmatize them as wrong. Because bribery, as we have seen, is a recurring problem and is as unlikely to be extirpated as are the human motives that give rise to it, the potential for antibribery campaigns will continue. I believe that bribery and other simple and easily comprehensible forms of white-collar corruption are more likely to be targets of popular crusades in the future than in the past. These crusades will serve as an outlet for tensions between governed and governors (and hence a useful, though potentially reflexive, weapon for would-be governors) and as ways of projecting responsibility for failures of social and other programs from government to equally visible targets. Above all, they will provide ready folk explanations for the discontents and crises of an increasingly complex and bewildering civilization, one in which roles are clearly defined but good and evil and cause and effect are becoming more and more difficult to unravel.

Chapter 5

Moralizing Bribery

"Listen, Professor. It's a rough world, and we've got a job to do." — An FBI Agent, Narcotics Division

THE dilemmas of bribery are not an extraordinary experience. Like adultery and betrayal, they are woven into the fabric of society with a potential, if not actual, universal incidence. All human beings who must make choices are caught between the high and often peremptory aspirations of their myth system and the need for accommodation and compromise that is an unyielding part of reality. Most manage the tension between myth and operation in a series of uneasy compromises, with deviations from the myth system accompanied by feelings of guilt and anxiety, requited by ritual penances and spasms of autopunitive behavior. Most people—particularly those who are reading this account and presumably gain a substantial part of their experience from that uniquely organized linear world of writing—"know" that bribery is wrong. Yet there are few of us who have not paid bribes at one time or another; virtually all of us have been in situations where explicit or indirect signals were saying "take care" of this man, while other signals were emphasizing the high and unjust costs of not doing so.

Whatever their general views of bribery, most people's evaluations of the propriety of a particular bribe will be influenced by features of the context. Who bribed whom, how, where, for what purpose, with what result? What was the law the bribe sought to circumvent and what were the

119

circumstances in which the law would otherwise have been applied? Were there alternatives to the bribery? What would have been the consequences of a refusal to bribe? There is a difference between bribing a Ugandan or a Russian official to secure the escape of someone threatened, or an antebellum judicial officer to prevent the return of a captured slave, and bribing an official of the Motor Vehicle Bureau for information that will help you steal cars. Yet even "good" bribes are bad and, when we pay or approve them, we may experience internal dissonance.

Moralizing is the personality's attempt to rationalize discrepancies between what you know you ought to be doing and what you know you are or will be doing. Moral discourse seeks to formulate a general theory for right behavior; the function of moralizing is to justify selectively *wrong* behavior. Obviously, the easiest justification for such norm-breaking is denial of the validity of the norm in question or, more subtly, asserting that the violation is aimed at creating a new prescription. The thief who honestly believes, like Proudhon, that property is theft, may moralize for tactical reasons, but he need not do it to assuage a sense of guilt; intention and conduct affirm a counternorm. In contrast, the merchant who steals yet, at the same time, upholds the norm he is violating is a prime candidate for moralizing. Indeed, what is distinctive and curious about the moralizer is that he always affirms the norm he violates. This feature accounts for the tortured and often casuistic character associated with moralizing and is one of the reasons we find moralizing so repellent when others do it.

As we have seen, common responses to discrepancies between myth system and operational code are discretion (doing things secretly), suppression of the discrepancy, and cultivated ignorance. When discrepancies are exposed or popularly protested, operators and their apologists, in their desire to retain the option of continuing them, must moralize. The styles and content of moralizing can provide insights into the varying intensity with which norms in a moral code are held, the ways people handle the tensions of myth system and operational code, the situations and ranges of tolerance for discrepancies between them, and some of the contingencies that will initiate crusades or reforms. In our society, bribery is a prime candidate for moralizing because it violates key norms in the myth system of liberal and popular democracy, yet sometimes seems compelled by the very social heterogeneity that such a system encourages.

There are societies in which obedience to authority is a fundamental strut of both personal morality and social order. Whatever their political rhetoric, such societies are profoundly undemocratic. In societies not characterized by this extreme of subordination, official decisions must be "implemented," for automatic obedience to an official order can no longer be assumed, perhaps no longer demanded. Some decisions may be effected by persuasion, but what of the decisions in which "reasonable" men (a generous but empirically untested generalization) differ?

Jeremy Bentham, writing from the perspective of the elite, classified the arsenal of influence at the disposal of any power holder as threats of deprivation for deviation from an order and promises of rewards for compliance: "carrots and sticks."[1] His contemporary, John Austin, whose theories still influence common law thinking, produced his "Province of Jurisprudence Determined" at the very beginning of English liberalism.[2] Writing from a profoundly Christian perspective, he struggled with the perennial problem of a man of conscience who finds his notion of right challenged by the law of the state. Breaking with Bentham, Austin argued that one could morally comply with the dictate of the state only if deviation from it would occasion the imposition of a severe sanction, or "evil," by the state. A Christian could defect from his conscience to escape an evil, but he could not defect in order to win a reward.

To an extent, the struggle between the perspectives of the

elite and that of the moral "legist" of the rank and file continues in our own political civilization. From the perspective of the elite, the technique of rewards for compliance, or patronage, is preferable to threats of coercion. While coercion may secure a temporary compliance, it alienates the target and may well generate opposition the moment the threat or actual coercion is withdrawn. Rewards, on the other hand, win friends and create complicities; long-term dependencies in a democracy, and particularly a pluralistic one in which elites will always need support for recurring electoral contests, may be as important as the momentary compliance for the reward. The Tolchins write that "the patronage system thrives as one of the occupational hazards of our democracy. In a land where most men have some degree of freedom of choice, incentives are often required to bestir them to public action, or to persuade them to change a course of action."[3]

From the perspective of the moral member of the community, in contrast, the elites' reward is a bribe, a payment to defect from the dictates of one's conscience, and it is viewed as wrong to give and as wrong to receive. Where the notion of personal conscience is built into the political system—for example, "each man votes his conscience"[4]— rewards, patronage, or official bribery seem particularly venal. Not surprisingly, the patronage process is obscured by elites and is accomplished surreptitiously.

An additional factor contributing to ambivalences about bribery derives from a fundamental dualism of our civilization. It encompasses two tendencies, perhaps two world views: capitalism's licit greed and republicanism's civic altruism and disdain for the material. In the political economy of America, these tendencies interlock, intersupport, and conflict at many points. Official and personal ambivalence about bribery, like the ambivalence about white-collar crime in general, relates to the incompatibility of capitalism and republicanism and the reluctance (if not practical impossibility) to choose, at last, one or the other. Those who believe that the dynamic of social process is always working toward unity will impatiently decry the ambivalence and dismiss techniques such as crusades, with their *lex imperfecta* and *simulata,* as cunning devices concocted by an elite to perpetuate itself and to avoid a final resolution; moralizing will be given similar treatment. Those who believe that social process is essentially dialectical, charged with conflict and change, will see these devices as mediating techniques, sometimes abused but essentially necessary and proper to establish and maintain the truces and coexistences on which civilization can be reared.

In bribery, as in politics in general, the controlled brutality and modulated dishonesty are often more apparent and shocking to the observer than to someone actually engaged in the operation. In theory, a person capable of purely economic calculations could view a bribal exchange as a pure economic transaction and with no need for moralizing. An American political commentator has written that "bribery is regarded as immoral by most Americans, but this is not the universal view, and there are many people, among them heads of some of our multinational corporations, who regard it simply as another form of taxation."[5] Long ago, Georg Simmel remarked that "the brutality of a man purely motivated by monetary consideration and acting . . . on the . . . axiom of greatest advantage and least sacrifice, often does not appear to him at all as a moral delinquency, since he is aware only of a rigorously logical behavior which draws the objective consequences of the situation."[6] But, like economics itself, this overstates the case. In many ways, these observations themselves are symptomatic of the inability to impose a unified morality on events that are evaluated by a variety of often discrepant codes. Gerth and Mills note that

due to the great weight which the economic order has in the American social structure, pecuniary motives tend to form a sort of common denominator of many other roles and motives. Other vocabularies are treated as shams, façades, and "rationalization," and "the wise guy" knows that *the real* motive is the desire for money which, as is commonly said, may not be everything but is almost everything.[7]

Because there is no entity such as rational or economic man, bribery, as understood by bribers, is more complex. The operator—the professional politician or the elite member—may be capable of viewing the wherewithal of bribery in cold and pragmatic terms—in contexts in which he knows the rules of the operational code. The dysphoria as well as the possible exhilaration may be greater for the occasional rather than the regular briber, but there is reason to believe that the complexities of subjective perception of bribery by its practitioners may show certain striking uniformities. In discussions with those informants who claimed that "payments" are a necessary and often customary practice, I have been struck by their frequent effort to defend and justify the behavior. This is a curious response for something "necessary" and "customary," and virtually belies its manifest justification. One-timers and recidivists may differ essentially in degree.

Most one-time bribers conduct the transaction with feelings of fear and guilt. The fear—often irrational—is of being apprehended, shamed, and sanctioned; the source of the guilt is more mysterious and complex, for one-time or infrequent bribers sometimes believe that they have no alternative, indeed that their action is "right" in the context.

In all human choices, rationality and explicit moral considerations interact and sometimes trade off with deep and usually unperceived psychological dynamics. The anguish over a moral defection may be more than requited by the deep satisfactions that can come from doing evil. Many of the psychological dynamics of the bribal relationship have generally been ignored in favor of a superficial moralizing or economizing that assumes the venality or opportunism of the briber and the cupidity and faithlessness of the bribee. These are often personal attributes of participants in bribery (as in other things), but the psychology of bribery is, I believe, more complex.

The multiple roles necessarily played by the individual in contemporary urban, industrial society will frequently create the double images or conflation of codes discussed in chapter 2. A businessman who may abhor bribery will nonetheless find that he is bribing for his firm. A landlord who protests the inflation that is eroding his wealth will nonetheless conspire to violate rent controls. Two empirical studies indicate that in such normative conflicts, the economic interest prevailed but did not completely replace its counterpart. In his study of government regulation, Lane found no "general anti-regulation animus"; rather, it was "the position of the firm, rather than any emotional qualities of its management, which led it to violate."[8] A study of rent-control violations reached a similar conclusion.[9] In this connection, Ball and Friedman write that "in the *Electrical Equipment Cases* many company officials who actively participated in the violations believed price fixing was wrong, and there is no evidence that any substantial numbers of the violators believed it was right (although for a variety of reasons many thought it necessary in the circumstances)."[10] The point here is not that the wealth drive is preeminent or more fundamental than others, but that in conflicts between competing codes, the norms of the most proximate and effective social group will dominate. Sutherland called this the doctrine of "differential association,"[11] but his approach assumed more of a "contamination of values" than the policing by an effective group of its norms. When another group and its norms become proximate, the dissonance will be resolved on the conscious level by individual moralizing.

At some level of consciousness, briber and bribee know that the payment demeans and corrupts a representative of authority or, indeed, the very conception of authority. If the briber's own attitudes toward authority are thoroughly disengaged, ambivalent, or even hostile, the act of bribery may provide him with a deep psychological gratification that may more than outweigh the material benefits the bribe appeared to seek. Certain personalities may thus seek opportunities to bribe even when the manifest objective of the interaction can be secured by lawful means: such personalities may possess, if you like, a psychogenic predisposition for bribery. It is not at all surprising to find, as Harold Lasswell observed, that people who seek out opportunities to bribe may also engage in some ritual of penance or autopunitive acts as a way of placating the authority they have challenged and still fear. The guilty have a special double-entry bookkeeping. Some of the biggest bribers may thus be the biggest givers;[12] ostentatious charity and attendant public recognition may render them idols and supporters of the myth system even as they practice the operational code.

Some studies[13] seem to assume that the bribe receiver generally acts out of a primary loyalty to a group other than that in which he is performing his public function, and that, as a consequence, bribery is a phenomenon of unintegrated societies. I am skeptical of the implication that the multiplicity of loyalties, prerequisite perhaps to bribery, is exceptional or that most people in "modern" societies have unitary or monolithic loyalty systems. The personality is a bundle of selves, each having its own loyalty system, and the selves compete for priority in different situations. The fact that the bribe taker rejects one self and its loyalties in taking bribes does not mean that he feels no loyalty and that the repudiation does not have psychic costs as well as gratifications. The bribe taker, like his counterpart, may thus act out some subsequent penitence. Finally, we should bear in mind that the bribe, like the lie, is in its profoundest sense an assertion of self through a rejection of the claims of another authority; if one's social goals include increased autonomy of the self, a bribe may be viewed, in some personal or social contexts, as a positive operation.[14] Thus the moral aspects of bribing or evaluating particular bribes may be very complex, requiring exploration not only of the transaction but of the phenomenal worlds of the actors as well.

There is a striking parallel in this respect between bribery and lying. R.D. Laing observes that lying, though an odious act, is a very important assertion of autonomous personality.[15] An individual who is unable to lie may be viewed as someone who is socially immature and undeveloped, for there are circumstances in which it is appropriate to lie, in which the insistence on a private reality separate from that held forth to others may be an important expression of autonomy as well as an exigent modality of survival. On the other hand, an individual who lies without compunction must be viewed as socially and psychologically defective as well as an obvious danger to those around him, for while the lie asserts the self, it also violates that basic norm on which all interaction rests: you ought to behave in ways you lead others to expect you to behave.

In a meaningful and responsible social sense, the key is not in learning never to lie, but when to lie, how to reinforce the code of honesty—for oneself and for others—even when one lies and, if necessary, how to manage one's detritus of guilt in cases of proper lying. Unfortunately, there is no single code to be put down to memory, for the question of when to lie depends upon a choice of identifications and loyalties. Most of us have many of these, and their relations and priorities are not always stable. Some are important to us in all settings, while some are important only in some settings. Sometimes the loyalties relate only to other group members. For example, with family members, one is truthful, about some matters, to a much higher degree than one is with outsiders. Some loyalties, without regard to their personal significance, are mandated by processes that severely punish defections, as people prosecuted for treason learn.

Lying runs some risks—exposure and punishment or offending the gods—but compared to bribery it is a much safer way to affirm the self. In contrast, the costs of constructing a personal reality through bribery may include severe legal sanctions whose likelihood of incidence is much increased, for you must incorporate one other human being when you construct a fragment of a private world with a folded lie. Ironically, bribery requires an act of trust in another who henceforth knows what you are about and, for a fee, shares part of your danger, your ecstasy, and your guilt. But though the risks are different, the moral questions are the same. If you accept this analysis with regard to lying, then the critical question with reference to bribery is under what circumstances is it appropriate to tender a bribe? Under what circumstance ought one to bribe? Answers to these questions will depend on the value system of the decider.[16]

The Relevance of Evaluative Criteria

Few people would gainsay the proposition that it is appropriate to bribe when (1) the official policy being subverted is one that is deemed grossly immoral and (2) the object of the bribe is to secure a result that is generally deemed to be moral or right and, for practical purposes, otherwise unattainable. One would have to be a pathological positivist to assume that Bertolt Brecht's bribe tendered to an immigration official in order to escape the Nazis during the Third Reich was wrong. Though certain moral philosophers might insist that any act of disobedience ought to be public if it is to be deemed to be moral,[17] this seems both impractical and unrealistic. In the more ruthless of our modern autocracies that prescription virtually assures that dissent will be a once-in-a-lifetime event. Irrational demands for publicity may derive from deep superstitions about the ultimate authority or sovereignty of the state or ruling elite. For people who believe that, whatever the merits, the state is ultimately right, it is quite plain that tolerated acts of civil disobedience should be followed either by voluntary exposure to personal dangers or by the initiation of acts inviting or assuring self-destruction. Socrates, for example, took on the state and, having made his point, participated in his own destruction; Socrates is not unlike the young Japanese who strikes a superior and then commits hara-kiri.

Evaluation presupposes criteria. Do you accept the idea that it is right to evade the incidence of a norm that requires immoral behavior or whose application would lead to consequences that are morally repugnant? Is it right to subvert a system that is basically "wrong"? If you accept such propositions, you must face the broader question of the content of the "higher," or, at least, other, code that justifies "illegal" acts. The important point here is that assessments of when it is appropriate to bribe will always be based upon a "higher," often unstated, code of preferences from which the state official who is the target of the bribe is allegedly deviating. From the standpoint of the moralist or his latter-day incarnation, the policy scientist, any attempt to develop a systematic code for evaluating the lawfulness of bribery must clarify a broader, transcending code of behavior against which the official behavior that is the target of subversion can be tested. Let us call this larger test one of general goal clarification.

In circumstances in which the briber is animated by natural law doctrines or by belief in supernatural laws reliably communicated by a divinity, goals and code are ready-made. There are tactical, but few moral, problems. A comparable function is implicitly performed by a highly ethnicized environment in which it is taken for granted that loyalty and substantially moral behavior are owed only to members of the family, tribe, race, dialect group, or sex group—whatever the unit of identification may be. In aristocracies, in which there are significant cleavages between rulers and ruled, the notion of primary loyalty to one's class simplifies the act of lying and bribing on behalf of the class; the act may, however, be just as complex when engaged in for other purposes.[18] The operational code of the elite in popular democracies is less clear-cut, as we have seen, for "vertical identifications," that is, identifications between ruler and ruled, may be more significant influences on behavior.

Where loyalties are clearly owed to your own state, bribing officials of another state on its behalf may expose you to personal dangers, but it is not wrong or unlawful under the terms of the effective loyalty system. The same "exemption" may apply with regard to bribes on behalf of one's corporation, though here bribers may encounter more internal dissonance, for apparently that social formation has yet to achieve a status fully comparable to the state's.[19]

In command systems, what one's superior orders is, by definition, right; at the very least, responsibility for the rightness or wrongness of the command is his alone. "We know enough," say the soldiers in *Henry V*, "if we know we are the king's subjects. If his cause be wrong, our obedience to the king wipes the crime of it out of us." For command systems in modern bureaucracies, staffed by less assured moralists, Hans Kelsen developed a more involved jurisprudential version. It essentially held that in the bureaucratic context, the only pertinent legal course was the command of a properly authorized superior.[20]

Some elites justify bribery, as we have seen, by shifting to a teleological rather than logical derivation of authorization. The bribe, though a violation of part of the formal code, is actually necessary to fulfill the larger objectives of the entire normative code.[21] Here and in circumstances in which the briber operates from more secure perspectives, the challenge is the creation or postulation of a set of principles or preferences that identify ultimate group or individual purposes and would warrant defections from the formal code when they are necessary to achieve these higher ends.

Instances of bribery that at first glance seem lawful or appropriate in their particular context are often deemed so because they effectuate a normative or loyalty system to which the observer is most committed. In highly ethnicized environments such as India, parts of Africa, the Middle East, or in any place or sector where the nation-state remains only an incipient social organization, the most intense loyalties relate to extended family, tribe, ethnic, or dialect group. For actors in such a system, nepotism imports laudable loyalty and not opprobrium. Individual members of a particular loyalty group (for example, the tribe) will view as lawful bribes paid to government officials to secure the application of tribal norms rather than discrepant national norms. What we encounter here are normative prescriptions more intensely demanded than the formal law. Individuals on the scene should, under the terms of *their* normative code, apply that code's pertinent norms, even though application might violate the formal law; but they cannot be applied because of the total political situation. The bribe vindicates people's deeper loyalties and the preferred normative system.[22]

Community Evaluation

In examples such as these, the notion of morality is that of the moral syntax of particular group members and not necessarily the code that an outsider or someone committed to a larger or more inclusive community would deploy to evaluate the propriety of particular bribes or of bribery in general. Within a particular legal viewpoint, bribery may be condemned absolutely, but it is more likely that the lawfulness of particular bribes will be evaluated, as we have mentioned earlier, in context: who bribed whom, how, where, for how much, for what purpose, with what result, and with what consequences flowing from refusal to pay the bribe. Even those who condemn bribery are likely to find that variations in the answers to some of these questions will influence their conclusions about lawfulness or, indirectly but equivalently, the severity of the sanction that they demand. In multiple code situations, whether or not a particular event is right or lawful depends on your legal viewpoint. But are there inclusive viewpoints with more transcending and durable standards by which anyone can recognize the violence and deceit of a bribe?

Crusaders and reformers usually insist that such standards exist. But many students of bribery question such faith. Some writers, for example, Professor Nye,[23] appear to assume that bribery is a neutral instrument. The test of its proper use in, let us say, national development is its cost-benefit ratio—the extent to which it contributes to preferred consequences. But the conclusion that bribery may be viewed strictly in instrumental terms and may thus aid development in some circumstances requires a very short-sighted and constricted focus of the issues. Obviously resistance to certain projects or proposed institutional changes that would contribute to development can be bought off. But a bridge or a road is not development. In the most profound sense, development involves and requires community power institutions endowed with sufficient rationality and predictability to enable them to perform the planning and implementing functions at the core of purposive social change. The effectiveness of such institutions requires internalization and compliance with a norm I call the "rule of role fidelity": fidelity to the expected behavior that is associated with a manifest role voluntarily undertaken. This might be taken as the corollary of a general norm of all social interaction that I mentioned earlier: behave in ways you lead others to expect you to behave.

Role fidelity is an inherent characteristic of any loyalty system. The degree of fidelity in different settings may account for different bribery and myth system patterns. Kinship ties of real or fictitious consanguinity are crystallized expressions, among other things, of identification. Loyalties in traditional societies are predetermined by such ties and their vigor often continues despite the superimposition of inclusive national symbols. Young and Willmott demonstrated the durability of family and kinship even in a modern metropolis.[24] Some scholars tend to characterize the durability of these identities as essentially pathological. Thus Wertheim writes:

> Corruption is essentially a sign of conflicting loyalties pointing primarily to a lack of positive attachment to the government and its ideals. In so far as corruption shows that the new government, with

its enormous task to fulfill in the new Asian world, is not yet sufficiently integrated in society and does not evoke full sympathy, enthusiasm and unfaltering loyalty from subjects and officials, it is a sign of weakness of the present political structure.[25]

Such evaluations posit by implication the values of the new state apparatus over traditional values and perhaps, more generally, the values of the state over those of nonofficial groupings.

In modernized societies, in contrast, kinship is generally believed to be a much more residual feature; the self system is believed to be acculturated to a capacity for developing many loyalties of varying intensities, contingencies, and durations. The modern personality, in contrast to its traditional counterpart, becomes a bundle of personalities, or, at least, a much bigger bundle, and one of its key features is the capacity to grow new personalities and loyalty systems. It is this acculturated capacity that permits organization and control in large-scale social systems in which people shuttle rapidly from family circle to on-the-job and corporation roles to army roles, and so on; in each context, appropriate loyalties can be activated to secure compliant behavior. At the same time, multiple loyalties increase the possibilities of internal conflict and supply some of the psychosocial prerequisites for bribery.[26]

Thus the bribe taker and bribe giver are not necessarily Simmel's *homo economicus*. They may well operate in a normative system that prescribes proper procedures for bribery and prohibits certain types of bribes. Ross describes

the St. Louis boodler, who, after accepting $25,000 to vote against a certain franchise, was offered a larger sum to vote for it. He did so but returned the first bribe. He was asked on the witness-stand why he had returned it. "Because it wasn't mine!" he exclaimed, flushing with anger. "I hadn't earned it."[27]

We have already noted that Jersey City's Boss Hague said that an honest politician is one who stays bought. That apothegm imports a context of modernization with its characteristic pattern of loyalties. In a traditional society, an "honest" politician" need not stay bought, for his frame of rectitude determining honesty is based on his kin group and does not include durable loyalties to outsiders. Hence, in intelligence gathering in traditional societies, the phenomenon of the entrepreneurial agent, as opposed to the double agent: the entrepreneur routinely sells the same pieces of information to a number of foreign intelligence agencies, though holding himself out to each of his customers as its exclusive agent.[28]

The traditional culture may change with the intervention of a charismatic leader, a process much more complex than Max Weber's brief account,[29] or with the intervention of a new belief or loyalty system that supersedes the kin group—for example, a national or international political or religious creed. Where such interventions have profound effects and replace rather than layer over previous loyalties, the system becomes, among other things, either nonbribal or bribal in the modern sense; at the very least, claims to bribe on behalf of residual identities such as the family or tribe will arouse more intense internal conflicts.

Conversely, a modern bribal culture or a nonbribal system can regain many of the characteristics of a traditional culture, bribal or otherwise, when the more inclusive loyalty patterns erode. Loyalty systems are sustained in part by expectations of the effectiveness of complex processes producing net gains of different values for the faithful; stress is put on loyalty systems when participants begin to believe they will no longer be requited in ways they have come to expect. If residual kinship systems are strong, they may bound back and fill the gaps in the crumbling modernism. If they have atrophied or have become irrelevant, functional loyalty systems may develop, such as gangs, secret societies, and the like;[30] some may be extremely nuclear, the quintessentially reduced maxim being "Every man for himself."

Virtually all societies have an intimation of a larger community of mankind, but for complex reasons involving personality dynamics and group formation, extension of the benefits of role fidelity to nongroup members ordinarily follows interactions supporting reciprocally amiable perspectives and, in effect, to the formation of another, larger, or more inclusive ingroup.[31] Before then, the application of the norm of role fidelity is limited to the subgroup; only later does it extend to members of the larger group. The creation and the maintenance of such an inclusive normative system, particularly in traditional societies characterized by more exclusive identification systems, is a major development task; bribery, even if it seems to offer short-run gains, always erodes role fidelity rules.[32]

Role Fidelity and the Bribal Society

Because role fidelity follows effective group identifications, the "social boundaries" demarking such groups are likely places for bribery to be deemed licit and even moral by one of the participants in the transaction. The likelihood will increase when one side of the boundary makes up what one might call a bribal society.

Some societies are distinctively bribal.[33] Whatever the express formulation of the normative code in a bribal society, there is a customary norm to the effect that anyone who performs an official act is entitled to a private recompense. In many cases, it is understood that the performer has himself paid for his official position, has been rewarded with it for past services, or pays a periodic "lease" fee and hence is entitled to dividends from his investment. The result is that no one expects any official act to be performed without a consideration to the performer; where a number of official acts must be performed simultaneously or sequentially, one may be obliged to pay the contact his bribe plus the bribes for the other officials as well as his agent's fee for distributing the bribe.

A bribal society need not be limited to politics or a regime of public acts: a private *quid* may be expected for all *quos* performed. Even routine religious sacraments, performed by a cleric, may call for a bribe. In a system in which "indulgences" are sold, the very gates of heaven are opened by bribes. These examples should occasion no surprise, for the official code of the government is only a part, and a very small part, of the total normative code of the community. In the ultimate bribal society, any time you seek performance of a norm, you pay a bribe of commensurate value.

Some societies and zones are not bribal. There the dominant ethic is that the performance of a public or official role is incompatible with the simultaneous performance of a remunerated private role; loyalties other than those owed to the official role are to be suspended during performance. The conception of a public role as a means of private enrichment is viewed as profoundly wrong. In nonbribal zones, informal social sanctions may be more severe and deterring than formal criminalization.

Inhabitants of a bribal zone may contemplate a nonbribal zone as different, curious, impractical, or quaint but rarely as "wrong." On the other hand, inhabitants of a nonbribal zone tend to view a bribal zone as amoral, or immoral, and wrong. Much of this is parochial, some is a misperception. Bribal zones are certainly not amoral. A classical bribal system such as the "amoral familism" that the Banfields[34] describe is not without morality; the boundaries of moral obligation are simply limited to the smallest unit of the system—the family—and not to larger units or the system itself. The ethic of role fidelity hews to the boundaries of meaningful groups.

Thus bribal zones may be quite organized and laced with special codes. The competence to collect bribes, for example, while against the formal code, is in fact allocated to certain families, each given an economic sector.[35] If you pay a bribe to the right person, you may conduct your business. Pay the wrong person and you and the recipient can expect severe sanctions if apprehended. Even if you are not caught, your bribe is not likely to secure the service you thought you were buying: *nemo dat quod non habet* (no one can give what he does not have). A bribal zone, in short, is not a zone of alegality or amorality, but of a different legality and morality.

Crossing Boundaries

When two or more codes prescribe conflicting behavior, the result is legal or moral "dissonance." Where bribery is the accepted modus operandi in societies or demarked zones therein, crossovers from a nonbribal zone will be accompanied by such dissonance. Even if the work is sensibly entrusted to an operator or specialist, the principal in the nonbribal zone may still find himself entangled in legal dissonances. Crossers resort to a variety of artifices to reduce dissonance and moralizing. Thus some of the moral sting of bribery can be anesthetized by the use of social and political boundary lines, those lines people draw in their minds and then project on the world. Marlowe's Barabas, when reminded of his fornication, dismisses it: "But that was in another country. . . ."

The tension and latent conflict characteristic of frontiers between groups is often an invitation and a justification to do to outsiders what may not be lawfully done to members of the ingroup. Outsiders may reciprocate in kind. Thus medieval Christians reserved one law for believers and another code for infidels; the Muslims, in like manner, divided the world into a *dar al-Islam* and a *dar al-Ḥarb*. The social forces underlying these boundary delimitations continue even today. The criminal law of many jurisdictions may recognize this by refusing to criminalize certain conduct that would be unlawful at home if it is committed abroad.[36] Social boundaries are key points for bribery; we will return to a more detailed examination of this point below.

Frontiers may emphasize or create the illusion of distance. Traditionally, legal systems have ascribed responsibility to those who directed their agents to do wrong: *qui facit per alium facit per se* (he who does something through another is deemed to have done it). But a *sense* of wrongdoing seems to diminish with the distance you can put between yourself and your agent. In 1907, Ross, the populist reformer and pamphleteer, assumed that much social iniquity was the result of mass society and the waning of face-to-face relationships. "Take the face-to-face element out of a relation," he said, "and any lurking devil in it comes to the surface."[37] The prospect of seeing the proximate consequences of your acts in the pain of a fellow human being can prick your conscience and perhaps restrain you from those acts. Complex organizations, in which the causal links between what you do and what the organization does are undetectable, can certainly slacken those bonds of conscience. This may be one of the advantages of the fiction of the corporation. Ross wrote in his alliterative style that "there is nothing like distance to disinfect dividends. . . . The saintly stockholders not only do not know what is going on, but so long as the dividends are comfortable they resent having inconvenient knowledge thrust upon them."[38] Modern life, with its increasingly complex organizations in which the individual has task responsibility but not outcome responsibility, may thus facilitate the violation of those basic social norms that the very fabric of traditional society sustained.

Boundaries and distance may ease the conscience but they do not always provide clear and persisting ethical guidelines for licit bribery. If boundaries were static we would know where licit bribery zones began and ended. But there are, alas, many competing boundaries.

As we saw earlier, Gerth and Mills suggest that a feature of the industrialized metropolis is that a person plays and is confronted with many roles, each of which has a different vocabulary of motives or justifications. One consequence is an enlargement of the activities of the self that must keep some situationally inappropriate sets of motives private from others. Another result is the secularization of the vocabularies of motive or justification and, with the increasing ideological twists and turns of the elite, a growing cynicism among people.

> In modern life there is often no stable or unquestioned vocabulary of motives available. And back of this is the fact that the institutional arrangements of roles demand that we rapidly give up and take on roles and along with them, their socially appropriate motives. Back of these "mixed motives" and "motivational conflicts" there is going on a competition of varying institutional patterns and their respective vocabularies of motives. Shifting and borderline situations, having no stable vocabularies of motive, may contain several alternative sets of motives originally belonging to different systems of roles.
>
> Such institutional conflicts are internalized and, accordingly, are revealed in the confusion and self-doubt of institutionally marginal persons. Institutional conflict, in short, threatens the sense of unity and even the identity of the modern self.[39]

We are members of a national community and a world community. Sometimes national boundaries are permeated by alliances, war communities, and so on. Moreover, there are many group and social boundaries within the state. Identification of key boundaries is perforce a complex operation.

"Fixers" and Boundary Mediators

The metaphor "the right side and the wrong side of the tracks" is used by participants to indicate sharply distinguished social and normative zones. Some societies appear to divide myth system and operational code into *spatial* zones and *appear* to have concordant bribal and nonbribal zones. There are supposed to be zones in which an accompanying private payment is considered an integral part of the performance of a normative act and other zones in which such payments will be deemed unlawful and even their mention a lapse of taste and discretion. I use the word *appear* because social boundaries, like all boundaries, have multiple, varying, and sometimes inconsistent meanings, dividing and retarding for some, increasing interaction for others, and, above all, creating the need for specialist groups, whom we might call, functionally, boundary mediators. Members of such groups— customs officials, lawyers, exporters and importers, insurers, smugglers of people and things—profit from their knowledge of, and skill in influencing the specialized social process a boundary really is.[40] The boundaries between bribal and nonbribal zones are social, and may have more sinuosities than Norway's coastline. The skill of the boundary mediator involves knowing the contiguities and, in particular, in which zones not to pay. He must also know the alliances, relationships, and agencies that link the two zones.[41]

Consider state X. If you want to arrange a pardon from the governor or secure a private bill through the intervention of your senator or get a favorable ruling from a judge, you had better not go to one of those individuals and suggest that you would be willing to pay for the favor. But you can "take care" of a local politician known to have ties, or an account may be opened with an advertising agency or an insurance agency, or you may seek the advice of a law firm that is still "compensating" the judge or senator for his past membership. The trick here is not the capacity to bribe but knowing the "bagman," knowing whom to fix.

Washington abounds with stories of boundaries and their porosities, but my favorite tells of a now-deceased senator who exploded in fury when a young man from his home state, seeking a favor, suggested an outright payment. "Young man, I ought to kick you right out of my office. I ought to kick you through the hall and right down the stairs. You know, I've got a mind to kick you right across Pennsylvania Avenue. What a nerve. I ought to kick you to _ Massachusetts Avenue and up to room 406, where my old law partner works. Now get out before I really get angry."

Those who have "know-who" are the effective boundary mediators. In transnational as well as national contexts, the mediators may be officials or nonofficials. Consider the experience of William Wearly, chairman of Ingersoll Rand. In 1972, he and some other businessmen who were planning a trip to the Middle East, stopped in Washington first.

> The Treasury briefed us on what payments were necessary on a country-by-country basis. Payments are required. It is considered politically benevolent by rulers of those countries for companies to distribute money. Both the Treasury and State Department Representatives were trying to keep us from spending money on the wrong people. They told us that as soon as we came into a country people would approach us, telling us that they had the right connections to get business. They said we had to find the guys who really were connected with the top people and use them as sales agent.[42]

Boundaries may, of course, shift in accord with larger social changes. In these circumstances, new specialists may supersede the veterans whose knowledge or contacts have become obsolete. The point is made graphically by Butler and Driscoll in a passage that also reveals the chagrin of old boundary mediators whose skills have been made obsolete by the demarcation of new social boundaries, for whose crossing others have monopolized the skills.

> Grafting used to be open and above board, like it should be if it's fairly honest. In the olden days, you paid the ward man in his saloon or right out on the street corner or on the church steps, wherever you happened to meet him. And the collector put the money in his sock or in his bank and thought no more about it.
>
> Most of the graft nowadays passes through the hands of lawyers, disguised as legal fees. If you want to get a favor from Tammany, just hire one of their leading lawyers and pay him five thousand dollars fee, part of which he keeps for himself and part of which he passes on to the boys who actually do the favor. You're safe then, because the courts are run by lawyers and lawyers stick together like the Forty Thieves. *Lawyers* can do no wrong.[43]

Boundary crossing requires an expert's guidance, for there are dangers to the novice. An official in the nonbribal zone who regularly, if indirectly, benefits from bribes may quite indignantly prosecute someone doing the "right" thing in the wrong zone. This is not simply because people are hypocritical and venal but also because people operate on many levels of consciousness and are quite capable of responses that seem inconsistent and self-contradictory if one fails to locate them in that network of expectations that divides social space and prescribes different codes for identical acts in different zones.

Two recent examples may emphasize the relations between bribal and nonbribal zones. The first involves former President Nixon's campaign, and the payoff effort has a certain refinement in its respect of boundaries and zones.[44]

The late Howard Hughes had apparently hoped to monopolize the Las Vegas Strip. On March 14, 1968, he sent a memo to his top assistant, Robert Maheu: "I want you to see Nixon as my special confidential emissary. I feel there is a valid possibility of a Republican victory this year ... that could be realized under our sponsorship and supervision every inch of the way." What he allegedly hoped for in this deal was an easing of the Justice Department's antitrust investigations of some of his operations; apparently Hughes felt that Nixon could influence then attorney general John Mitchell. Rather than carry the money to Nixon himself, Hughes delegated the task to Maheu. Maheu, perhaps understanding the necessity for using the "appropriate" zones and people for such a transaction, did not go directly to the president but called on Richard Danner, a longtime friend of Charles "Bebe" Rebozo and the then manager of the Frontier Hotel in Las Vegas. Danner delivered two $50,000 donations in hundred-dollar bills to Rebozo in Key Biscayne, Florida. The Dunes Hotel, in what appears to have been a quid pro quo for the cash, became available to Hughes. Although his purchase of the hotel fell through, Rebozo kept his $100,000. (There is conjecture, however, that the Nixon forces, rather than Hughes, initiated the idea of a large campaign donation from Hughes.)

A second example involves securing trade licenses in Ghana, as described by Professor Verbit:

By statute "the power to grant licenses and to create exemptions is vested in the Minister of Trade." Regulations are administered in behalf of the Minister by the Controller of Imports and Exports, the senior civil servant in the Ministry. . . .

In order to apply for a special license, an importer had to be registered with the Ministry of Trade. If he were registered, he could apply to import a product for which the Controller had announced . . . that applications were being received. The application would be mailed to the Controller. An applicant could request an interview to discuss his application for a license. In such a case, his request was to be sent to the Chief Commercial Officer, Ministry of Trade. Licenses were distributed based "on the amount of foreign exchange available for each class of commodity." Applicants were notified of the decisions on their applications by "printed standard letters." Apparently, however, the procedures outlined in the statute and notice presented only the formal structure. For it was evident from the testimony taken by the Ollennu Commission that some import licenses were issued according to a different procedure.

J.K. Khubchamdani, managing director of the Glamour Garment Factory in Accra, filed an application for import licenses of a value of £ 1 million for 1965 pursuant to the regulations. Two months went by without Khubchamdani hearing from the Ministry. Finally he received a telephone call in January 1966 from a Mr. Inkumsah, Deputy Speaker of the National Assembly, asking him to stop by the latter's office. At the meeting, Inkumsah indicated that he knew about Khubchamdani's application for an import license and he (Inkumsah) would "help."

Mr. Inkumsah, after speaking with the minister of trade, informed Khubchamdani that he had to pay a "commission"—10 percent of their value—in order to receive the licenses. Because this was a substantial sum, Khubchamdani tried to have the price lowered by seeking a personal interview with the minister of trade. He was unsuccessful.

Finally, he met the Minister at a cocktail party and indicated to him that he would like to see him at the office. The Minister responded that it would be very difficult. Khubchamdani then said, "I know Inkumsah well." To this the Minister replied, "If you know Inkumsah, then it is not necessary for you to see me."[45]

After further negotiations Khubchamdani received his licenses, and portions of his "commission" were divided up within the Ghanaian government.

These cases are not forwarded as examples of a universal proposition that there is always a secret channel between bribal and nonbribal zones. There are certainly nonbribal zones in which the tender of money or a money substitute to secure the performance of an official act will be viewed as illegal, tasteless, a violation of the gentleman's code, or worse. On the other hand, anyone who studies bribery becomes sufficiently cynical to note the proximity of bribal and nonbribal zones, the utility of official power to all, and the attractions of money to many. In light of past evidence it seems more realistic, if less pious, to hypothesize the likelihood of a cash flow until empirical evidence refutes it.

The relationship between bribal and nonbribal zones tends to challenge the popular notion that the zones are self-contained and hierarchically located: the higher you go, the cleaner things are supposed to get. Some studies of the hierarchical ordering of the legal profession have indeed assembled data that seem to show that the lower you go, the more prevalent the fix as a fixture of professional activity.[46] But at the present stage of my own research, I am inclined to reject the notion of progressive hierarchical cleanliness and, if anything, to assume that the higher one goes and the greater the stakes, the larger, but considerably more refined, will be the bribery. Just as pernicious as the myth of big badness is the populist myth of small business probity: the smaller the firm and the more direct the proprietary control, the less the predisposition for, and practice of, bribery. An official at the Department of Justice charged with bribery prosecutions has said that

despite the varied nature of these prosecutions, certain generalizations can be ventured. First there are just as many cases involving firms which are not giant multinational corporations as there are cases in which such firms are involved. The large international firms do not seem to have any monopoly at all of the tendency to violate the antitrust laws.[47]

In his very valuable study of the Chicago bar, Jerome Carlin found "a relatively low order of professional skill exercised by individual lawyers because, at this level of practice, more than at any other, results are obtained for clients less on the basis of manipulating legal doctrine than of manipulating officials."[48] Carlin thought this was so "because the individual practitioner tends, by and large, to be at the bottom of the status hierarchy of the metropolitan bar, he, more than other practitioners, is likely to be a bookkeeper, broker, and/or fixer."[49]

While I cannot marshal empirical data to counter Carlin's conclusion, I am skeptical of its implications. It is very difficult to purge oneself of status bias; even after the recent revelations of multinational bribery, it is still hard for many to imagine silken and aristocratic American law firms engaging in "that sort of thing." But there should be no surprise. Every firm has a "tough guy," and all large organizations develop specialist roles. It would appear that someone will be willing, pleased, and even anxious to show his courage, toughness, or grit and do "the job that has to be done." Superiors may not wish to know, but they are not necessarily unappreciative. In reply to the question whether he would fire a worker for paying bribes abroad, Charles Bower, chairman of Booz, Allen & Hamilton Consultants, replied, "Hell, no! Why fire him for something he was paid to do?"[50]

Bribers and Administrators

From the standpoint of an administrator *within* an organization, unauthorized and undelegated bribery is an organizational pathology because it retards the accurate execution of directions and orders from above. A bureaucracy, in whatever value process, may be understood as a social process hierarchically designed as an authority system for the execution of the orders of a superior. Its effectiveness depends, in addition to factors such as design, personal competence, and adequate numbers, on the submissive loyalty of the bureaucrat to orders coming directly from above. This loyalty is established by contract, by general cultural norms, by careful recruitment of personality types, by contingent criminal sanctions, and by quasi-religious invocations, such as oaths of office.[51]

Bribery, like Plato's noble lie, is a useful, perhaps indispensable, elite instrument. But it depends on who's doing it. Where unauthorized variance and outright purchase bribes are practiced, bureaucracy fails pro tanto. While the failure is usually explained in moralistic terms of the "corruptability" or "venality" of the bureaucrat and the briber, an observer, outside of the administration, will often discover that the briber was offered or accepted the bribe at the behest, or in the interests, of another organization or administration to which one of the participants owed and practiced loyalty.[52] Despite moralistic imprecations, the administrative response at some level takes this into account by escalating the available techniques already being used to police loyalty: more explicit contract terms, more onerous oaths, more selective personnel procedures, more internal controls and policing. There is no reason to assume that the counterpart organizations and administrations are not themselves undertaking comparable programs, the result of all of which is probably reciprocal neutralization. Insofar as red tape slows up bureaucratic functions and time is of value to the erstwhile purchaser of them, the administrative response is likely to generate more and more expensive bribery. It is also likely to generate more centralized control.

The key factor in bribery, one probably characteristic of all social life, is the coexistence of competing organizations and communities, each with its own loyalty system. In periods during which the constellation of superordination and subordination is clear—backed both by authority and by the relative control bases of the superordinates and the subordinates—circumstances for bribery may still arise, but the notion of what's right is comparatively pellucid. In periods in which the constellation of intergroup relations is more fluid or unstable and coarchical, guidelines as to bribery behavior are also less clear in terms both of authority and of effective power. Those in conflicting loyalty situations do not know if it is *more* right or wrong to bribe in concrete circumstances or if they are more likely to be sanctioned (or sanctioned more severely) by one of the competing organizations if they do or don't bribe. Even the normative guidelines are not clear. To Jesus' message to the Herodians, "Render therefore to Caesar the things that are Caesar's, and to God the things that are God's," Thoreau added tersely, "leaving them no wiser than before as to which which was which: for they did not wish to know."[53]

The major focus of the current antibribery campaign is on the growth of the multinational corporation, not merely as a commercial unit but as a competing political and loyalty system, with departments of external affairs, press attachés, welfare programs, internal police, and house clericals or "ethicists." The claims these neo-behemoths can make on their employees are, as we have seen, enormous and may, in the phenomenal world of the employee, be virtually impossible to reject. But there are many other competitors for loyalty: nations, regions, religions, language and dialect groups, tribes, particular government departments or agencies. Indeed, any focus for loyalty may become the basis for some group organization. Even the demand for personal gain at the expense of a larger group—the quintessential bribe—reflects a normative and loyalty system.

In circumstances in which the power relations between groups and communities are coarchical, elites will often be driven to establish certain norms for indispensable activities between diverse groups: norms of nonaggression, respect for the zones of other groups, norms about restraint in the use of violence, of bribery, propaganda, and so forth. Such norms may be widely promulgated and become part of the myth system but need not necessarily be self-executing because of the tension between myth systems and operational codes and the social distances generated between the governors and the governed.

Rolf Dahrendorf has added a rather bleak corollary to Robert Michel's "iron law of oligarchy": the inexorable stratification between governing and governed.[54] When governors view themselves as somewhat distinct from the rest of the community, tensions between myth system and operational code are generated. And as long as governors say "This is wrong" but indicate to a limited and elite audience by words or deeds that it is right to do it (albeit discreetly) in the instant case, bribery, among other myth discrepancies, will continue to enjoy selective toleration. Hence, even where bribery is prohibited in interelite agreements, it may continue operationally and, more significant, continue to be morally ambiguous, the ultimate conclusion as to its rightness depending on context, value, and the special calculus of the effective loyalty system of the appraiser.

Even assuming that every group could become absolutely coarchical, without role specializations, elites, rank and file or masses, myth systems and operational codes, the very existence of a plurality of groups would continue to generate bribery. The proliferation of usury, as Nelson showed, was a product of large-scale social and personality changes: a transition from visions of "tribal brotherhood" to "universal otherhood."[55] A termination of usury would require a reversal of that transition and a world of universal brotherhood. Similarly, bribery will stop when every man loves his brother as himself. Its ultimate elimination would require a massive social and psychopersonal reconstruction in which a single loyalty system would be reared, with no competitors. For bribery, seen in broadest context, is not an evil in itself;

virtually nothing is. Bribery is an epiphenomenon of a pluralistic world community and the constant process of exclusive
group and loyalty formation. The price of completely eliminating bribery is actually the termination of this ongoing
process of individuation, group formation, and self-deter-
mination and the replacement of the old philosophical radical
conception of pluralism and the dialectical character of truth
with a single, unchallengeable authority. Is this the type of
world order and psychopersonal organization we desire?

Epilogue

The Current Bribery Campaign

All that having been said, there is still a pressing need for a national debate on the question of what we expect a business executive to do in places like Iran.
— "No Saints Available," *Wall Street Journal*, February 28, 1978

IS there a consensus among our elite to reform the commercial practices of bribery? It would be quite inaccurate to say that the United States "government," as a single entity, is conducting either a crusade or a reform against bribery. Every demonology has its own scientific method and a bribery campaign is no exception. To paraphrase Harold Lasswell, *some* private rewards by *some* actors in *some* circumstances have been characterized as bribery. Others have not. The discrepancy is interesting and enlightening. The government in Washington is many governments, in shifting patterns of conflict and alliance. In addition, the governmental process of the United States includes many nonofficial participants. For many of these "governments" or their constituencies, bribery of a private or mixed nature has been a convenient and perhaps indispensable tool for social influence. Though hard evidence is elusive, it would take an extraordinary faith in either the virtue or the stupidity of our officials to believe that the massive transnational commercial bribery currently being attacked was effected without the knowledge or advice, let alone the facilitation and even participation, of some officials.

Bribery is, as we have seen, a variant of one of the

fundamental techniques of politics: the tendering of actual or promised indulgences in order to secure certain desirable behavior. Part of the current scandal over the bribery activities of multinational corporations may be viewed as a struggle between competing social organizations for the ultimate authority to use this particular technique. Most operators would accept as appropriate, if not necessarily "nice," that officials, overt or covert, of one nation-state might tender bribes to officials of others in the line of duty.[1] Thus Secretary of State Cyrus Vance, when pressed in a public forum to distinguish Korean bribery of United States congressmen from United States bribery of Korean politicians, claimed that he could "draw a clear distinction between a government-to-government operation and one that deals with individuals, such as the Korean situation." Theirs, he said, "was not a government-to-government kind of operation" and that rendered it unlawful.[2] All governmental bribe operations are, of course, not automatically lawful, but most operators would be somewhat uneasy with the assertion that any other social organization operating in the international arena might just as properly use the bribe technique as a way of securing its objectives. A member of the Church committee remarked that the question involved in certain Lockheed activities was whether the United States had a foreign policy or Lockheed had a foreign policy.

At the center of the issue is a species of social organization that is rapidly becoming a major factor in world politics and will perhaps rival and succeed the nation-state as a focus for loyalties. That organization is demanding for itself the same competence to bribe that is already available to the nation-state. In response, nation-state officials are trying to protect a competence that was formerly exclusively theirs by using criminal sanctions against the multinational enterprise. Thus the issue is not that bribery in a transnational context is viewed as unlawful per se but that *some groups ought not to be bribing.* Plato's "noble lie" is available only to the rulers, and, after all, who *are* the rulers? From this perspective, the rash of multinational corporate disclosures concerning "questionable payments" assumes a more portentous political significance. Both the national and international proposals aimed at regulating these transnational corporate practices amount to efforts by one elite group to curb the rapidly rivaling power of a competing group.[3]

Official attitudes about bribery vary, according to the role or responsibility of the official concerned in the governmental system. For those charged with responsibility for the balance of payments or the balance of power, "extraordinary payments" may be viewed as a necessary evil, if an evil at all; in intelligence activities and in foreign trade,[4] all sorts of things that may not be done at home can be done abroad if they are properly approved. But other officials view bribery as an intolerable evil. As the newspapers make manifest, a number of senators and congressmen and some staff members, as well as the enforcement division of the Securities and Exchange Commission, are active in investigating and exposing corruption. In short, parts of our government may be reforming while others are crusading.

Attitudes in the nonofficial sector of our national elite appear more uniform. I have not conducted a survey of the attitudes of opinion-formation groups, such as clergymen, but money changers are often close to the temple, and marketplace indicators suggest a lack of popular agitation against payoffs. Stockholder suits, for example, are not necessarily an indicator of popular discontent but quite often of lawyers' enterprise. As the *New York Times* reported, "The corporate payoff revelations are triggering an unprecedented wave of stockholder lawsuits. . . . Gulf Oil Company has been sued by seven, Exxon Corporation by three, and Lockheed Aircraft Corp., Tenneco Inc., and others have already been hit with one or two suits at the latest count . . . but more will come as lawyers find plaintiffs and fill out forms." Traditionally the legal remedy, and hence the legal incentive, for corporate misbehavior is suit for money damages. The settlements reached in the shareholder suits involving Northrop Corporation and Phillips Petroleum Company, however, "provided for some repayment of money and also for significant structural changes in the companies' board of directors, and executives committees."[5] This may act as a disincentive for further suits.

The *Wall Street Journal* reported in April, "Bribery scandals aren't turning off job-seekers at the companies involved. Exxon, Grumman and other concerns that admitted to questionable foreign payments say job applications are strong and most applicants haven't even raised the payoff issue in interviews." Job-seekers aren't asking questions, according to an official from Northrop, "because most of the applicants are aerospace people and understand the system." A slightly different explanation was offered by another official of an unnamed company: "So many companies have acknowledged payments that an applicant would have to be very selective to avoid one."[6]

A crucial and perhaps basic reason for the lack of popular concern, even among many shareholders, over corporate practices may be the fact that disclosures of corporate misconduct have had minimal to negligible impact on the stockmarket value of those corporations involved in the disclosures and may be viewed as responsible for business gains.[7] Roderick Hills, then chairman of the SEC, publicly noted that stockholders and even judges may not be particularly concerned over how "their" company makes a profit. He quoted from a comment sent to him by a state circuit judge: "I read your bureaucratic blurb in the *Wall Street Journal* today [about foreign payments]. You are out of your mind. Stockholders don't give a good damn."[8]

There appears to be little ambivalence among the shareholders of Northrop stock about the company's practices. Thomas V. Jones, the chairman of Northrop Corporation who pleaded guilty to felony charges of making illegal contributions to the reelection campaign of former president Nixon, was "warmly applauded" at a stockholder's meeting when he said that Northrop revenues would easily surpass $1 billion this year.[9] Lockheed shareholders have apparently fared well despite, or perhaps because of, their company's commercial extraordinaries. Lockheed Aircraft Corporation, perhaps the most renowned of transnational corporate bribers, completed, in the wake of the entire Japanese-Lockheed scandal, their largest single foreign sale ever. With the smell of the scandal still lingering in the air, Canada purchased eighteen Lockheed antisubmarine planes, the largest peacetime military purchase in Canadian history. This transaction would appear to indicate that a close ally is willing to disregard the sensational bribal escapades of America's number-one defense contractor.[10]

Modalities of Political Confrontation

A political confrontation is by definition an absence of consensus. Whether the current campaign will emerge as a reform or a crusade will depend upon power, mode, and context. Four major modalities have been pursued: international agreements, federal legislation, state legislation, and self-regulation or corporate housecleaning.[11] Each presents a different visage, but in each the basic elements of crusade and reform can be detected.

International Agreements

Though the antibribery campaign is essentially American in origin, it is perforce exported to all corners of the globe thanks to United States preeminence in international commerce. Some United States officials and traders contend that the elimination of corporate bribery rather than United States traders can be achieved only if a general international prohibition of bribery is prescribed and enforced.[12] Thus a

United States representative, speaking to the Intergovernmental Working Group on Corrupt Practices in 1976, said:

> Our experience has brought the conviction that the illicit payments problem can only be solved by collective international action based on a multilateral treaty to be implemented by national legislation. We have also come to believe that the traditional criminal laws cannot solve the problem by themselves.[13]

The actual proposal made by the United States only sketched a disclosure system and, even then, was somewhat reticent and ambiguous as to what was to be disclosed.

A related argument contends that if United States legislation alone prohibits what is a widespread multinational practice, the result will only be prevention of American firms from competing; bribery will continue. Hence, they insist, an international agreement eliminating bribery should come first, followed by national implementing legislation in all relevant jurisdictions. There has thus been strong support in the executive branch for the Organization for Economic Cooperation and Development's code of conduct and hearty noises of approval about an international agreement.

Antibribery campaigns are not the sort of thing that government officials anywhere openly oppose. If the resolution of draft law is lofty and general enough and if the section on enforcement "will be dealt with later," everyone will vote aye. In 1975, the General Assembly of the United Nations adopted a resolution that condemned all corrupt practices, including bribery by transnational and local corporations, intermediaries, and anyone else who might be involved and called upon everyone (but no one *in particular*) to take all necessary and appropriate measures to prevent the corrupt practices.[14] The resolution was adopted by consensus. On June 21, 1976, the OECD issued a policy statement exhorting that firms

> (i) not render—and they should not be solicited or expected to render—any bribe or other improper benefit, direct or indirect, to any public servant or holder of public office;

(ii) unless legally permissible, not make contributions to candidates for public office or to political organizations;

(iii) abstain from any improper involvement in local political activities.[15]

The United States has moved within GATT, the General Agreement on Trade and Tariffs, for an accord prohibiting bribery.[16] Yet another working group has been established in the United Nations[17] and certain general guidelines have been drafted provisionally by the new Commission on Transnational Corporations.[18]

It is difficult to see how an international agreement will actually change the operational code with regard to bribery. The formal code of virtually every country in the world already prohibits bribery.[19] Hence an international agreement might win quick acceptance but result in no more enforcement than is currently secured under the different, quite ineffective, domestic laws it replicates. An international prosecutor and an international court whose writ ran to all corners of the world could make an international agreement effective; but neither exists nor is likely to be created, and it is, hence, idle and diversionary to speculate on them. To date, the international efforts that have been mounted seem more on the order of crusade than reform. Their major contribution appears to be the feeling that something laudable is being done.

Federal Legislation

United States legislative exercises that the current campaign has stimulated have been particularly interesting for their fierce competitive redundancy. Bribery has been illegal for a long time. In 1918 the commissioners of the Federal Trade Commission wrote to Congress in crusading terms almost identical to those we now hear that "bribery is criminal per se."[20] From a legislative standpoint, there is really little more to say on the subject. There is a complex of legislation, much of which, in one form or another, prohibits bribery: the Sherman, Clayton, Robinson-Patman, and Fair Trade Commission Acts,[21] the fraud and antiracketeering laws,[22] key decisions by the Federal Trade Commission,[23] and antitrust and fair trade legislation enacted in many of the fifty states.[24] In many circumstances bribery is criminal. Though the Internal Revenue Code is not a penal statute, it has indicated official disapproval by barring the deduction of bribes as "business expenses."[25] Nor is new legislation required to legitimize the projection of United States law abroad. United States courts have evolved a code for extending our jurisdiction, key parts effected, ironically, in the aftermath of the Teapot Dome scandal.[26] While some official action might require the cooperation of foreign governments, the SEC's enforcement division has demonstrated that results can be won by vigorous domestic prosecution. When enforcement agencies are exposed as lax, one of their defenses is the claim that the law was inadequate: they need more authority. A review of the legislation suggests that is not the case.

Congressional investigations of corporate bribery stimulated bills and counterbills from the Hill and the White House. Several representative examples may be profitably examined. The Ford administration's proposals[27] called for no more than disclosure, by corporations making extraordinary payments, of the amounts and the recipients. The information, disclosed to the secretary of commerce, would be kept confidential for a year, then given to other executive departments and government agencies on what appear to be basically discretionary grounds. The information could still be suppressed if the secretary of state or the attorney general indicated foreign policy or other prosecutorial reasons. Nondisclosure would be penalized by fines. The Ford bill was hardly a creative breakthrough. Some congressional legislation has, in fact, incorporated disclosure requirements. The Arms Export Control Act of 1976,[28] for example, required reports of payments related to the sales of arms abroad. The Internal Revenue Service has also become more insistent on receiving information about payments.[29]

Disclosure requirements may also be disarmed by conditioning the obligation on "knowing." For example, Senate Bill 3379 provided criminal sanctions for failure to keep books.

> Whoever, unless prevented by foreign law (a) knowingly fails to file a statement required by this section, (b) knowingly files a false statement or (c) knowingly fails to obtain from any agent all information for any disclosure statement shall, upon conviction, be fined not more than $25,000 and imprisoned for not less than one month and not more than two years.

Moreover, it prescribed personal liability for violations:

> Any person who signed the disclosure statement required, any person who is a director or partner in the company required to file such disclosure statement, and any other person who, with his consent, has been named as having prepared or certified any part of such disclosure statement, and who, unless prevented by foreign law, (a) knowingly fails to file a statement, (b) knowingly fails to obtain information required, or (c) knowingly files a false statement shall, upon conviction, be fined not more than $25,000 and imprisoned for not less than one month and not more than two years.

But the requirement of knowledge in both of these provisions is a virtual invitation to ignorance.

There is a curious circularity in the legislation employing the disclosure technique. Even before the legislation, bribery was unlawful and hence was always accomplished surreptitiously. Why the legislature, in its abundant wisdom, should assume that its demand for disclosure of illegal activities will now be complied with and will somehow prevent bribery is baffling.[30] It is hard to escape a suspicion of cynicism in these proposals. As we saw in chapter 1, the executive has, in the past, resorted to the "disclosure" technique to scotch more effective legislation. If bribery is a problem, the Ford proposal is essentially a simulated response.

A different approach was taken in the Proxmire bill,[31] which would dictate criminal penalties for corporate bribers, even if the bribery were conducted abroad. Though some critics, notably from the executive branch, raised evidentiary and jurisdictional questions,[32] this sort of legislation could be made effective. The real question would be the degree of executive commitment to consistent and vigorous enforcement, which is, of course, the key to the enforcement of antibribery laws and indeed to any meaningful response to white-collar crime. There is law aplenty on the books.[33]

The function of sanctions is to maintain or restore public order. No more. No less. As a general matter of sanction theory, severe and painful sanctions that deprive in a measure beyond the apparent injury to society, so-called *in terrorem* penalties, are effective if they in fact deter potential perpetrators from engaging in acts deemed harmful to public order. If such sanctions do not deter, but serve only to intimidate and cause anxiety among perpetrators who nonetheless continue to engage in the prohibited activities, the sanctions may be deemed a failure from the standpoint of public order. Indeed, they may be as noxious to public order as the behavior they are supposed to prevent. Selective enforcement, as we saw in chapter 3, can be a device for intimidation of opposition and aggrandizement of executive power,[34] ultimately eroding the fiber of democracy. Communication of a real commitment to control bribery would require little more than an opinion by the attorney general of the pertinence of existing law coupled with the ample funding of an enforcement program. Alas, if the prosecution of bribery proves similar to the prosecution of other forms of white-collar crime, it will be sporadic at best.

The ultimate legislative product of these efforts was the Foreign Corrupt Practices Act of 1977 (FCPA).[35] Briefly stated, the act obliges accounting methods that will provide an accurate record of, among other things, bribe transactions. But the act discharges suppressions of information in matters concerning national security.

(3) (A) With respect to matters concerning the national security of the United States, no duty or liability under paragraph (2) of this

subsection shall be imposed upon any person acting in cooperation
with the head of any Federal department or agency responsible for
such matters if such act in cooperation with such head of a department or agency was done upon the specific, written directive of the
head of such department or agency pursuant to Presidential authority to issue such directives. Each directive issued under this paragraph shall set for the specific facts and circumstances with respect
to which the provisions of this paragraph are to be invoked. Each
such directive shall, unless renewed in writing, expire one year after
the date of issuance.[36]

The result is an almost amusing self-indictment, for FCPA
confirms foreign suspicions that the United States government has used corporations operating abroad for intelligence
purposes, and will continue to do so. The legislative Report
of the Senate Banking, Housing, and Urban Affairs Committee, the architect of the act, emphasizes its concern for
"the reputation and image of all U.S. businessmen."[37] But
the need to accommodate the committee's high moral tone
with a low reality authoritatively tarnishes United States
business's reputation and integrity and provides legislative
reasons for suspecting *all* American firms abroad prima facie.

FCPA prohibits all "domestic concerns," those subject to
the Securities Exchange Act and those not, from using the
mails or other means of interstate commerce

corruptly in furtherance of an offer, payment, promise to pay, or
authorization of the payment of any money, or offer, gift, promise
to give, or authorization of the giving of anything of value to—
    "(1) any foreign official for purposes of—
        "(A) influencing any act or decision of such foreign official in
    his official capacity, including a decision to fail to perform his
    official functions. or
        "(B) inducing such foreign official to use his influence with a
    foreign government or instrumentality thereof to affect or influ-
    ence any act or decision of such government or instrumentality,
    in order to assist such issuer in obtaining or retaining business for or
    with, or directing business to, any person;
    "(2) any foreign political party or official thereof or any candi-

date for foreign political office for purposes of—

"(A) influencing any act or decision of such party, official, or candidate in its or his official capacity, including a decision to fail to perform its or his official functions; or

"(B) inducing such party, official, or candidate to use its or his influence with a foreign government or instrumentality thereof to affect or influence any act or decision of such government or instrumentality,

in order to assist such issuer in obtaining or retaining business for or with, or directing business to, any person; or

"(3) any person, while knowing or having reason to know that all or a portion of such money or thing of value will be offered, given, or promised, directly or indirectly, to any foreign official, to any foreign political party or official thereof, or to any candidate for foreign political office, for purposes of—

"(A) influencing any act or decision of such foreign official, political party, party official, or candidate in his or its official capacity, including a decision to fail to perform his or its official functions; or

"(B) inducing such foreign official, political party, party official, or candidate to use his or its influence with a foreign government or instrumentality thereof to affect or influence any act or decision of such government or instrumentality,

in order to assist such issuer in obtaining or retaining business for or with, or directing business to, any person."[38]

A "foreign official" is defined as

any officer or employee of a foreign government or any department, agency, or instrumentality thereof, or any person acting in an official capacity for or on behalf of such government or department, agency, or instrumentality. Such term does not include any employee of a foreign government or any department, agency, or instrumentality thereof whose duties are essentially ministerial or clerical.[39]

The Senate report specifically excludes "grease payments":

The statute covers payments made to foreign officials for the purpose of obtaining business or influencing legislation or regulations. The statute does not, therefore, cover so-called "grease payments" such as payments for expediting shipments through customs or placing a transatlantic telephone call, securing required permits, or obtaining adequate police protection, transactions which may involve even the proper performance of duties.[40]

The definition of *grease* is ecumenical, and a good many sins may slide through that category. The bite of FCPA is further blunted by the requirement of a "corrupt purpose." As the Senate report puts it:

> The word "corruptly" is used in order to make clear that the offer, payment, promise, or gift, must be intended to induce the recipient to misuse his official position in order to wrongfully direct business to the payor or his client, or to obtain preferential legislation or a favorable regulation. The word "corruptly" connotes *an evil motive or purpose,* an intent to wrongfully influence the recipient. It does not require that the act be fully consummated, or succeed in producing the desired outcome [emphasis added].[41]

Imagine the following scenario. Yours is the better product, qualitatively or pricewise (could it be otherwise?). The Minister of Development agrees, but adds apologetically that he cannot award you the contract you should rightfully have unless "certain other matters" are arranged discreetly. Is your payment "corrupt," accompanied by an "evil motive or purpose" or "an intent to wrongfully influence the recipient"? It is a question that need not have been asked, for the legislation might simply have said that payments, without regard to corrupt intent, are unlawful.

The story is told of a diplomat at the United Nations General Assembly who had marked his speech in the margins, almost like a musical score. In one place the marginal notation read: "Weak point. Speak loud." The penalties established by the FCPA are severe: up to $1 million for the firm violating it and up to $10,000 or five years' imprisonment for an officer or director in willful violation.[42] This is a comparatively high if not excessive penalty and, given the hedging in the act and the difficulties of enforcement, it may be largely symbolic: the weaker the legislation, the louder the accompanying threat. In its report, the Senate committee explained that "the committee believes that legislation is appropriate to make clear that cessation of these abuses is a matter, not merely of SEC concern, but of national policy."[43] Criminalization is, of course, a most emphatic indication of community opprobrium. The Senate report sought to explain why it chose this route: "Direct criminalization entails no reporting burden on corporations and less of an enforcement burden on the Government. The criminalization of foreign corporate bribery will to a significant extent act as a self-enforcing, preventative mechanism."[44] This is a curious statement, to say the least. With no reporting burden on the corporation and no enforcement burden on the government, the act is indeed self-enforcing. Of course, if it were truly preventative, all police could beat their swords into plowshares, for the law alone would suffice to secure conforming behavior. If it is not, FCPA is a broad congressional wink.

The Securities and Exchange Commission's voluntary disclosure program[45] has won much more publicity, but it is a curious phenomenon in its practice, its result, and even in its reference. Under the Securities Exchange Act, corporations under its jurisdiction must file a so-called Form 8K[46] in any month in which an event of stockholder interest has occurred. If bribes are or were of interest to shareholders or are material to investors, they must be filed. From 1974 to 1976 alone, almost two-hundred corporations made such disclosures. But their motives, criteria of internal decision, and the longer-range consequences of the voluntary disclosure program remain questionable. The fact that payments in the past were effected surreptitiously indicates that executives making them knew they were prohibited. Why a voluntary disclosure program will retard payments in the future when business judgments would seem to require them is, once again, obscure. Consider the strange case of the Northrop

Corporation. Northrop settled an SEC suit and agreed not to engage in foreign bribery. It later admitted that more than $100,000 had been paid in foreign bribes after it signed the decree.[47]

As of October 11, 1976, the SEC had sued twenty-two companies in connection with corporate bribes and payoffs. All twenty-two companies settled these suits through the technique of consent settlements. In these deals, defendants agree to an injunction and sometimes other sanctions, while neither admitting nor denying guilt. The information from such settlements cannot be used as evidence in private stockholder suits following SEC action. An attorney for private plaintiffs said: "A consent settlement to my clients is as if nothing happened at all." August Bequai, a former SEC trial lawyer now practicing privately and teaching at George Washington University, asks, "How do you think the SEC enforcement division was able to grow from just a handful of people in the 1950's to where it is today? It's because the S.E.C. has been firing blanks. Who gets hurt in consent settlements? The S.E.C. gets a notch on its gun. The law firm gets money, the public is happy because they read 'fraud' in the newspaper and think criminality right away. The company neither admits nor denies anything. It's the perfect accommodation. And it's all one big charade."[48]

Shareholder suits against corporation executives who may have bribed customers or made unlawful payments to national politicians seem, at first impression, to be an ideal form of control of commercial bribal propensities and, indeed, a number of favorable judgments have been secured.[49] What could be more durable than shareholder self-interest? Shareholder activities have taken two forms: resolutions at meetings and court actions. It is difficult to gauge the impact of shareholder resolutions on subsequent corporate practices.[50] Suits would seem to promise greater effectiveness. But in fact, much depends on sternly disapproving judges. A judge who expresses understanding and sympathy for the dilemmas of the merchant is unlikely to create an unshakable expectation of enforcement. In a shareholder suit against Gulf Oil Corporation, federal judge Joseph P. Wilson characterized the defendant's actions as "just humanity." "You can't," he said, "blame them too much." Though Gulf had added only one new member to its board, Judge Wilson pronounced that the company was "what the new President would call 'reborn.' "[51]

State Legislation and Prosecution

Most of our states have their own antitrust and fair trade practices laws, which can, under principles of contemporary federal jurisdiction, be projected to activities occurring outside the states but affecting citizens or events within the state.[52] Thus a substantial number of states enacted or extended legislation to prohibit and punish participation in some aspects of the Arab boycott[53] despite the fact that much of the precipitating conduct originated in the Middle East. It is quite likely that an enterprising and ambitious attorney general in one of the states will set his sights on a multinational corporate briber. The most recent tendency of the federal courts has been to view activities such as these as essentially preempted by the federal government and hence prohibited to the states.[54] Even if such preemption is not declared, however, state enforcement will, by its nature, be selective and sporadic. It will intimidate but not deter.

Housecleaning

To be sure, crime does not pay. Our prisons are filled with wrongdoers. But certain groups in our pluralistic system, endowed with power and status, can defer punishment when caught in malefactions by offering promises of self-reform. One of the responses of multinational businessmen to the antibribery campaign has been the promise to clean house themselves.[55] The International Chamber of Commerce, for example, has created an Unethical Practices Commission and a code of corporate conduct.[56]

Self-reform may be serious and honest or it may be no more than a way of parrying official efforts at reform.

There have been a few times when Wall Street has done more than slap the wrists of its elite, and investors have not had to do the job that assigned regulators should be doing. But any observer or chronicler of such exceptional periods—which is what they were—would do well to look beneath the surface. Vigorous prosecution has come about almost only when the Street has feared that inaction would result in the loss of a privilege or a prerogative, or worse, result in action by an angry Congress.[57]

Good intentions notwithstanding, it is always important to ascertain whether key and effective group members are actually committed to reform. Even if they are, self-reform is possible only if the self-reforming group has sufficient decision articulation and centralized power to make its nostrums effective. International business does not; ironically, it cannot lest it violate antitrust policies. Moreover, its incorporation in the competitive nation-state system makes cooperation in securing the reforms sought even more unlikely. In the current bribery campaign, promises of self-reform, though they may be made in good faith, do not seem fulfillable. Self-reform here will accomplish no more than reaffirmation of the pertinent norms of the myth system.

Many corporations have initiated internal campaigns to determine the extent of bribery practices and to formulate policy statements and prescribe procedures for the future. A study by the Council on Economic Priorities reported:

The effectiveness of such policy statements is uncertain; theoretically honored, they are often ignored in practice. Xerox, for example, had an impressive anti-bribery policy in effect while an operating group was making $100,000 in questionable payments abroad from 1971 to 1975. The elaborate and detailed policies drawn up since disclosure by such firms as Northrop and Control Data remain to be tested. Still other companies, such as Abex (I.C. Industries) have made merely perfunctory statements proscribing illegal payments and the falsification of records, but provide their employees with no detailed guidelines.[58]

Problems in the application of an internal code derive from different perceptions of what is right held by different types and roles in an organization whose raison d'être is not poverty, abstinence, nor altruism. Corporations are social organizations designed to maximize wealth; performance pressures and promises of reward and advancement are likely to outweigh ethical claims that are costly and, moreover, may be viewed as essentially hypocritical. Early in 1977, *Business Week* reported on surveys conducted among business executives that seemed to confirm that a majority of those consulted felt pressure to compromise personal ethics to achieve corporate goals. Significantly, *BW* reported, "Almost all respondents felt that business ethics, however imperfect, were as good or better than the ethics of society at large."[59]

Interviews I have conducted with attorneys from firms who participated in the in-house investigations confirmed general seriousness of purpose, but several of the lawyers remarked on the difficulties of sustaining effective prohibitions in those foreign countries where "extraordinary payments" were apparently part of the local monetary unit. One in-house attorney who participated in the drafting of an internal code regarding payments witnessed the dismissal of an executive who ignored it in favor of the older practice. The harsh punishment failed to persuade him of the continuing efficacy of the new code. In particular, he commented on the difference in personality of the lawyer and the sales executive in larger corporations and their differing attitudes toward bribery. According to him, many of the lawyers tended to be apprehensive about violating the code prohibiting payments, even if potential sales might be lost. Sales executives in contrast thought in "bottom-line" terms and tended to evaluate payments in terms of their contribution to securing sales. As with other areas of regulation, there comes a point when commercial factors loom large and, as the saying goes, "the lawyers leave the room."

Where companies have gone out of their way to establish

effective internal monitoring procedures, capable of uncovering wrongdoing that might otherwise have gone undetected, the rewards appear to have proven dubious. A colleague of mine who is researching the area of corporate compliance reports an interesting experience. He telephoned the general counsel of a multinational that had responded to the current anticorporate crusade with a "model" internal compliance program distinctive for its thoroughness. In the course of their conversation, he congratulated the counsel on his achievement. The counsel's response, after a year's experience with the program, was bitterness: "Some laws are made to be broken. We're monitoring things the regulators didn't know about—and don't want to know about. It prevents us from doing things that have always been done in this business, that everybody else is doing; we've increased our liability exposure and put ourselves at a competitive disadvantage, all at one stroke."

Robert Merton has written that "certain phases of social structure generate the circumstances in which infringement of social codes constitutes a normal response."[60] Delicately reminiscent of that insight, several interviewees commented on the problem of conflicting messages. The company's legal department drafts a no-payment statement, which is sent out over the signature of the president. One lawyer suggested the following scenario. The president tells the vice-president for Latin American sales that sales must be boosted by 10 percent. The vice-president begins to explain, but the president interrupts. "If I have to take a hand in day-to-day management, I don't need a vice-president for sales." Even in the absence of explicit conflict, the degree of aggressiveness of a sales executive may tone and color one of the messages. The problem of corporate housecleaning is essentially a micro-replication of the operational code of the larger system. "Of course we don't bribe. But our business is selling and there are times. . . ."

Self-reform of those who *service* the neo-behemoths of

modern commerce may be more plausible; they are in fact
more organized and, through the application of codes of
professional ethics, they can exercise certain sanctions over
their members.[61] Self-reform by lawyers, however, is re-
tarded by the adversarial ethic of that profession. In a liberal
state, the lawyer serves his client and not the state, a view
easy to criticize but in many ways fundamental to a coarchical system. Some lawyers feel that their professional role
requires suspending their own judgments about what clients
do and providing them with their best advice and, where
necessary, their most effective defense. Moreover, lawyers
who service the great multinational enterprises operate within
distinct organizations with their own codes, of which a major
norm is to secure the continuity of the organization. One
exchange with the partner of a prominent firm may serve as
an example.

> Q. Suppose your corporate client explained that it was involved in
> such a country and asked for your advice on whether it should
> make the payments.
> A. It's unlikely they'd ask me.
> Q. Supposing they did.
> A. I would tell them not to make the payment.
> Q. And if they did?
> A. If I found out about it, I'd resign. [That is, respondent and his
> firm would no longer work for that corporation.]
> Q. But you said that there are countries where such payments are
> regularly made.
> A. I've got to protect my firm.

Lawyers will simply not be consulted, or not be consulted on
the record. Accountants might prove to be more "account-
able" since they must review and certify disbursements; their
conclusions and identities are basic parts of the public record.
Unless it develops usages and euphemisms that permit the
concealing of payments, the accounting profession may be
transformed into a means for reforming the operational code.
Some recommended legislation addresses this possibility.[62]

Yet, as testimony by a representative of the American Institute of CPA's made clear, "the abuses usually involved circumvention of internal accounting controls." Hence changes in the law are unlikely to be effective.[63]

The Real Costs of Simulation

Rather early in the bribery campaign and with the prospect of a presidential election looming, some incumbent officials naturally considered an exercise in *lex simulata*: the enactment of a statute that would seem to deal with the problem but would prove unenforceable or unenforced, yet would steal the opposition's thunder. A number of drafts, some no more than airy affirmations of purpose, were internally circulated and discussed, but were not acted upon. After the presidential election, with the bribery campaign waning, there again seemed to be governmental interest in putting a tidy end to the episode with some innocuous legislation. Would it not provide public catharsis, yet impose minimum restraint on productive economic and influential political forces? In fact, it could have serious costs.

While the enactment of a simulated law provides a short-term catharsis for those strata who feel something wrong was done, in the longer term its very nonenforcement will undercut popular belief in the efficacy of government in general. In the next campaign, nonenforcement will be an additional issue leveled against incumbents. From the government perspective, *lex simulata* is a defensive weapon with an unprogrammed self-destruct mechanism that can cause great harm to its own designers.

Despite the fact that it was designed to be ineffective, a *lex simulata* may also act to paralyze traders in situations in which they would otherwise operate freely. The calculation that the law *might* at some future moment be activated to satisfy a new or renewed public outcry will often deter the prudent trader from bribing or escalating the going bribal rate. If the law requires new record keeping, all traders will be obliged to meet these standards. Hence the inevitable grafting of a new layer of regulatory dermis through which commercial activity must seep. The likelihood of the application of some part of the new law—simulated or not—will increase with the complexity of the program and the number of agencies charged with its application; if several do not act on it, one zealous or ambitious attorney in another may still begin an enforcement program. In short, the simulated law provides certain short-term popular releases but is likely in the longer term to prove expensive for the operator as well as for general public order.[64]

It may be actual or even preferred policy to eliminate bribery, but if those in power were serious about limiting the types of commercial bribery exposed as endemic to sectors of transnational and national commerce, new legislation would not be the urgent issue. What would be required would be a strong indication of executive policy about prosecuting such bribery. There is, of course, a selectivity in the enforcement of all norms, and no norm is enforced in every case of violation. So-called prosecutorial discretion is exercised in choosing cases that promise maximum returns in norm vindication and reinforcement, address the most serious threats to community order, and provide the greatest deterrence to potential future violators. Hence prospective law-breakers (often with advice of counsel) will always be able to calculate the risks and costs of apprehension. But this fact does not mean that the law thereby ceases to exist or is weak. The critical element is the set of expectations of the business community that certain types of commercial bribery are wrong. This is a socially important expectation and one that will require some indication of real enforcement intention and not, as in the past, unenforced or capriciously enforced law. Whether that expectation will be created by a new enforcement program remains to be seen.

Thurmond Arnold wrote: "Most unenforced criminal laws

survive in order to satisfy moral objections to established modes of conduct. They are unenforced because we want to continue our conduct, and unrepealed because we want to preserve our morals."[65] Unless the business community comes to believe that a strong enforcement program, with sufficient funding and allocation of able personnel, is going to be mounted, it will believe, and indeed will be entitled to believe, that the current campaign is a crusade and not a reform and that public obeisance to the myths without changes in operations is sufficient.

Notes

Prologue: **Studying Bribery**

1. The term *operational code,* as far as I have been able to learn, was first used by Nathan Leites in his *Operational Code of the Politburo* (1951) and then in his more expanded work, *A Study of Bolshevism* (1953). Leites was interested in capturing what he described as "the spirit of a ruling group." For a discussion of the different meaning that I have given the term, see W.M. Reisman & G. Simson, "Interstate Agreements in the American Federal System," *Rutgers Law Review* 27 (1973), pp. 70, 72, n. 5. In *The Operators* (1960), Frank Gibney defines his subject, "operators," broadly; his work "is about how everybody *is* doing it" (p. 4, italics in original). Gibney explores much of the behavior I am concerned with here, but his definitional conclusions that these activities are "dishonest" (p. 4), "legal but immoral sharp practices in business, labor and politics" (p. 4), or "crooked" (p. 5) tend to skirt one of the central issues that I wish to explore in this book. Joseph Bensman and Israel Gerver's superb essay "Crime and Punishment in the Factory: The Function of Deviancy in Maintaining the Social System," *American Sociological Review* 28 (1963), p. 588, though it does not use the terms *myth system* and *operational code,* comes much closer to the way I have used those concepts.

2. Where class distinctions have emerged sharply and the criminal justice system tends to be oriented toward the control of lower classes, the very inclusion of a "white-collar crime" in the criminal code may indicate its "mythic" quality. Social conditioning operating on the police will make it less likely that they will focus on that species of crime as sufficiently important, dangerous, or urgent to draw attention from street crime. Other indicators may be quantity of budget, quality of personnel assigned to white-collar crime, and the like.

3. The common-law crime of bribery was restricted to the corruption of public officials and this pattern was carried over into federal statutes. See, for example, 18 United States Code, §§201–224, especially §201. Commercial bribery was generally treated under the rubric of the law of "master and servant" since it involved deceit of the employer practiced jointly by the external briber and the employee as well as contractual violations by the employee. But the Federal Trade Commission viewed commercial bribery as an unfair trade practice:

> The Commission has applied the term "commercial bribery" to the practice of sellers of secretly paying money or making gifts to employees or agents to induce them to promote purchases by their own employers from the sellers offering the secret inducements. The vice of conduct labeled "commercial bribery," as related to unfair trade practices, is the advantage which one competitor secures over his fellow competitors by his secret and corrupt dealing with employees or agents of prospective purchasers.

See *American Distilling Co.* v. *Wisconsin Liquor Co.,* 104 F. 2d 582 (1939).

In a judgment of a federal district court in Massachusetts in 1942, the installation of commercial bribery as a form of fraud within the meaning of federal criminal statutes was rather thoroughly explained. See *United States* v. *Procter & Gamble Co. et al.,* 47 F. Supp. 676 (1942). Procter & Gamble and others had been indicted for allegedly paying bribes to Lever Brothers' employees in order to get secret processes, formulas, and so on. Among other things, Procter demurred to the characterization of its alleged acts as criminally fraudulent. But the court responded:

> The normal relationship of employer and employee implies that the employee will be loyal and honest in all his actions with or on behalf of his employer, and that he will not wrongfully divulge to others the confidential information, trade secrets, etc., belonging to his employer. . . . When one tampers with that relationship for the purpose of causing the employee to breach his duty he in effect is defrauding the employer of a lawful right. The actual deception that is practiced is in the continued representation of the employee to the employer that he is honest and loyal to the employer's interests. The employee, in using the employment relationship for the express purpose of carrying out a scheme to obtain his employer's

confidential information and other property, as alleged in the indictment, would be guilty of deliberately producing a false impression on his employer in order to cheat him. Such conduct would constitute a positive fraud. . . .

In 1975 the Court of Appeals of the Fourth Circuit went further, directly assimilating commercial bribery to criminal bribery. "We discern no reason why the Congress, in using the term 'bribery,' intended that it be limited to the corruption of public officials." See *United States* v. *Pomponio,* 511 F. 2d 953 (1975). Many states have criminalized commercial bribery (see, for example, New York Penal Law, McKinney's Consolidated Law, c. 40, Article 180," "Commercial Bribing"), and their characterization is carried directly into federal law, where the definition of the crime derives from state law. Thus, 18 United States Code, §1952, establishes fines of $10,000 and up to five years imprisonment for anyone traveling or using any facility in interstate or foreign commerce, including the mails, to, among other things, "promote, manage, . . . any unlawful activity," including "extortion, bribery or arson in violation of the laws of the State in which committed or of the United States. . . ."

4. E.A. Ross, *Sin and Society* (1907), p. 137.

5. W. Riordan, *Plunkitt of Tammany Hall* (1948), p. 3.

6. Sunday *Times* (London), April 11, 1976, p. 6.

7. R.M. Hills, "Doing Business Abroad: The Disclosure Dilemma," *Yale Law Report* (Fall 1976), p. 6. See also R. Hershey, "Files of S.E.C. Show Slush Funds in Use Decades before Watergate," *New York Times,* May 18, 1977, pp. A-1, D-16. For a similar characterization of the behavior of contemporary public officials, see the remarks of Richard Thornburgh, the head of the Justice Department's criminal Division, in W. Rawls, "Indictments on Rise for Public Officials," *New York Times,* Feb. 11, 1977, p. A-1.

8. T. Arnold, *The Folklore of Capitalism* (1937); V. Aubert, "White-Collar Crime and Social Structure," *American Journal of Sociology* 58 (1962), p. 263.

9. See L. Fuller, *Legal Fictions* (1967), for a review of the literature.

10. M. Kadish & S. Kadish, *Discretion to Disobey: A Study of Lawful Departures from Legal Rules* (1973), chaps. 2 and 3.

11. H.L.A. Hart, *The Concept of Law* (1961).

12. K.C. Davis, *Discretionary Justice: A Preliminary Inquiry* (1969).

13. R. Dworkin, "Is Law a System of Rules?" in R.S. Summers, ed., *Essays in Legal Philosophy* (1968).

14. W.M. Reisman, *Nullity and Revision* (1971); idem, "Private Armies in a Global War System," *Virginia Journal of International Law* 14 (1973), p. 1; idem, "A Theory about Law from the Policy Perspective," in D. Weisstub, ed., *Law and Policy* (1976); Reisman & Simson, "Interstate Agreements."

15. M.S. McDougal & H.D. Lasswell, "Legal Education and Public Policy: Professional Training in the Public Interest," *Yale Law Journal* 52 (1943), p. 203.

16. See, generally, R. O'Day, "Intimidation Rituals: Reactions to Reform," *Journal of Applied Behavioral Science* 10 (1974).
    A recent and flagrant example of this phenomenon involved Henry Durham, a production-control supervisor at Lockheed Aircraft Corporation's plant in Marietta, Georgia. Durham spoke out about mismanagement, false documentation, and waste in Lockheed's production of the C-5A military-transport aircraft. An intense intimidation campaign began, following his charges. "Kill Durham" signs appeared on bulletin boards at the Lockheed plant. He received threatening phone calls. As Durham recalled, "They had murder on their minds." One caller warned, "The only way you'll go to Washington is in a pine box." Durham did testify before a Senate committee and has since resigned. Lockheed will not comment on his job performance and he can't find a safe place to live in Marietta. Mr. Durham, a former marine, comments, "There's certainly a defect in our society when people who call attention to wrongdoing are ostracized, fired, criticized and virtually abandoned. I have become disillusioned with the virtues I used to believe in." See J. Lubin, "Spilling the Beans, Disclosing Misdeeds of Corporations Can Backfire on Tattlers; Whistle Blowers Lose Jobs, Face Ostracism, Threats, Yet Many Take the Risk, Maalox and Sleepless Nights," *Wall Street Journal*, May 21, 1976, pp. 1, 19. This article includes two other stories of men who discovered that loyalty is valued more than conscience. A similar report is found in N. Zacchino, "Bribe Case Informant Has Regrets," *Los Angeles Times*, Aug. 6, 1976, pt. 1, pp. 1, 3, 25. See

also T. Branch, "Courage without Esteem: Profiles in Whistle-Blowing," *Washington Monthly* (May 1971).

Contrast some executives who have lost their jobs because of the recent disclosures of corporate misdeeds. Their lives haven't suffered in the ways depicted in the previous example. The *Wall Street Journal* comments: "They haven't suffered financial hardship. Their egos may be bruised more than their bank accounts. They are active, but miss their old jobs. Socially, they aren't quite as popular as they used to be." See H. Byrne, "An Executive Dropped in Fund Scandal Finds Life Is Different Now," *Wall Street Journal,* Aug. 31, 1976, p. 1. See also M. Jensen, "Outside Directorships Also Lost in Scandals," *New York Times,* May 7, 1976, p. D-3; H. Watkins, "Lockheed Suspends Fees to Former Top Executives," *Los Angeles Times,* Aug. 6, 1976, pt. 3, p. 15.

17. For a general discussion of the relationship between business and the media, see J. Poindexter, "The Great Industry-Media Debate," *Saturday Review,* July 10, 1976, pp. 17–24.

18. C. Trillin, "Reflections: Political Moderates," *New Yorker,* March 21, 1977, pp. 85, 86.

19. In its most institutionalized form this is encountered in the government-controlled press. See, for example, T.E. Kruglak, *The Two Faces of Tass* (1962) and, generally, J. Reston, *The Artillery of the Press: Its Influence on American Foreign Policy* (1966), pp. 20–22, 30–31; the latter is a study prepared for the Council on Foreign Relations. See also "The Press and Foreign Policy," in J. Reston, *Sketches in the Sand* (1967), p. 177.

20. M. Tolchin & S. Tolchin, *To the Victor: Political Patronage from the Clubhouse to the White House* (1971), p. 9.

21. Another source of distortion is the possible hostility of press personnel to businessmen, a charge often heard in business circles. Louis Banks, professor at the Harvard Business School and former managing editor of *Fortune* magazine, claims that the public is being "fed [by the press] a daily diet of authoritative ignorance, most of which conveys a cheap-shot hostility to business and businessmen. Here is where the nation sees a persistently distorted image of its most productive and pervasive activity, business." See Poindexter, "Industry–Media Debate," p. 18. Of course, one technique of defense against unpleasant exposure is to draw attention to

some impropriety in the exposure itself. By way of response, the need for a business press is succinctly stated by editor James W. Michaels of *Forbes* magazine: "It's human to want to conduct your business quietly and not have to explain everything. But . . . in a world in which a rise in the price of steel is a political act, corporations can no longer hide from public scrutiny." Ibid., p. 22.

Chapter 1: Myth System and Operational Code

1. Most, but not all. Even the most general and fundamental postulates of a culture may be held by different members with varying degrees of intensity. A psychopathic or sociopathic personality, as these terms are used, seems to learn the external forms, but there is no accompanying sense of rightness and hence no possibility for autopunitive mechanisms, a most effective method for policing group uniformity. Marginal group members and "minorities" are distinguished by their multiple acculturations and, hence, a certain capacity for a more "objective" view of the official picture of the group.

2. Where an operational code deviates from a myth system, part of the support that will be necessary and demanded will be collaboration in suppressing information about the existence of the code. As great a challenge to the integrity of the code as the muckraking journalist is the "squealer" or "stool": someone who tells the truth to myth system advocates. A part of the sanctioning system of the operational code is directed against precisely these actors; the expectation of sanction serves to police loyalty.

3. And perhaps more, for each segment of the control process may have its own operational code. Lawyers entering a particular judge's court for the first time are struck by the extraordinarily different ways the rules may be applied there; to all intents and purposes there is a different code. A protest to the judge that what he is doing is a violation of the rules of procedure is not likely to be successful: "This is the way it's done in *my* court." Similarly, someone beginning to work in a government office will be told that "of course there are the rules, but this is the way we do things here."

4. A brief necessarily superficial note on ethnolinguistics. Different strata and lay and specialist groups use the same terms differently. (Where the terms are normatively charged, the different uses indicate different codes and possibly different authoritative decision processes.) Unless one believes that words have inherent meanings, one must accept that divergent uses are equally meaningful in their social contexts; one is not more correct than another.

In this regard, note that the popular use of the term *illegal* may be different from the specialist use of the term. As Vilhelm Aubert writes:

> The public's and the violators' perceptions of crime in general are frequently not congruent with legal definitions, the implication being we may find important differences in motivation and other causal mechanisms within even very specific legal categories. Consequently, we find differences to an even higher degree within broader concepts such as white-collar crime.

See V. Aubert, "White-Collar Crime and Social Structure," *American Journal of Sociology* 53 (1962), pp. 263, 271. Specialists will often pull rank and insist that a situation is legal, hence appropriate for their expertise, and insist on using their definitions. In myth system and operational code tensions, operators may answer popular charges of illegality by explaining patiently that what is being done is technically legal. The social observer, however, should be careful not to be overawed, for the popular meaning of "misunderstandings" can be an important indicator of the social perspectives of a key group in the process. Which meaning, and hence which value allocation, becomes dominant depends, of course, on the disposition of authority and control in the context. But rejected meanings continue to be important social and political factors, indicating degree of group integration and of resistance to implementation as well as the type and likelihood of future conflicts.

5. R. Pound, *Interpretations of Legal History* (1923), p. 4; M. Cohen, "Jurisprudence as a Philosophical Discipline," *Journal of Philosophy, Psychology and Scientific Method* 10 (1913), p. 225, quoted in L. Fuller, *Legal Fictions* (1967), p. ix.

6. H. Maine, *Ancient Law* (1963), p. 25.

7. Fuller, *Legal Fictions,* p. 5, n. 5.

8. Bentham's animus against fictions seems to have derived from his

conviction that they obscured what the twentieth-century scholar would call the policy of the norms in question, the issue to which Bentham gave preeminent attention.

9. Fuller, *Legal Fictions,* p. 7, n. 5, and passim.

10. See, generally, G.R. Driver & J.C. Miles, *The Babylonian Laws,* vol. 1 (1952; corrected reprint, 1956). For a more extreme position, see J.J. Finkelstein, "Ammisaduqa's Edict and the Babylonian 'Law Codes,'" *Journal of Cuneiform Studies* (1961), p. 91.

11. M.S. McDougal, H.D. Lasswell, & W.M. Reisman, "The World Constitutive Process of Authoritative Decision," *Journal of Legal Education* 19 (1967), pp. 253, 403; reprinted in C. Black & R. Falk, *The Future of the International Legal Order,* vol. 1 (1969), p. 73. See also M.S. McDougal, H.D. Lasswell, & W.M. Reisman, "Theories about International Law: Prologue to a Configurative Jurisprudence," *Virginia Journal of International Law* 8 (1968), p. 188.

12. W.H.R. Rivers, "Survival in Sociology," *Sociology Review* 6 (1913), p. 295.

13. See, generally, chapter 4.

14. H. Gerth & C.W. Mills, *Character and Social Structure: The Psychology of Social Institutions* (1953), p. 122.

15. L. Pospisil, "Legal Levels and Multiplicity of Legal Systems in Human Societies," *Journal of Conflict Resolution* 11 (1967), p. 2.

16. *Republic* 459, trans. B. Jowett.

17. *Republic* 389.

18. D.D. Eisenhower, *The White House Years,* vol. 2 (1965), p. 551. Interestingly, Eisenhower felt his only mistake in the affair was his concurrence in the initial cover story. Ibid., p. 558.

19. B. Moyers, "Open Letter to Arthur Schlesinger," *Wall Street Journal,* July 20, 1977, p. 15.

20. United States, Senate, Select Committee to Study Governmental Operations with Respect to Intelligence Activities, *Alleged Assassination Plots Involving Foreign Leaders: An Interim Report* (Nov. 20, 1975), pp. 314–15.

21. See, generally, K. Popper, *The Open Society and Its Enemies* (1944), chapter 8.

22. For further discussion, see the epilogue.

23. M. Tolchin & S. Tolchin, *To the Victor: Political Patronage from the Clubhouse to the White House* (1971), p. 9.

24. J. Rawls, *A Theory of Justice* (1971), p. 363, and see the very perceptive comment on this point by Simson in his review of Rawls's book, "Another View of Rawls' *Theory of Justice*," *Emory Law Journal* 23 (1974), p. 473.

25. See, for example, T. Arnold, *The Folklore of Capitalism* (1937).

26. T. Szasz, *Ideology and Insanity* (1970), pp. 218-45.

27. *Republic* 514-15.

28. See the discussion of S. Ranulf, *Moral Indignation and Middle Class Psychology* (1938; reprint, 1964) in chapter 5. See also A. Hochman, *Marijuana and Social Evolution* (1972), pp. 169 ff, and L. Grinspoon, *Marijuana Reconsidered* (1971), pp. 331-43.

29. J. Piaget, *The Moral Judgment of the Child,* trans. M. Gabain (1932; reprint, 1965).

30. As virtually any post-mortem of a failed effort at social change reveals, *informal* modes of acculturation are extremely important. In an earlier note, I had occasion to observe that "cultures as well as civilizations must find ways of instilling components of the social code which are not appropriate for direct discourse. Often a way must be found to provide dramatic illustrations of how people balance the 'do's' and 'don'ts' of group life in those dynamic situations which seem so much more complicated than the normative code. Stories [folktales] can be a particularly useful social carrier. . . ." See W.M. Reisman, "Folktales and Civic Acculturation: Reflections on the Myths in Dinkaland," in F. Deng, *Dinka Folktales: African Stories of the Sudan* (1974), p. 13.

31. See chapter 4.

32. M. McLuhan & Q. Fiore, *War and Peace in the Global Village* (1968), p. 4.

33. Indeed, the United States system of criminal trials may itself exemplify the point. See A. Blumberg, "Practice of Law as a Confidence Game: Organizational Cooptation of a Profession," *Law and Society Review* 1 (June 1967), p. 15. The Justice Department's investigation of the Central Intelligence Agency's twenty-

year-old program of opening mail in transit between the United States and Communist countries supplies another telling example. Despite the fact that under federal law, tampering with first-class mail in this country is a criminal offense, the Justice Department lawyers have recommended against criminal prosecution of CIA officials involved in the mail-opening operations. See Crewdson, "Inquiry Is Said to Oppose Prosecuting C.I.A. Aides," *New York Times*, July 27, 1976, p. 1, and July 30, 1976, p. A-20 (editorial). But see, in regard to FBI activities, A. Marro, "Ex-F.B.I. Man Indicted by U.S. in Mail Openings," *New York Times*, April 8, 1977, pp. A-1, A-12; *New York Times*, "Bell Standing Firm on F.B.I. Indictment; Hears Complaints on Damage to Bureau Morale but Indicates Prosecution Will Go Forth," April 26, 1977, p. 14; E. Ashbury, "300 F.B.I. Agents Mass in Support of Indicted Aide," *New York Times*, April 15, 1977, p. A-17; A. Marro, "New York F.B.I. Men Said to Link Justice Department to Break-Ins," *New York Times*, April 28, 1977, pp. A-1, A-16; *New York Times*, "Bell Is Urged to Pursue Inquiry into F.B.I. Action," May 5, 1977, p. 19; M. Seigel, "Mail-Opening Trial Using Advisory Jury; C.I.A. Accused in Federal Court of Invasions of Privacy," *New York Times*, May 10, 1977, p. 8; and M. Seigel, "Jury Bids C.I.A. Pay 3 in Mail Case," *New York Times*, May 13, 1977, p. A-28.

34. While *secrecy* may be used to refer to serious efforts to conceal from all others practices deemed to be wrong and even sanctionable, *discretion* may be used to refer to the concealing of practices that though discrepant from the myth system are known to be widely done and most infrequently sanctioned. In Connecticut until recently, "law-abiding citizens" broke the law by buying and selling contraceptives in pharmacies; let us refer to this practice as discreet rather than secret. The use of discretion indicates a tension between myth system and operational code, but not necessarily unlawfulness.

35. P. Rosenberg, *Contract on Cherry Street* (1975), p. 134.

36. Thus, a most effective defense to deferred prosecutions is the threat to tell too much about the operational code and hence to compromise the future effectiveness of the operational code for the zealously prosecuting elite. Consider, in this regard, the conclusion of the prosecution of Richard Helms, former director of the

CIA, for allegedly lying to Congress about the agency's activities in Chile. See A. Marro, "Helms, Ex-C.I.A. Chief, Pleads No Contest to 2 Misdemeanors," *New York Times,* Nov. 1, 1977, p. 1, col. 6; and N. Horrock, "Helms Accord: Sense of Relief," ibid., p. 23. At sentencing, Judge Barrington Parker said, "You dishonored your oath and now stand before this court in disgrace and shame." But Helms later told reporters that he considered the conviction "a badge of honor." See A. Marro, "Helms Is Fined $2000 and Given Two-Year Suspended Prison Term," *New York Times,* Nov. 5, 1977, p. 1, col. 2. Attempts to regulate or control the transnational practices of United States-based corporations will be confronted by this condition. Many commercial operators believe that conformity with foreign standards and practices, which may include bribery, is absolutely necessary for commercial success. Consider the following excerpt from a recent study:

> An executive of a chemical firm sums up this point: "I believe that American companies must comply with the commercial modes of the countries in which they do business or forget trying to do business in certain countries. The competitive consequences of not complying would, in many cases, make it impossible for the American company to complete certain transactions. I have found that business people from most of the major exporting countries do not hesitate to meet the conditions required to do business."

See the Conference Board, "Unusual Foreign Payments: A Survey of the Policies and Practices of U.S. Companies," by James R. Basche, Jr., Report No. 682, 1976, p. 28. See also *Wall Street Journal,* "Baker International Lists Payments Abroad, Will Continue Practice," Dec. 23, 1976, p. 2.

37. See, generally, J. Reston, *The Artillery of the Press: Its Influence on American Foreign Policy* (1966), pp. 20–22, 30–31.

38. *Blutkitt* means "blood-cement." The technique of irredeemably "cementing" a person into an organization by having him commit a criminal act is well known in criminal organizations. Participation in the operational code may itself function as blood-cement. Leo Alexander writes:

> We know that in the SS, as in any other criminal organization, if a man did anything which put his loyalty to that organization into a questionable light, he was either liquidated—

that means killed—or he had to undertake a criminal act which would definitely and irrevocably tie him to that criminal organization. We say in such a case the man was put "on the spot." Such an act must include murder, according to the age-old custom of criminal gangs. In the SS this was specifically called *blutkitt* (blood cement). I first learned of the existence of this special German term from Dr. Wanda von Baeyer, a German psychologist, who also told me that Hitler himself introduced the idea and the word *blutkitt,* which he had discovered in a book about Genghis Khan in which it was emphasized that the crimes which the Khan's hordes committed served as "blood cement" ("blutkitt"), holding the organization together. He was supposed to have read that book as early as his Landsberg Prison days.

The concentration camps were the main places within the confines of Germany where SS members were expected to acquire blood cement, until they were considered reliable enough to be sent abroad into the occupied countries where they could then be relied upon to perform similar crimes inside and outside the confines of specific camp areas.

See L. Alexander, "War Crimes and Their Motivation," *Journal of the American Institute of Criminal Law and Criminology* 39 (1948), pp. 300–301.

39. On *omertà* see F. Ianni & E. Ianni, *A Family Business: Kinship and Social Control in Organized Crime* (1972), pp. 34–35.

40. 2 United States Code §455.

41. V.O. Key, "The Techniques of Political Graft in the United States" (Ph.D. dissertation, University of Chicago, 1934), pp. 81–86, 361–69.

42. Tolchin & Tolchin, *To the Victor,* p. 12.

43. A recent example may be the 1976 draft of a code of guidelines for multinational corporations prepared by the OECD. See Organization for Economic Co-operation and Development, "International Investment and Multinational Enterprises," Declaration by the Government of OECD Member Countries Decisions of the OECD Council on Guidelines for Multinational Enterprises, National Treatment, International Investment Incentives and Disincentive Consultation Procedures Declarations of June 21, 1976. *Business Week,* June 14, 1976, p. 43, asserted the code "has rubber teeth when it comes to enforcement." A similar journalistic characterization was given to the Ford administration (S.R. 3741) and the

Proxmire drafts (S.R. 3664) dealing with bribery abroad by United States corporations. See *Time* magazine, June 28, 1976, p. 58; for a discussion of the drafts, see the epilogue.

44. See R. Chatov, *Corporate Financial Reporting* (1975); G. Stigler, "Public Regulation of the Securities Market," 37 *Journal of Business* 117 (1964); I. Friend & E. Herman, "The SEC through a Glass Darkly," ibid., p. 382; and G. Benston, "The Effectiveness and Effects of the SEC's Accounting Disclosure Requirements," in H. Manne, ed., *Economic Policy and the Regulation of Corporate Securities* (1969), p. 23.

45. §146, P.L. 94–141: 25 U.S.C. 2576.

46 Subsection (a).

47. Subsection (b)(3).

48. Subsection (c). This provision cannot be taken as merely shifting enforcement from the courts to the executive branch. The genesis of the amendment was the inability of ACDA, a comparatively small agency, to secure data from that Goliath of government, the Department of Defense. The amendment could be meaningful only if its implementation were to be shifted from the Byzantine politics of the executive branch, where the fact that ACDA had already been bested gave rise to demands for new law, to a more equalizing arena such as the courts. But see G. Berdes, "Congress' New Leverage," *Center* magazine 9:4 (1976), p. 76.

49. Internal Revenue Code §162(c)(1).

50. In many ways, the entire prohibition of deductions for illegal bribes may be viewed as a simulation. My colleague Boris Bittker believes that the sanction is ordinarily so minimal as to have power neither to deter nor to act as an incentive for self-correction. Indeed, where legislation is supported by ludicrously mild sanctions, the total effect may be to communicate that there is no real official intention to change behavior.

51. As of the time of this writing, only one federal case was reported interpreting §162(c)(1); none had been reported on §162(c)(2). In *United States* v. *Rexach,* 331 F. Supp. 524 (D.P.R. 1971), the district court allowed deductions for payments to Trujillo in connection with a building project in the Dominican Republic, ruling that §162(c)(1) was inapplicable because Trujillo *was* the government, not an official of the government. On appeal, the First Circuit reversed on other grounds, but in a somewhat confusing dictum said that there was no point in subsidizing dictators if the same sorts of payment are disallowed to elected officials, a point hardly self-evident in logic or national practice. See 482 F. 2d at 11, n. 8.

Regulations to implement §162(c) as written in 1958 went into effect in 1959 and stayed in effect until 1975. Proposed regulations to implement the 1969 amendments were published in 1971, 36 F.R. 9637, but were not approved because the 1971 Tax Reform Act made certain of those proposed regulations obsolete. New proposed regulations were published in 1972, incorporating the changes to §162(c) made in both the 1969 and 1971 acts. See 37 F.R. 25936. These proposed regulations were finally approved in 1975. See 40 F.R. 7437. The regulations define some of the terms, such as *indirect payment, official or employee,* and *generally enforced,* but otherwise add nothing of real importance to the law itself. The delay in implementing regulations to enforce the 1969 and 1971 amendments to §162(c) leads to the suspicion that, until recently, the section was not considered important and was seldom enforced.

This suspicion is given added weight by the fact that in the spring of 1976 the IRS announced "new" stringent guidelines for its field agents investigating suspected incidents of corporate bribery and other illegal corporate payments. See BNA Taxation and Finance (DER 95), 5-14-76, J-3 to J-9. The guidelines were designed to help identify schemes to establish "slush funds" that might be used for bribes and that could circumvent the tax laws by reducing the amount of taxable income (that is, by unjustified deductions). Agents were sent a set of eleven questions to be asked in audits of returns of every large corporation and of those small corporations whose circumstances warranted closer scrutiny. The questions asked whether the corporation or an agent made bribes or kickbacks to any person, corporation, government, or other organization. The questions also inquired about any foreign bank accounts that might have been used to house slush funds and about loans or contributions to any government, political party, or candidate, domestic or foreign. Whenever any of the eleven questions were answered in the affirmative, a further investigation was to be made to secure all details of the transaction. False statements provided in answer to any of the questions could subject the individual to criminal penalties under Titles 18 and 26 of the United States Code. Further, any information concerning nontax violations uncovered by the answers to these questions could be forwarded to the appropriate state or federal agencies.

52. Export Control Act §2 (4)(B).

53. See *Hearings to Amend Section 2 of the Export Control Act of 1949*, 89th Cong., 1st sess. (1965); hearings before a subcommittee of the Senate Committee on Banking and Currency.

54. 15 C.F.R. §369.

55. Export Control Act §3(c).

56. See "U.S. Exporter's Report of Request Received for Information Certification or Other Action Indicating a Restrictive Trade Practice or Boycott against a Foreign Country, Form 1a-1014," reprinted in A. Lowenfeld, *International Economic Law: Trade Controls for Political Ends,* vol. 3 (1977), p. 470.

57. Lowenfeld, *International Economic Law,* vol. 3, p. 116.

58. Ibid., p. 126.

59. J. Bensman & I. Gerver, "Crime and Punishment in the Factory: The Function of Deviancy in Maintaining the Social System," *American Sociological Review* 28 (1963), pp. 597–98.

60. M. Walzer, "Political Action: The Problem of Dirty Hands," *Philosophy and Public Affairs* 2:2 (Winter 1973), p. 160.

61. Some reasons for the differential rates of change are examined with regard to territorial title in L. Chen & W.M. Reisman, "Who Owns Taiwan? A Search for International Title," *Yale Law Journal* 91 (1972), pp. 599, 601–603.

62. See, generally, E. Hughes, "Good People and Dirty Work," *Social Problems* (1962), p. 10; L. Coser, "The Visibility of Evil," *Journal of Social Issues* (1969), p. 25. See also in this regard the intriguing remarks of Walter Mondale in "Nobody Asked: Is It Moral?" *Time* magazine, May 10, 1976, pp. 32, 34.

63. See Alexander, "War Crimes," p. 298.

Chapter 2: **Myth System and Bribery**

1. The phrase *control apparatus* is used to refer to the decision structures of value processes that may be based on any value, including power. In the market, for example, the control apparatus may be a centralized authority as in a command economy or the coarchical activities of buyers and sellers who act in fidelity to certain role norms, as, for example, in a free market. Participants in each structure can be "bribed" to defect from that role norm in much the same manner that officials in the power process can be bought.

2. See note 34 to chapter 1.

3. The McCloy report on Gulf's bribe payments, which for some reason has been held up as a model of disciplined self-revelation, is a good example of the use of extortion as a defense. Descriptions of payments abroad are accompanied by hints of official extortion. But a number of cases of apparent extortion take on a different cast when put in a time perspective. In Korea, for example, Gulf appears to have rather voluntarily initiated payments as a way of entering the local political economy on preferred terms. Subsequent claims, characterized by McCloy as extortionate, may have been viewed by the Koreans as continuations of a pattern that was jointly and consensually established and in which new services were entitled to new payments. See J. McCloy, *The Great Gulf Oil Spill: The Inside Report; Gulf Oil's Bribery and Political Chicanery* (1976). On the use of "extortion as a defense," see V.O. Key, "Techniques of Political Graft," in A.J. Heidenheimer, ed., *Political Corruption: Readings in Comparative Analysis* (1970), p. 47.

4. See chapter 3.

5. C. Shifrin, "Justice Official Says Price-Fixing Is a Common Practice in Business," *Washington Post,* Feb. 27, 1976, p. C-9.

6. J.R. Laing, "U.S. Study of Soybean Trading Is Seen Leading to Tax-Law, Other Indictments," *Wall Street Journal,* Aug. 9, 1976, p. 16.

7. *Los Angeles Times,* "U.S. Forms Team to Probe Chicago Board Price-Fixing," Aug. 10, 1976, pt. 3, p. 9.

   For a review and appraisal of antitrust cases filed with the Federal Trade Commission and the Justice Department, see R.

Smith, "Administration and Critics at Odds on Antitrust Laws; White House Drops Support on Some Stricter Bills, Denies Any Weakening of Enforcement," *New York Times,* Apr. 26, 1976, p. C-43. For specific references and media commentary, see *Los Angeles Times,* "Antitrust Investigation of Auto Makers Authorized: GM Considered Prime Target of FTC Inquiry; Pricing Policies, Distribution to Be Examined," Aug. 4, 1976, pt. 1, p. 1; *New York Times,* "Breakup Opposed of Oil Companies; U.S. Official Says It Might Lead to Higher Prices," June 4, 1976, p. D-15; *Los Angeles Times,* "14 Box Firm Officials Plead No Contest in Pricing Case," July 30, 1976, pt. 3, p. 20; *Wall Street Journal,* "No Contest Pleas Filed by Last of 48 Persons in Carton-Pricing Case," July 28, 1976, p. 9; S. Penn, "Little Data Company Charges That IBM Spread False Rumors of Link with Mafia," Wall Street Journal, July 8, 1976, p. 30; L. Kohlmeier, "Snap, Crackle and Divestiture: The F.T.C. v. the Four Cereal Giants; 'Shared Monopoly' Case Goes to Trial," *New York Times,* April 25, 1976, sec. 3, p. 1; I. Barmash, "Price-Fixing Study in Apparel Quickens: Manufacturers and Retailers Face More Inquiries from Several Sources," *New York Times,* May 31, 1976, p. C-21; *New York Times,* "Indictment Lists 7 Oil Companies: Independent Units Charged with the Illegal Fixing of Gasoline Prices; Others Named in Case-Trade Group and Officials of 3 of Concerns Also Are Said to Have Conspired," June 2, 1976, p. C-49.

8. A. Auerbach, "Secret Cartel to Control Uranium Prices Reported," *Los Angeles Times,* Aug. 30, 1976pt. I, p. 1; W. Carley, "Justice Unit's Study of Uranium Industry Turns into Hunt for Price-Fixing Scheme," *Wall Street Journal,* July 7, 1976, p. 3; and *Time* magazine, "Scandals, Darkening Storm over Gulf," June 27, 1977.

9. *Economist,* "The Best Form of Defence Is Defence," Feb. 21, 1976, p. 83.

10. R.T. McNamar, "Regulation versus Competition," *Wall Street Journal,* Aug. 9, 1976, p. 8.

11. Commercial Bribery: Letter from the Federal Trade Commission, May 15, 1918, 66th Cong., 2d sess., Senate, Document No. 258, March 20, 1920, p. 3.

12. Ibid., p. 4.

13. See Commerce Clearing House, *Trade Regulation Reporter* para.

7903.14.

14. *New Jersey Asbestos Co.* v. *Federal Trade Commission,* 264 F. 509 (1920).

15. Ibid., 510–11.

16. For example, *Federal Trade Commission* v. *Grand Rapids Varnish Co.,* 41 F. 2d 996 (1929), but compare that decision with *Winslow* v. *Federal Trade Commission* and *Norden Ship Supply Co.* v. *Federal Trade Commission,* 277 F. 206 (1921).

17. See F. Klein, "Brewing Scandal: Beer Firms Are Target As Agencies Extend Bribery Probes to U.S.; Evidence of Alleged Payoffs to Beer Buyers Is Sought by SEC, Alcohol Bureau; Free Taps, Stools & Glasses," *Wall Street Journal,* June 10, 1976, pp. 1, 22. Payoffs to individual bars take many forms, including cash rebates or free beer in excess of that allowed by law, free glassware and other supplies, remodeling allowances, or free tap and cooling equipment. One Chicago distributor of a major beer says, "For about three years in the middle sixties, I'll bet not a bar opened in Chicago that didn't get its taps equipment paid for by a beer distributor" (p. 22). He commented that the bill for such installation can run to almost $1,500. The extent of such bribal practices is captured in the "well-established etiquette governing bar owners' handling of loans from wholesalers, which are illegal under federal law. An individual who has owned campus bars in two southern cities comments, "If you get a loan from a distributor, and you decide to switch beers, the guy handling the new brand is supposed to pick up your loan" (p. 22). One federal investigator summed up the situation, "Price rigging and payment of illegal inducements are carried on in the beer industry to such a scale that they have become a way of life." See *Business Week,* "Corporate Cash, Hot on the Scent of Payoffs at Home," March 8, 1976, p. 29. For more details on bribery in the beer industry, see the following articles: R. Hershey, "S.E.C. Bribery Suit Names Emersons: Charge Is First Domestic One of Its Kind over Corporate Payments; Beer Promotions Cited; Food Chain and 2 Former Officers Allegedly Took Gifts from Brewers," *New York Times,* May 12, 1976, p. 57; W. Waggoner, "Head of Jersey Senate Denies Guilt," *New York Times,* Oct. 20, 1976, p. 49; *Wall Street Journal,* "President of Senate in New Jersey Pleads Innocent to Bribery," Oct. 20, 1976, p. 26.

18. H. Lawson, "Boeing Ex-Salesmen Recall Job's Pressures and Foreign Intrigues: They Say Firm Didn't Bribe but Knew Its Rivals Did; Company Denies It Knew a Customer Gets a Bear Hunt," *Wall Street Journal*, May 7, 1976, pp. 1, 23. For a different perspective on Boeing's participation in transnational bribery, see H. Lawson & R. Immel, "Using Agent with Family Tie to Buyer, Boeing Sold Jets to Pakistan Airline," *Wall Street Journal*, June 15, 1976, p. 2. In this article, the *Journal* commented, referring to a former financial officer of Boeing, "he decided to tell his story to the *Wall Street Journal* because 'the industry practice was to pay off' in many foreign areas, and he considers it unfair that Lockheed Aircraft Corp. 'was taking the fall' for the entire aircraft industry." Apparently the former financial officer at Boeing was correct. Boeing has since admitted to having made $70 million in questionable overseas payments. Of the 288 companies that have disclosed such payments from 1970 through 1976, Boeing's sum is the single largest amount. Other top disbursers of corporate cash include Exxon Corporation, $46 million; Northrop Corporation, nearly $32 million; Lockheed Aircraft Corporation, $25 million, and Armco Steel Corporation, $17.5 million. See *Wall Street Journal*, "Questionable Payments Total Put at $4.2 million," Jan. 21, 1977, p. 5. As these figures are supplied by the companies themselves, according to criteria they have formulated, the degree of credence to be invested in them must be decided by each reader.

19. *Wall Street Journal*, May 7, 1976, p. 23.

20. The construction of Bethlehem Steel Corporation's Burns Harbor Plant, described by Bethlehem as the largest construction job in the world, produced an elaborate scheme where all parties significantly benefited from the exchange of such tangible things. The scheme largely involved Walsh Construction Company, now a division of Guy F. Atkinson Company, and employees of Bethlehem Steel. Walsh was the major contractor on the project, which took thirteen years to complete.

Edward J. Hofstetter, a former Bethlehem office manager, testified that between 1967 and 1969, in addition to the transfer of cash, "Walsh employees, among other things, paneled, remodeled and carpeted the lower level of his house, and built him a patio and a 96-foot long fence. They removed a large oak tree from his yard and, in doing so, accidentally tore up his driveway. So they built a new driveway. Also, they gave him a color television set, a washer, a dryer, whiskey, gasoline for his car, and tickets for 'three or four' plane trips for himself and his family to Baltimore, his hometown. After his father-in-law died, the Walsh employees managed to have the family piano, an heirloom, shipped from Baltimore." See E. Morgenthaler, "How a Fraud Scheme and Steel Mill Arose Together in Indiana: Contractor's Employees Kept Payouts Flowing Freely As Bethlehem Built Plant; Lettuce in the Cabbage Patch," *Wall Street Journal,* June 8, 1976, pp. 1, 16. Mr. Hofstetter in return would sign bogus work forms for the Walsh people. Straightforward dispersals of cash were also common. "Walter Cox, Walsh's former master mechanic and self-described bag- man for about six years, estimated that between 1966 and 1972 (when he was fired) he handed out $300,000 to $500,000 of Walsh money. He said that 'lots of times I had $20,000 in my pocket.' " Tom Walsh, Jr., Walsh's former chairman, had given Cox on three occasions $275,000. He told Cox to "spread it around where it will do the most good." Cox commented that he would distribute it "like candy out of a bag." No one knows just how much money was involved. Bethlehem and Atkinson "figure it was in the 'hundreds of thousands of dollars' while the government considers $50 million a 'reasonable' estimate." Despite the fact that twenty men have been convicted or pleaded guilty to federal charges, Bethlehem and Atkinson insist that there are no ill feelings between them over the affair. In fact, a Bethlehem spokesman commented that Walsh "might well do work for the company in the future."

21. This appears to be particularly the case with United States national defense contracts. Yet defense contractors frequently seem to entertain, against Defense Department regulations, those civilians and military personnel responsible for both the determination of what equipment is to be produced as well as the companies who will do the producing (that is, get the contract). See the following section in this chapter, "Modern Representative Government and Its Myths"; see also J. Finney, "Rockwell Names Pentagon Guests: Concern Says Ex-Head of Joint Chiefs Was One of Visitors to Lodge," *New York Times,* March 18, 1976, p. 1; J. Finney, "6 More Officers Northrop Guests: Proxmire Releases List and Complains to Rumsfeld," *New York Times,* March 24, 1976, p. 57.

22. A. Bozeman, *Politics and Culture in International History* (1960), pp. 402–403.

23. S. Raab, "Payoffs to U.S. Meat Inspectors Are Found Common in City Area," *New York Times,* April 5, 1976, sec. C, pp. 1, 60.

24. J. Kwitny, "Massive Indictments of Meat Inspectors Is Seen in New York," *New York Times,* Aug. 5, 1976, p. 7.

25. *Wall Street Journal,* "Inquiry into Scandal in Grain Inspection Spreads to 15 States," Aug. 4, 1976, p. 24; W. Robbins, "Inquiries into Grain Find New Data on Gratuities," *New York Times,* Aug. 4, 1976, p. 11; but see *Los Angeles Times,* "Grain Inspection Bribe Charges Called False," Aug. 6, 1976, pt. 1, p. 23.

26. *Los Angeles Times,* "Medicaid Invites Fraud, Convicted Chiropractors Claim," Sept. 1, 1976, pt. 1, p. 8.

27. S. Auerbach, "Medicaid Examiners Cite Fraud Findings, Senate Team Visits Health 'Mills' in Five States, Uncovers Errors, Cheating," *Los Angeles Times,* Aug. 30, 1976, pt. 1, p. 1; see also *Time* magazine, "Uncle Sam Strikes Back," Oct. 18, 1976, pp. 66–67.

One of the more sensational and even ironic cases involved Dr. Louis Cella. He embezzled $2 million from the Medicaid program in California, spent much of the money in the 1974 California political campaigns, was apprehended and sentenced to five years in federal prison for major fraud. Assistant U.S. Attorney Stephen V. Wilson, who headed the prosecution, said that Cella's crime amounted to trying to "buy the political system with money." (Cella was the single largest political contributor in the 1974 California political campaigns.) Wilson continued, "It would have been bad enough to buy it with his own money but the evidence shows he attempted to buy the political system with the government's money, with Medicare's money." See R. O'Reilly, "Cella Sentenced to 5 Years for Hospital Fund Fraud," *Los Angeles Times,* July 20, 1976, pt. 1, p. 1. See also T. Wood, "Inquiry on Cella Contributions to Politicians Opens," *Los Angeles Times,* Aug. 5, 1976, pt. 2, p. 1.

28. R. Hershey, "Special Task Force Will Press Charges in Corporate Bribes: S.E.C. Expected to Aid Team; Justice Department's Operation Linked at Growing Possibility of Prosecutable Offenses," *New York Times,* Oct. 14, 1976, p. 53. For a detailed list of the first 99

companies to disclose "questionable payments," see *National Journal,* "Corporate Bribery: Something's Wrong, but What Can Be Done about It?" May 15, 1976, p. 660. From May 15 to November 1 of 1976, 126 more companies disclosed "similar" payments at a rate of one disclosure per working day.

29. J. Brooks, "Annals of Business: Funds Gray and Black," *New Yorker,* Aug. 9, 1976, p. 28.

30. P. Nehemkis, "Business Payoffs Abroad: Rhetoric and Reality," *California Management Review* 18 (Winter 1975), p. 15.

31. *Business Week,* "The Global Costs of Bribery," March 15, 1976, p. 23. "Ironically, the U.S. aircraft makers that paid the biggest bribes to government officials were mostly competing not against foreigners but against each other." Ibid., p. 24. For example, in Japan, the Lockheed payments to Japanese officials were inducements to purchase the Lockheed L-1011 Tristar Airbus rather than a similar aircraft manufactured by McDonnell Douglas. See S. Jameson, "Japan's Lockheed Affair, Political Fallout Uncertain," *Los Angeles Times,* Aug. 15, 1976, pt. 4, pp. 3, 4.

32. *Business Week,* "The Corporate Rush to Confess All," Feb. 23, 1976, p. 22.

33. The Conference Board is an independent research organization financed largely by American companies. See J.R. Basche, "Unusual Foreign Payments: A Survey of the Policies and Practices of U.S. Companies," 1976, Report No. 682. See also M. Jensen, "Many U.S. Executives Reported in Favor of Overseas Bribes," *New York Times,* Feb. 13, 1976, p. 49.

34. Ibid.

35. R. Nader & J. Seligman, "Curbing Corporate Bribery," *Washington Post,* June 13, 1976, p. C-1.

36. Ibid.

37. J. Berry, "Tenneco Executive Accused in Payoff," *Washington Post,* June 19, 1976, p. A-1.

38. In the case of multinational corporate bribery, every regulatory suggestion, whether it be from Elliot Richardson (see *Time* magazine, "The Double Damn," June 28, 1976, p. 58); Roderick Hills (see "Doing Business Abroad: The Disclosure Dilemma," *Yale Law*

Report [Fall 1976], pp. 4-9); or Lloyd Cutler (see *Trialogue*, "The Payoff Muddle and How It Grew" [Summer 1976], no. 11, pp. 8-11) is dependent upon the business community's ability and desire to police and reform itself. All of these suggestions center around the concept of "disclosure." Ironically, legislation forcing or suggesting private and/or public disclosures of corporate practices (questionable and otherwise) could produce more clandestine behavior, not less, for there could be far fewer written, recorded discussions, far more private verbal discussions, far more tacit rather than explicit decisions. See W. Bennis, "Have We Gone Overboard on 'The Right to Know'?" *Saturday Review,* March 6, 1976, pp. 18-21.

39. L. Brandeis, *Business: A Profession* (1914). In this speech, Judge Brandeis, in tones reminiscent of Robert Owen, exhorts the graduating class of Brown University to follow the examples of William McElwain and the Filene brothers, all of Boston, whose financial success as businessmen was due to "the greater efficiency of their employees," which, in turn, was fueled by "industrial democracy and social justice." When all business follows the methods used by McElwain and the Filenes,

> "big business" will lose its sinister meaning, and will take a new significance. "Big business" will then mean business big not in bulk or power, but great in service and grand in manner. "Big business" will mean professionalized business as distinguished from the occupation of petty trafficking or mere moneymaking. And as the profession of business develops, the great industrial and social problems expressed in the present social unrest will one by one find solution.

See ibid., p. 12.

40. Internal Revenue Code 1977, §162(a), but see §162(c)(1).

41. *Kelley-Dempsey* v. *Commissioner,* 31 United States Board of Tax Appeals Reports 351 (1934).

42. Ibid., p. 354.

43. Ibid. See also *Frederick Steel Co.* v. *CIR,* 42 T.C. 13 (1964), *rev'd. on other grounds,* 375 F. 2d 351 (6th Cir. 1967), *cert. denied* 384 U.S. 901 (1967); *United Draperies, Inc.* v. *CIR,* 340 F. 2d 936 (1965).

44. 31 United States Board of Tax Appeals Reports 355 (1934). The

civic obligation of businessmen to fight corruption, apparently without regard to cost, is urged in *United States* v. *Kahn,* 472 F. 2d 272 (2d Cir. 1973), p. 278. "The proper response to coercion by corrupt public officials should be to go to the authorities, not to make the pay-off."

45. Ibid., pp. 355-56.

46. 14 Tax Court of the United States Reports 1066 (1950): 188 F. 2d. 269; 343 U.S. Reports 90.

47. Remington's Wash. Rev. Stat. 1949; Supp. §10185-14; Deering's Cal.; Business and Professional Code, 1951, §§650, 652; N.C. Law 1951, C. 1089 §§21, 23.

48. 14 Tax Court 1077.

49. Ibid., p. 1080.

50. Ibid.

51. Ibid., p. 1087.

52. There have been varied judicial responses as to how "sharply defined" the policy must be. Apparently, expression of the national policy in the form of a criminal law is sufficiently sharp to bar deductions, even if the severity of the penalty is minimal and, it would seem, even if violation of the policy is accepted calmly by the enforcement agency. *Tank Truck Rentals* v. *CIR,* 356 U.S. 30 (1958), involved the attempted deduction by a trucking company of fines incurred in Pennsylvania for overweight trucks. The weight limit in Pennsylvania was 45,000 pounds, considerably less than the 60,000 pounds allowed in neighboring states. The petitioner was unable to operate profitably at the low limit and therefore deliberately operated overweight. The IRS would not allow the company to deduct the fines, and the Tax Court, the Third Circuit, and Supreme Court all affirmed. The Supreme Court said that the policy of Pennsylvania with regard to protection of highways from damage and to the safety of users was evidenced by the penal statute on weight limit (ibid., p. 34). The fine incurred was punitive action, and the deduction, if allowed, would encourage a business enterprise to violate the declared policy of the state. The Court cautioned that "the test of nondeductibility always is the severity and immediacy of the frustration (of public policy) resulting from allowance of the deduction" (p. 35). In the case of a fine,

the frustration resulting from a deduction is apparently quite direct, and so the deduction was not allowed (pp. 35-36). Even though Pennsylvania raised its maximum weight to 60,000 pounds in 1955, the fact remains that the truckers were fined by the state as a penal measure in support of public policy as it stood in 1951, and it is that public policy that controls the case (p. 36).

It is, of course open to question whether the *form* of a law is always a decisive indicator of the degree of community concern about its violation. In *Dixie Machine Welding and Metal Works, Inc.* v. *United States*, 315 F. 2d 439 (5th Cir., 1963), the court disallowed deductions for kickbacks that violated the Louisiana bribery statute. *Lilly* was distinguished because no law or stated policy had outlawed the optician's payments. In *Textile Mills Security Corp.* v. *CIR*, 314 U.S. 326 (1941), lobbying expenses were judged not deductible. A Treasury regulation that prohibited their deduction, given previous cases warning against "insidious influence in legislative halls," was considered a reasonable interpretation of "ordinary and necessary." In three cases, *Easton Tractor & Equipment Co.* v. *CIR*, 35 BTA 189 (1936), *Flanagan* v. *CIR*, 47 BTA 789 (1942), and *Nicholson* v. *CIR*, 38 BTA 190 (1938), the Tax Court refused to allow deductions for money used to influence the decisions of government officials. Such payments, stated the court in *Flanagan*, are "commonly regarded" as contrary to the public interest, even though "not repugnant to express provisions of law." Finally, in dicta to *Kelly-Dempsey* v. *Commissioner*, the Tax Court hinted that it would invalidate deductions for "grease" payments to a private company as contrary to public policy because allowing the deductions would encourage graft and extortion.

In those cases where allowance of deductions was ruled consistent with public policy, the activity whose expense was sought to be deducted was less directly connected to an activity sought to be prevented. For instance, in both *CIR* v. *Heininger*, 320 U.S. 467 (1943), and *CIR* v. *Tellier*, 383 U.S. 687 (1966), the Supreme Court allowed deductions for legal expenses incurred in defending against criminal fraud charges. The Court reasoned that a contrary finding would help prevent a person from presenting a good defense and would be a punitive measure not intended by the criminal fraud statute.

In *Sterling Distributors, Inc.* v. *Patterson,* 263 F. Supp. 479 (N.D.Ala., 1965), a deduction for rebates given by Sterling to induce purchases was upheld, even though such rebates constituted a misdemeanor under Alabama law. Since the laws were not enforced by the state and thus were not good evidence of state policy, the IRS should not have attempted to revive those laws through the tax code. In *Fiambolis* v. *United States,* 152 F. Supp. 10 (E.D.S.C., 1957), the court allowed deductions for kickbacks in the ship chandlery business. It found that such kickbacks were customary in the industry and that a state statute that appeared to prohibit the payments actually referred only to corrupt business agents and secret payments. The ship chandlery payments, being both open and customary, did not frustrate the public policy evidenced by the antikickback law.

53. 343 U.S. 97.

54. F. Klein, "Brewing Scandal: Beer Firms Are Target As Agencies Extend Bribery Probes to U.S.," *Wall Street Journal,* June 10, 1976, pp. 1, 22 (quote is from p. 22).

55. Many of these operations usually involve the misuse or clandestine use of public funds. V.O. Key refers to such behavior as "autocorruption." He distinguishes between bribery, extortion, and state-bribery and autocorruption: "In bribery, extortion, state-bribery . . . relationships between two or more individuals are involved. In autocorruption the public official or person exercising the power of such official, boss or whatever he may be, in a sense plays the role of both parties in the other situations involving two or more persons. He secures for himself the administrative privilege which would be secured by an outsider by bribery. He awards contracts to himself . . . appropriates public property, etc." See Key, "Techniques of Political Graft," p. 48. See also R. Getz, "Congressional Ethics and the Conflict of Interest Issue," in A.J. Heidenheimer, ed., *Political Corruption* (1970), pp. 434–39. A trivial but telling congressional example is the stationery allowance: $7,500 a year for each house member and about $7,000 for reproduction of newsletters and special-delivery stamps. Withdrawals from these accounts do not have to be specified. Says one committee member, "Some guys never spend it." See *Newsweek,* "Capitol Capers," June 14, 1976, pp. 18–27 (quote is from p. 26).

One congressman took $23,611 of accumulated stationery funds with him when he retired. See J. Gannon & J. Landauer, "Ethics in Congress: Despite Sex Scandals, Self-Serving Actions Are the Major Problems; Lawmakers Vote Pay Rises, Other Benefits, Ignore Own Conflicts of Interests," *Wall Street Journal,* June 15, 1976, pp. 1, 20. Travel provides another opportunity for publicly financed private congressional enjoyment. See *Boston Globe,* "Spain, Greece, Egypt, Israel: Join Congress and See World," July 6, 1976, p. 32; and B. Nelson, "If It's Tuesday, It Ought to Be Chicago," *Los Angeles Times,* Aug. 4, 1976, pt. 2, p. 5. The itineraries usually have minimum relevance to the legislative function.

Staffing practices provide a continuum of abuses ranging from the absurd to the criminal. A 1976 *Newsweek* story gave examples: one "congresswoman has her male aide serve as a chauffeur and escort at parties, but also sends him shopping for pantyhose and other personal items"; "there are reports that a few congressmen give raises to staffers, then demand that part of the money be kicked back in political donations or other contributions"; other committee staffers, hired and paid to work on legislation, engage in election-year campaigning. See *Newsweek,* "Capitol Capers," June 14, 1976, p. 26.

56. M. Miller, *Plain Speaking: An Oral Biography of Harry S. Truman* (1973), pp. 199–201. Truman was particularly miffed by the fact that Kennedy got West Virginia so cheap . . . $14,500, or just enough to pay off the mortgage on the home of the most influential member of the West Virginia delegation.

57. Ibid., p. 70.

58. Ibid.

59. Ibid., p. 69.

60. Tolchin & Tolchin, *To the Victor,* p. 94.

61. Preferential legislation, for private groups, companies, or individuals, is largely effected by knowing someone in a key post or by hiring an influential lawyer or lobbyist, preferably someone with some government experience of his own. See D. Rosenbaum, "Tax Breaks for the Few Hinge on Access to Power: Knowing Someone in Key Post or Hiring Influential Lawyer or Lobbyist Helps with Preferential Legislation," *New York Times,* July 19, 1976, pp. 1, 13; see also J. Pierson, "Lobbying for Loopholes: Southern Scrap

Saga Shows How Firms Press Congress for Special Tax Relief Amendments," *Wall Street Journal,* July 19, 1976, p. 22. "And while lobbyists for business groups have drawn most attention in recent years, there are also those who effectively plead the tax interests of such groups as lawyers, doctors, and other professionals, universities, hospitals, even labor unions. The objective is always the same: to keep what you have and get what you can." See R. Rosenblatt and Paul Steiger, "Tax Reform Punctured by Loopholes," *Los Angeles Times,* Aug. 22, 1976, pp. 1, 24, 26 (quote is from p. 24). Whatever is mainly responsible—the efforts of lobbyists, a weak Treasury Department, the tax fairy, or simply the desire of congressmen to do favors for key constituents and for one another—"the fact remains that what started out four years ago as a major effort to tighten America's tax laws has all but broken down into a free-for-all raid on the Federal purse." Ibid., p. 1. There are presumably limits to this behavior. In some cases, the self-dealing becomes so flagrant that congressional operators may try to restrain one of their colleagues. See *Los Angeles Times,* "House Reprimands Sikes Financial Misconduct," July 30, 1976, pt. 1, p. 1; see also *New York Times,* "House Panel Asks Reprimands For Sikes in Stock Ownership," July 27, 1976, pp. 1, 10.

House majority leader Thomas O'Neill successfully lobbied "the Department of Housing and Urban Development into granting $88 million in Federal rent subsidies to a corporation headed by James Wilmot," a Democrat "who not only contributes to O'Neill campaigns but heads up fund-raising for all Congressional Democrats." See W. Safire, "The Do-Anything Congress," *New York Times,* June 24, 1976, p. 33; see also *Washington Post,* "Would-Be Speaker O'Neill Amasses $142,000 Nest Egg," Oct. 9, 1976, p. A-2.

Senators Robert T. Stafford, J. Glenn Beall, Jr., and John V. Tunney voted for national no-fault auto insurance in 1974. After voting against no-fault insurance in March 1976, Senators Stafford and Beall received $5,000 from a trial lawyers' political campaign committee. Senator Tunney, who missed the vote, also received $5,000 from the Attorneys Congressional Campaign Trust. After some questions from a few puzzled senators, all participants denied any impropriety, and politics went on as usual. See M. Mintz, "Senators Change Votes, Get Funds," *Los Angeles Times,* Aug. 30, 1976, p. 1, p. 14.

The $15 million appropriation for a new and more powerful engine for the navy's F-14 interceptor plane was the result of the lobbying energies of "the United States Navy, the Grumman Aerospace Corporation and Pratt & Whitney combined . . . with strategically placed Congressional committee members." See T. Wicker, "The Most Pervasive Corruption," *New York Times,* Oct. 19, 1976, p. 39. The navy wanted the engine, Grumman needed to build more F-14s, Pratt & Whitney wanted the engine contract, and the members of Congress wanted jobs for their constituencies. For other questionable behavior involving Grumman, former President Nixon, and arms sales to Iran, see S. Hersh, "Senate Unit Hears Nixon Rejected Pentagon Advice on Iran Jet Sales; Hearings Suggest the Ex-President Might Have Bowed to Grumman Sales Pressure," *New York Times,* Sept. 28, 1976, p. 3.

62. J. Austin, *The Province of Jurisprudence Determined* (1832), reprint of 1861 edition in 3 vols. (1971).

63. J. Douglas, "Boss Tweed's Revenge," *Wall Street Journal,* June 30, 1976, p. 16.

64. Tolchin & Tolchin, *To the Victor,* p. 94.

65. Ibid., p. 190.

66. "Nepotism, strictly speaking, has been prohibited by various rules in the Senate and—to a lesser degree—in the House. But in both chambers members get past the restrictions by hiring each other's relatives or those of important contributors and other VIPs, particularly for summer jobs. And with payroll vouchers almost as well kept a secret as travel vouchers, it is difficult to figure out whose back is being scratched by whom. 'It's just a cute game they're playing,' says one lobbyist. 'There's still a lot of nepotism. It's just harder, sometimes impossible, to track down.' " See *Newsweek,* "Capitol Capers," June 14, 1976, p. 27. For the details of l'affaire Delaney, see R. Hersey, "Rep. Delaney Is Criticized As Son Seeks an S.E.C. Job," *New York Times,* June 11, 1976, pp. A-1, D-5; *Wall Street Journal,* "Ford Affirms Choices for SEC; Comptroller Picks FTC Candidate," July 21, 1976, p. 4; C. Falk, "Ford to Nominate Patrick Delaney to SEC despite the opposition of Agency's Chief," *Wall Street Journal,* July 20, 1976, p. 2; and *Wall Street Journal,* "Delaney Is Again Nominated by Ford for Seat on the SEC: Move, Which Isn't Expected to Succeed, Could Place

Carter in Delicate Spot," Jan. 7, 1977, p. 2.

On federal regulatory agencies, see A. Kneier, *Serving Two Masters: A Common Cause Study of Conflicts of Interest in the Executive Branch* (1976). Congress's own "watchdog," the General Accounting Office, reports that potential conflicts are almost the norm. See *New York Times*, "Potential Conflict Almost the Norm," Aug. 15, 1976, p. 4, and A. Levin, "U.S. Agency Conflict of Interest Charged," *Los Angeles Times*, Aug. 11, 1976, pt. 3, p. 12. President Carter has issued an executive order detailing a code of ethics concerning conditions of conflicting interests for members of his administration.

67. On the role of favoritism, cronyism, and nepotism in local government, see the discussion of civil service promotions in Los Angeles County in D. Shuit, "Civil Service Promotions: Knotty Game; County Merit System Is Increasingly Being Challenged as a Sham," *Los Angeles Times*, July 23, 1976, pp. 1, 25, 26. See also Tolchin & Tolchin, *To the Victor*, and L. Hershkowitz, *Tweed's New York: Another Look* (1977).

68. Headlines calling for reform are scattered across the pages of most major newspapers: see J. Gannon, "House 'Reform' Plan Speedily Approved by Chief Democrats, Shaken by Scandals," *Wall Street Journal*, June 23, 1976, p. 3; P. Steiger, "Panel Acts to Control Vacation Tax Abuses," *Los Angeles Times*, Aug. 26, 1976, pt. 1, p. 1; R. Madden, "More Disclosures on Lobbying Reported," *New York Times*, June 16, 1976, p. 11; R. Soble, "Some Tax Shelters Are Falling Down," *Los Angeles Times*, Aug. 29, 1976, pt. 5, p. 1; and C. Mohr, "Carter Assails Role of Lobbyists in Bloated Mess of Government," *New York Times*, Sept. 28, 1976, p. 1. The last headline is arresting considering that Carter's campaign was helped immeasurably by labor unions and the American Federation of State, County, and Municipal Employees. See E. Conine, "Public Employees View Carter with Hope: He May Plan to Pare Bureaucracy, but He'll Be Beholden to Its Unions," *Los Angeles Times*, Aug. 13, 1976, pt. 2, p. 7.

Nor is there any dearth of governmental reassurances. "The Justice Department boasts that since 1970 its prosecutors have convicted more than 1,000 public officials (just under 3 officials per week)—including one Vice-President, two U.S. Senators, six

Congressmen and one Governor. There may be more." See *Time* magazine, "Going after a Governor," Oct. 4, 1976, p. 63. See also T. Goldstein, "Keenan Takes Oath As Special State Prosecutor," *New York Times,* July 1, 1976, p. 19. But see R. Lyons, "Charges of Wrongdoing Being Ignored in Congress Races," *New York Times,* Oct. 27, 1976, p. 21; and R. Silver, "Lag in Nassau Case Involving Kickbacks Held Disillusioning," *New York Times,* Nov. 28, 1976, p. 67.

69. J. Finney, "Furor over Missile Decision Reflects Pitfalls of Policy-Making Jobs in Pentagon," *New York Times,* April 15, 1976, p. 50.

70. Had Dr. Currie visited Rockwell's fishing lodge as an employee of the Hughes Aircraft Company no one would have alleged impropriety. "The public's 'right to know' is a phrase much bandied about these days, though it has a sketchy standing in a court of law. There is a greater legal right to know, for example, about the behavior of Government officials than about businessmen in general, though the conduct of one might just as surely affect the public's well-being or pocketbook as the other." See T. Griffith, "Scandal That's Fit to Print," *Newsweek,* June 14, 1976, p. 72. See also S. Hess, "A Congressional Quiz on Ethics," *Wall Street Journal,* July 9, 1976.

71. See details of note 69.

72. J. Finney, "Rumsfeld Clears Pentagon Aide of Conflict of Interest in Missile Program; Eagleton Charges a 'Whitewash,' " *New York Times,* June 9, 1976, p. 9. For other Defense Department investigations of conflict of interest violations, see J. Finney, "Schlesinger Is Looking into Entertainment of Aides," *New York Times,* Oct. 18, 1975, p. 13; and idem, "Rockwell Names Pentagon Guests; Concern Says Ex-Head of Joint Chiefs Was One of Visitors to Lodge," *New York Times,* March 18, 1976, p. 1.

73. See details of note 72, *New York Times,* June 9, 1976.

74. Ibid.

75. J. Finney, "Aid to Contractor by Currie Reported; Pentagon Official Cooperated on Missile Plan with Rockwell, Congressional Unit Says," *New York Times,* Oct. 15, 1976, p. A-9. See also U.S. Congress, Joint Committee on Defense Production, Subcommittee

on Investigations, *Conflict of Interest and the Condor Missile Program,* 94th Cong., 2d sess., 1976.

76. *Los Angeles Times,* "Official Resigns Defense Position," Jan. 6, 1977, p. I, p. 10; and W. Rawls, "Ex-Pentagon Aide Joins Hughes Aircraft to Oversee Missile He Promoted," *New York Times,* Feb. 15, 1977, p. 53.

77. Augustine, *The City of God against the Pagans,* Book I, preface.

78. W.M. Reisman, "Private Armies in a Global War System: Prologue to Decision," *Virginia Journal of International Law* 14:1 (1973), pp. 7-8.

79. M. Copeland, *The Game of Nations: The Amorality of Power Politics* (1969), p. 264.

80. P. Agee, *Inside the Company: CIA Diary* (1975); M. Copeland, *Without Cloak or Dagger,* The Truth About the New Espionage (1974). For CIA specifics, see *New York Times,* "Senate Intelligence Panel Calls for a Law to Curb Covert Action As Implement of Foreign Policy," April 27, 1976, pp. 1, 25; L. Gelb, "Wider Congress Role; Committee Goes Further Than Ford in Moving toward Tighter Oversight," *New York Times,* April 27, 1976, pp. 1, 24; *New York Times,* "Excerpts from Report of Intelligence Unit: Document Recommends Broader Authority for the Director of Central Intelligence; Committee Says U.S. Paramilitary Operations 'Frequently Amounted to Making War,' " April 27, 1976, pp. 21-24; J. Crewdson, "C.I.A. Secretly Owned Insurance Complex and Invested Profits in Stock Market; Business Success Cited in Report," *New York Times,* April 27, 1976, p. 25; J. Treaster, "Report Says C.I.A. Agents Picked Up Bar Patrons for LSD Experiments," *New York Times,* April 27, 1976, p. 25; D. Rosenbaum, "C.I.A. to Retain More Than 25 Journalist Agents; Personnel Not Covered by Pledge Bush Made," *New York Times,* April 27, 1976, p. 26; *Time* magazine, "Nobody Asked: Is It Moral?" May 10, 1976, pp. 32, 34; G. McGhee, "CIA Reform: How Much Is Enough?" *Saturday Review,* May 29, 1976, pp. 5, 59; J. Reston, "Reporters As U.S. Agents," *New York Times,* April 28, 1976, p. 37; *Los Angeles Times,* "Mobster Roselli, Key Figure in CIA Plot to Kill Castro, Found Slain in Bay at Miami," Aug. 9, 1976, pt. 1, pp. 1, 19; *Los Angeles Times,* "Roselli Tied Castro to Kennedy's Death," Aug. 22, 1976, pt. 2, p. 2; B. Nelson, "Authorities Ponder Possible

Link between Mobster Slayings, Plot to Kill Castro," *Los Angeles Times,* Aug. 9, 1976, pt. 1, p. 19.

81. See the following articles for public condoning of CIA behavior: B. Gwertzman, "Vance Supports C.I.A. Payments As Appropriate," *New York Times,* Feb. 28, 1977, pp. 1, 7; A. Marro, "C.I.A. Money Flowed, but U.S. Aides Insist It Was for Intelligence," *New York Times,* March 1, 1977, p. 8; J. Crewdson, "Inquiry Is Said to Oppose Prosecuting C.I.A. Aides," *New York Times,* July 2, 1976, p. 1; *New York Times,* "Government of Laws?" July 30, 1976, p. A-20; R. Calamaro, "The Way the Government Is Going," *New York Times,* 17, 1976, p. 41; and especially the *New York Times* editorial "To Bribe or Not to Bribe," Feb. 23, 1977, p. A-28.

See also M. Biederman, "Illegal Guns to South Africa," *New Haven Advocate,* Oct. 20, 1976, pp. 4–7; M. Jensen, "U.S. Checking Mobil's Role in Rhodesia," *New York Times,* Aug. 2, 1976, pp. 1, 36. And from the United Kingdom on the same topic: B. Nossiter, "British Glimpse Goings-On at the Top in Juicy Government Report on Lonrho," *Los Angeles Times,* July 25, 1976, pt. 8, p. 9; *Wall Street Journal,* "Some Top Lonrho Executives Criticized in U.K. Report on Dealings in Early '70s," July 7, 1976, p. 10; J. Collins, $60 Million Payoff Charged to Leyland in Bid for Exports, Britain Orders Investigation, London Paper Says State-Owned Auto Manufacturer Formed a 'Worldwide Bribery Web,' " *New York Times,* May 20, 1977, p. D-1; and *Wall Street Journal,* "U.K. Paper Says Leyland Made Payoffs Overseas with Approval of Government," May 20, 1977, p. 4.

82. R. Calamaro, "The Way the Government Is Going," *New York Times,* March 17, 1976, p. 41.

The CIA exercised influence even during the investigation of itself. "At the urgent request of C.I.A. officials, some 200 pages of material on secret overseas operations were deleted from the final version of the Senate Intelligence Committee Report and many portions of the surviving text were heavily censored." See *Time* magazine, "Nobody Asked: Is It Moral?" May 10, 1976, p. 34. Senator Philip A. Hart of Michigan, then senator Walter F. Mondale of Minnesota, and Senator Gary Hart of Colorado, all members of the Senate Intelligence Committee, professed "that in preparing the report the committee 'bent over backwards' to insure that no intelligence sources, methods or other classified materials were disclosed. . . . Some of its [the report's] most important implications are either lost or obscured in vague language." See *New York Times,* "3 Senators Score C.I.A. over Report; Some Security Objections Are Called Outlandish," April 27, 1976, p. 26.

83. Copeland, *Without Cloak or Dagger* (1974), p. 147. See also Agee, *Inside the Company,* pp. 64-65.

84. K. Teltsch, "Moynihan Cites U.N. Vote-Buying, Says He Knew of Payments in Key Assembly Ballots," *New York Times,* May 30, 1976, p. 10.

85. Ibid. The *Los Angeles Times* described a purported confrontation between two CIA agents and an aide to the Soviet Union's U.N. ambassador, Yakov A. Malik. The agents allegedly cornered the aide in his hotel room. They wanted to know how serious the Soviet government was in conducting the policy of detente. They offered, in return, to give the aide information of use to his superiors. When he refused, the agents told him "that the only way out of the room was through the window." The agents backed off; the aide reported the incident to his superiors and headed for the Soviet Union. See *Los Angeles Times,* "Russians Say CIA Threatened U.N. Aide," Aug. 4, 1976, pt. 1, p. 23. The U.S. has accused the Soviet Union of comparable tactics.

86. H. Maidenberg, "Administration Stockpile Plan Expected to Lift Copper Prices," *New York Times,* Oct. 14, 1976, p. 33. "Zambia, Zaire, Peru and Chile are the leading foreign copper producing countries in the non-communist world, Zaire is reportedly in dire financial straits, along with Peru." See also J. Valentine, "Copper Futures Prices Rise As GSA Intends to Increase U.S. Stockpile," *Wall Street Journal,* Oct. 5, 1976, p. 38.

   In some countries the government often pursues its "national interest" through the economic arm of state-run or state-supported enterprises. In such cases the relations between the trading corporations and the government are close—consultation, coordination of policy, exchange of personnel—and may be considered as effective elite units. In some countries, external corporate bribery may have been undertaken with the knowledge of the company's government, with its aid or counsel, and perhaps even through its functionaries. See also *Business Week,* "The Global Costs of Bribery," March 15, 1976, p. 23; *Economist,* "Controlling the Multinationals," Jan. 24, 1976, p. 68; *New York Times*, "2 Oil Companies Admit Payments: British Petroleum and Shell Paid $7.9 Million to Italian Coalition Parties," April 14, 1976, p. 13; and S. Masterman, "£6 Million Dutch Bribes to Argentines Alleged," Sunday *Times* (London), March 13, 1976, p. 4.

87. See *Economist*, "The Best Form of Defence Is Defence," Feb. 21, 1976, p. 38. See, in general, S. Melman, *The Permanent War Economy: American Capitalism in Decline* (1975); idem, *Pentagon Capitalism: The Political Economy of War* (1970); idem, *The Defense Economy: Conversion of Industries and Occupations to Civilian Needs* (1970).

88. "The Grumman Aerospace Corporation of Bethpage, L.I., for example, has been advised by the Defense Department that it can try to sell its E2C radar plane in Israel and Japan. But Grumman has been told by the Defense Department to stay out of the European Market, where the Pentagon is trying to sell a Boeing radar plane to the North Atlantic Treaty Organization." See J. Finney, "Rumsfeld Trying to Help Lockheed Save Japan Sale, Urges Defense Department as Contracting Agent for $250 Million Plane Deal, Assurances for Tokyo; Unusual Intercession Meant to Overcome Uneasiness of Japanese on Bribery," *New York Times*, May 27, 1976, pp. 1, 53 (quote is from p. 53).

There are currently three methods for transacting military sales: government-to-government sales, military grants, and commercial sales. "Such government-to-government sales have shot up from a level of $1.5 billion a decade ago to the current $9 billion to $10 billion a year. Meanwhile, military grants assistance has fallen to around $750 million, while commercial sales, which have been gradually growing, are around $600 million a year. The Pentagon has become the middleman in promoting and arranging foreign military sales. In its military advisory groups in 54 countries, the Pentagon has its sales teams advising the foreign country on what arms are available and should be bought." See J. Finney, "Selling Arms Is a Pentagon 'Mission,' " *New York Times*, June 20, 1976, p. E-4.

Where an advisor promotes unnecessary purchases, his behavior may be characterized as an anterior or preinvestment type of bribery. When a military assistance group persuades the local military that it needs "modern" equipment, it secures the commitment of a substantial part of the national wealth for an indefinite period. An advisor is in something of a fiduciary capacity and when he convinces his charges to make purchases (which can be very important for his own national treasury and career advancement), he may violate a fundamental duty. Subsequent bribes by United States companies A and B to sell their own varieties of the sought and essentially fungible product seem trivial in comparison with the preliminary decision to buy them at all.

In the Senate hearings on Lockheed's "payments" in Japan, Senator Frank Church wondered whether "Lockheed had been pursuing one foreign policy by supporting a leading right-wing nationalist while the United States had been pursuing another by supporting a moderate Japanese Government that opposed the ultraright. Actually, Lockheed made its payments to Yoshio Kodama, Lockheed's secret agent in Japan, precisely because behind the scenes, Mr. Kodama was tremendously influential with the leaders of the Liberal Democratic Party, having helped, with our blessing, to put them in power." See J. Cohen, "Lockheed Cover-Up?" *New York Times,* March 29, 1976, p. 29.

89. J. terHorst, "Bribery or 'Compensation,' It Smells Bad," *Los Angeles Times,* Sept. 2, 1976, pt. 2, p. 7:

> Most top U.S. diplomats, including former Secretary of State Kissinger, fret more about the continuing disclosure of overseas payoffs than the practice itself. The revelations concerning Japan, Holland and Italy are said to have had an adverse impact on U.S. relations. Good. Maybe that's what it will take to produce a change. Ever since World War I, we've been taught that communism was the real threat to the free countries of the world. It would be more than ironic if Asia's biggest democracy and our allies in Europe were done in not by leftists but by Lockheed and other bag men of Yankee big business.

90. A.C. Flannery, "Multinational 'Payoffs' Abroad: International Repercussions and Domestic Liabilities," *Brooklyn Journal of International Law* 2:1 (1976), pp. 111–13.

91. *New York Times,* "I.T.T. Elaborates on Funds in Chile; Geneen Discloses $350,000 Possibly Was Sent in 1970 for Political Purposes," May 13, 1976, p. 51.

92. Flannery, "Multinational 'Payoffs.' " Related to the United Brands–
Honduras episode was the charging, in May 1976, of the president
of five major stevedoring companies "with fraud and deceit in
accepting a $100,000 bribe to unload ships of the Standard Fruit
and Steamship Company during a longshoremen's strike in 1971."
These charges stemmed from the SEC investigation of three United
States fruit and steamship companies that were allegedly "conspiring against Central American banana exporting countries to
keep them from raising export taxes." See R. Tomasson, "Stevedore Cited in $100,000 Bribe," *New York Times,* May 10, 1976, p.
48.

93. Flannery, "Multinational 'Payoffs.' " For one in-depth examination of transnational corporate bribery and domestic bribery in the
form of illegal campaigns contributions, see McCloy, *The Great
Gulf Oil Spill.* For a two-page summary of this report, see *Economist,* Intelligence Unit, "The Cautionary Tale of Gulf Oil," *Multinational Business,* no. 1 (1976), pp. 43–44; see also J. Brooks,
"Annals of Business, Funds Gray and Black," *New Yorker,* Aug. 9,
1976, pp. 28–44.

94. G. Hodgson, "Pay-Off for the Oil Companies' Handouts: £500
Million," Sunday *Times* (London), April 18, 1976, p. 6. See also G.
Hodgson, "The Secret Power, Buying Italian Favours: The Role of
BP and Shell," Sunday *Times* (London), April 11, 1976, p. 6; and
Economist, "Italian Oil Scandal, Big Deal," April 17, 1976, p. 86.
   For Exxon's role in this affair, see *Economist,* Intelligence Unit,
"Bribery, Corruption, or Necessary Fees and Charges?" *Multi-
national Business,* no. 3 (1975), pp. 11–17; and see note 25,
Nehemkis, "Business Payoffs," pp. 11–13. Nehemkis contends that
there are parallels between Italian and American politics: These
facts would have portrayed Italian politics as not greatly different
from American politics. Special interest groups in Italy slip cash to
politicians in the same way that milk producers in the United
States, for instance, finance Democrats and Republicans to fix milk
prices, or the unions finance Democrats to see things labor's way."
Ibid., p. 13. See also W. Carley, "Loose Reins: How Exxon Missed
Red Flags That Signaled Secret Money Deals in Its Italian Subsidiary," *Wall Street Journal,* May 24, 1976, p. 30. For the perspective of Exxon management, see Exxon Corporation "Notice of
Annual Meeting," May 20, 1976, and Proxy Statement, Exxon

Corporation, 1251 Avenue of the Americas, New York, New York 10020, March 31, 1976.

95. No other multinational corporation has received so much press as Lockheed regarding its transnational practices. Among the most pertinent reports are the following.

In Japan: "Japan's Lockheed Affair; Political Fallout Uncertain," *Los Angeles Times,* Aug. 15, 1976, pt. 4, pp. 3, 4; S. Jameson, "Former Lockheed Executive Gives Details of $9 million in Japan Secret Payments," *Los Angeles Times,* Aug. 23, 1976, pt. 1, p. 4; *Business Week,* "Japan: An Aftershock on the Lockheed Affair," April 12, 1976, p. 43.

In Europe: *Time* magazine, "The Lockheed Mystery (*contd.*)," Sept. 13, 1976, pp. 31-32. Included in this article, Lockheed and Netherlands, Lockheed and West Germany, Lockheed and Britain, Lockheed and Japan, and Lockheed and Italy.

In Italy: *Newsweek,* "Who Is 'Antelope Cobbler'?" May 3, 1976, p. 31.

In West Germany: M. Getler, "Lockheed Documents Missing in Bonn," *Los Angeles Times,* Sept. 18, 1976, pt. 1, p. 9. This article includes the public statement for Ankara that the Turkish government reportedly is investigating Lockheed payoffs in Turkey.

In Australia: *New York Times,* "Whitlam Says Lockheed Paid Australian Official," April 30, 1976, p. A-10.

In general: *Economist,* "Lockheed's Iceberg," Feb. 14, 1976, pp. 13-14, 52, 55.

Public reaction to Lockheed: *Los Angeles Times,* "Dutch Flock to Buy Lockheed Report," Aug. 28, 1976, p. 1, p. 4.

96. T. Griffith, "Business Morality Can Pay," *Los Angeles Times,* Aug. 24, 1975, pt. 8, pp. 1, 4 (quote is from p. 4).

97. H. Watkins, "Effects of Aerospace Payoffs: U.S. Firms Add Up the Balance Sheet," *Los Angeles Times,* Feb. 15, 1976, pt. 6, pp. 1, 4 (quote is from p. 1).

98. R. Nader & J. Seligman, "Curbing Corporate Bribery," *Washington Post,* June 13, 1976, p. C-1.

99. But see L. Clark, "Innocents Abroad? How a Multinational Avoids Paying Bribes Overseas—Probably," *Wall Street Journal,* April 14, 1976, pp. 1, 22 (quote is from p. 22). See also A. Crittenden, "C.I.A. Said to Have Known in '50s of Lockheed Bribes; Data on

Japanese Reportedly Were Not Passed On to State Department or Grumman, Whose Fighter Lost Out to F-104," *New York Times,* April 2, 1976, pp. 1, 44; A. Crittenden, "McCloy Says Governments and Officials Must Share in Corporate Bribery Blame," *New York Times,* June 11, 1976, p. D-2; and J. Landauer, "CIA May Have Encouraged Firms to Pay Foreign Political Figures, Probe Shows," *Wall Street Journal,* March 1, 1977, p. 2. A more ambiguous situation developed in Haiti, where a Dallas company responded to a bribe request from Haitian officials by seeking assistance from the American embassy. The company, Translinear, Inc., refused to pay $250,000 and was forced to give up an initial $3 million investment in the development of a free port in Haiti. William H. Crook, chairman of the board, hoped that American officials at the embassy would publicly protest the extortionate demands. There was no response. Says a reflective Crook, "The result is to have your pride and go bankrupt." See R. Smith, "Bribe Requests Alleged in Haiti, Dallas Realty Concern Says Refusal to Comply Cost It $3 Million Investment, Little Help from American Embassy Cited at Hearing before Senate Panel," *New York Times,* March 3, 1976, pp. 1, 46 (quote is from p. 1).

100. These included, in addition to a $1.3 billion order for Lockheed's P-3C anti-submarine-warfare plane, an equally large order for a new jet fighter—Grumman's F-14 or McDonnell-Douglas's F-15 or General Dynamics's F-16. See J. Stenzel, "Fallout of Bribery: Lockheed Aids Japan Militarists," *Nation,* March 6, 1976, p. 264.

101. See J. Finney, "Rumsfeld Trying to Help Lockheed Save Japan Sale, Urges Defense Department as Contracting Agent for $250 Million Plane Deal, Assurances for Tokyo; Unusual Intercession Meant to Overcome Uneasiness of Japanese on Bribery," *New York Times,* May 27, 1976, pp. 1, 53. For a similar case regarding Boeing, see J. Landauer, "Boeing Escalates Court Fight with SEC on Data about Overseas Sales Payments," *Wall Street Journal,* Dec. 16, 1976, p. 5; J. Landauer, "State Department May Help Boeing Keep 'Consultants' Secret in Payoffs Inquiry," *Wall Street Journal* Dec. 28, 1976, p. 4; *Wall Street Journal,* "U.S. Seeks to Withhold Names in Boeing Inquiry," Dec. 31, 1976, p. 16; *Wall Street Journal,* "SEC Avoids Clash over Identifying Boeing Consultants," Jan. 18, 1977, p. 14; and *Wall Street Journal,* "Boeing Is Upheld in Sealing of Names of Overseas Agents," March 1, 1977, p. 2.

Chapter 3: **Operational Codes and Bribery**

1. For a general presentation of both the incidence and the evaluation of corrupt practices in various types of societies, see A.J. Heidenheimer, ed., *Political Corruption: Readings in Comparative Analysis* (1970), p. 24.

2. In a 1976 report to the U.N. General Assembly, the newly formed Commission on Transnational Corporations classified corrupt practices, including bribery, in the following general way: "In the international context the primary concern is focused on three types of corrupt practices: those involving improper participation by foreign interests in the political process, payments to public officials either directly or through middlemen, in order to obtain favourable decisions, and facilitative payments to achieve speedy action, which is not necessarily illegal." See United Nations Economic and Social Council, Report of the Secretary-General, "Transnational Corporations: Measures against Corrupt Practices of Transnational and Other Corporations, Their Intermediaries and Others Involved," E/5838/, June 11, 1976, p. 6. The commission has, for various reasons, decided to examine only those "payments to public officials either directly or through middlemen, in order to obtain favourable decisions."

   In a 1977 report the Commission on Transnational Corporations further distinguished three types of illicit payments: expediting payments, decision-altering payments, and political contributions. See United Nations Economic and Social Council, Report of the Secretariat, "Corrupt Practices, Particularly Illicit Payments in International Commercial Transactions: Concepts and Issues Related to the Formulation of an International Agreement," E/AC.64/3, Jan. 20, 1977, pp. 8, 9. The second report is closer to the categorization I use, but "political payments" are not included here because they refer to the recipient rather than to the type of bribe.

   Officials in Washington engaged in transnational bribery investigations have indicated considerably less interest in "facilitative" payments, or what are here called transaction bribes. This cannot be attributed to a reverence for the maxim "De minimis non curat lex," the law does not bother with trifles, for some TBs can be quite substantial. For further discussion, see T. Griffith, "Business

Morality Can Pay," *Los Angeles Times*, Aug. 24, 1975, pt. 8, pp. 1, 4.

3. There may be other, more subtle, reasons, such as the cementing of friendship for nonbusiness purposes, or even psychopathological reasons, such as the delight the briber may take in corrupting authority. For discussion of these aspects, see chapter 5.

4. See note 34 to chapter 1.

5. There is, to be sure, an economic distribution function to TBs, for the functionary who receives the bribe gets a "piece of the action": See D. Bayley, "The Effects of Corruption in a Developing Nation," *Western Political Quarterly* 19:4 (Dec. 1966), p. 727. The more business his clients have, the more he receives. But this does not mean that TBs are eufunctional, acting in some way as an incentive to better bureaucratic work. There is no reason to assume that TBs contribute to a qualitative amelioration of the performance of the bureaucratic function, for the bureaucrat, who has an effective monopoly of his service, has no incentive to do a better job in order to get more TBs.

6. See in general V.O. Key, "The Techniques of Political Graft in the United States" (Ph.D. dissertation, University of Chicago, 1934); and J. Gardiner & D. Olson, *Theft of the City* (1974).

7. In cases where public officials charge a standard percentage for the performance of their duty and their assistance is necessary for the successful completion of a large project, transaction bribes can become exceedingly large. I refer here not to those cases where a public official or sales agent uses influence to assist in the winning of a contract but to those instances where a contract, already awarded, still requires special assistance "in connection with importation of materials, customs, tax and other regulatory matters [as well as] for a general goodwill in connection with contracts." See *Wall Street Journal*, "GE Discloses Units Abroad Made $550,000 of Dubious Payments," Nov. 1, 1976, p. 18. This is apparently a common occurrence with multinational corporations where contracts and projects often run into millions of dollars. In such cases a six-figure transaction bribe, while seeming unreasonable, may be considered standard fare by all participants to the transaction. See P. Nehemkis, "Business Payoffs Abroad: Rhetoric and Reality," *California Management Review* 18 (Winter 1975), pp. 7–9.

8. Many societies use their own distinct expressions for the event I call transaction bribery. In Mexico, a TB is known as *mordida* (the bite); in Honduras, *pajada* (a piece of the action); in Brazil, *jeitinho* (the fix); in West Africa, *dash*; in France, *pot de vin* (jug of wine) *baksheesh* in the Middle East; *la bustarella* (little envelope) in Italy *kumshaw* (literally, "thank you"), or tea money, in Japan and other Asian countries; and, of course, "a little grease" in the United States. For specific examples of these bribes in their home contexts, see Nehemkis, "Business Payoffs," pp. 7–9.

9. Another factor that may induce moderation in the prices set for TBs is the desire of the bureaucrat taking transaction bribes to avoid making the activity so lucrative that larger fish will either take it over or insist on providing "protection."

10. C.V. Vaitsos, *Intercountry Income Distribution and Transnational Enterprises* (1974), pp. 130–31.

11. C. Elias, *Fleecing the Lambs* (1971), p. 203.

12. Rather than speeding up the procedures, transaction bribes may produce the opposite effect. As the Santhanam committee noted: "Certain sections of the staff concerned are reported to have got into the habit of not doing anything in the matter till they are suitably persuaded. It was stated by a Secretary that even after an order had been passed, the fact of the passing of such an order is communicated to the persons concerned and the order itself is kept back till the unfortunate applicant has paid appropriate gratification to the subordinate concerned. Besides being a most objectionable corrupt practice, this custom of speed money has become one of the most serious causes of delay and inefficiency." See Report of the Committee on Prevention of Corruption, published by the Government of India, Ministry of Home Affairs, New Delhi, 1964 reprinted in United Nations Economic and Social Council, "Transnational Corporations," June 11, 1976, p. 7. In other words, the whole harm of TBs may be greater than the sum of its parts.

13. For an analytic discussion of this condition, see S. Huntington, "Modernization and Corruption," in *Political Order in Changing Societies* (1968), p. 59; for a description of a society where bribery is almost a behavioral norm, see E.C. Banfield, *The Moral Basis of a Backward Society* (1958), p. 85.

14. See United Nations Economic and Social Council Report E/AC.64/3 Jan. 20, 1977, p. 8, para. 30.

15. J.C. Scott, "Corruption, Machine Politics and Political Change," *American Political Science Review* 63:4 (1969), pp. 1142–59; Bayley, "The Effects of Corruption," pp. 719–32; Huntington, "Modernization and Corruption," pp. 59–71; Key, "Techniques of Political Graft," p. 52.

16. In regard to the appointment of appellate and district court judges, see J. Wooten, "Carter Establishes Merit Selection of Appellate Judges, but Yields to Senators on District Courts," *New York Times,* Feb. 18, 1977, p. A-28; and N. Miller, "The Merit System vs. Patronage," *Wall Street Journal,* Feb. 28, 1977, p. 14.

17. J. Gardiner, *Traffic and the Police: Variations in Law-Enforcement Policy* (1969), pp. 118–23; and *New York Times,* "L.I. Judge Guilty of Ticket Fixing," Dec. 17, 1976, p. B-2. Professor Davis opines that this sort of thing is an example of "injustice." But its persistence leads me to speculate on the existence of an "operational" norm. Se K. Culp Davis, *Discretionary Justice in Europe and America* (1976), pp. 1–2.

18. Every community and group with a recognized normative code is subject to the suspension or transformation of its code through the techniques of variance bribery. This needs to be clarified because many writers unduly restrict their discussion of this type of bribery to activities in the political arena. For a precise discussion of this point, see H.D. Lasswell, "Bribery," *Encyclopaedia of the Social Sciences* (1931), vol. 2, p. 690.

19. See S. Raab, "Payoffs to U.S. Meat Inspectors Are Found Common in City Area," *New York Times,* April 5, 1976, sec. C, p. 1; J. Kwitney, "Massive Indictment of Meat Inspectors Is Seen in New York," *Wall Street Journal,* Aug. 5, 1976, p. 7; and *Wall Street Journal,* "Federal Jury Charges 2 Defunct Meat Firms in Sales to Pentagon," Feb. 3, 1977, p. 11. If the meat inspectors were paid for speeding up the work and not for varying from substantive norms, these would be transaction bribes. Meat and grain inspection provide good examples of the gray areas between bribery and extortion, since their operations provide many opportunities for dilatory practices that can stimulate bribes.

20. See W. Robbins, "Inquiries into Grain Find New Data on Gratuities," *New York Times,* Aug. 4, 1976, p. 11; *Wall Street Journal,* "Inquiry into Scandal in Grain Inspection Spreads to 15 States," Aug. 3, 1976, p. 24; *Los Angeles Times,* "Grain Inspector Bribe Charges Called False," Aug. 6, 1976, pt. 1, p. 23; *Los Angeles Times,* "U.S. Sues Cook for $24 Million in Grain Scandal," Dec. 23, 1976, pt. 3, p. 9; and *Wall Street Journal,* "Cook Industries Inc. Sued for $23.9 Million by Justice Department," Dec. 23, 1976, p. 4.

21. See in general J. Gardiner & D. Olson, *Theft of the City,* (1974), chapter 4. Specific examples of bribes designed to suspend a norm and ensure special treatment include payoffs on the waterfront between union leaders and businessmen interested in "labor peace," avoiding the costs of strikes, and in price fixing. See *Wall Street Journal,* "United Brands Report Indicates Payoffs to Labor; High ILA Aide Is Indicted in New York on Charges of Racketeering Activity," Dec. 13, 1976, p. 8; L. Dembart, "U.S. Summons 350 in 2-Coast Inquiry on Pier Kickbacks," *New York Times,* Jan. 27, 1977, pp. 1, 70; *Wall Street Journal,* "U.S. Subpoenas Transway International; R.J. Reynolds Unit in Dock Crime Probe," Jan. 28, 1977, p. 4; and N. Gage, "Corruption Is Broad on the Waterfront, An Inquiry Indicates; 2 Grand Juries Hear Evidence; Federal Cases Reported to Involve 'Majority' of Longshoremen's Union Executive Council," *New York Times,* Feb. 7, 1977, pp. 1, 34. For an example of this type of variance bribe in the broadcasting industry, see *Wall Street Journal,* "FCC Hearings on 'Payola' and 'Plugola' by Broadcasters Planned for Early 1977," Dec. 24, 1976, p. 4; and in the New York City School System, see L. Buder, "Queens School Custodian Investigated on Kickbacks," *New York Times,* Feb. 11, 1977, p. B-3. A final example is supplied by Metromedia Inc.'s outdoor advertising division. Regular payments were made to domestic government employees in order to influence their decisions concerning the division's failure to comply fully with certain laws. See *Wall Street Journal,* "Metromedia Discloses Payoffs by Unit in U.S. to Government Aides," Jan. 14, 1977, p. 18. This type of variance bribe can, of course, occur in a transnational context. See A. Crittenden, "Business Bribery Abroad: A Deeply Etched Pattern," *New York Times,* Dec. 20, 1976, pp. D-1, D-3.

22. Most recent examples of this phenomenon include Brooklyn Democrat Frank Braso, who was convicted in 1974 of taking a bribe from a local trucking company, allegedly controlled by the Mafia, for which he had helped obtain a Post Office contract. And, four months later, another Brooklyn Democrat, Representative Bertram Podell, pleaded guilty to a charge that he had received money for helping a Florida airline win federal authorization to fly more profitable routes. See *Newsweek*, "Capitol Capers," June 14, 1976, p. 22. See also T. Robinson, "Graphic Arts Firms under Payoff Probe," *Washington Post*, Feb. 27, 1976, p. 1. In reference to shipping contracts, see W. Robbins, "Passman Is Said to Face Inquiry on Coercion of Aid Recipients," *New York Times*, July 11, 1976, sec. 1, pp. 1, 42; and related to the preceding article, see W. Robbins, "Agriculture Aides Queried in Inquiry Linked to Korea," *New York Times*, Nov. 1, 1976, p. 3. For a British caper of similar design, see B. Weinraub, "British Officer Linked to Bribes, Arrested in an Inquiry into Corrupt Arms Sales," *New York Times*, March 15, 1976, p. 7. In this account the officer allegedly fixed defense contracts, mostly for sale to Oman, by passing money to officials in the Ministry of Defence.

23. A recent example involved Representative Henry Helstoski, indicted for, among other things, soliciting and accepting bribes from aliens in the United States on whose behalf a congressman may introduce a special bill authorizing citizenship. Helstoski denies all charges. See R. Sullivan, "Helstoski Indicted by U.S. in Extortion on Alien Bills," *New York Times*, June 31, 1976, p. 41. Another recent example involved Massachusetts state senators Joseph J.C. DiCarlo, the Democratic majority leader, and Ronald C. Mac-Kenzie, a ranking Republican. Both were indicted on eight counts of bribery and extortion following a two-year investigation. The indictments charged the two with conspiring to extort $40,000 from a New York management consultant firm for whitewashing a legislative report investigating a $3 million contract awarded to the firm. See *Los Angeles Times*, Aug. 13, 1976, pt. 1, p. 2.

24. Cyril Neiderberger, a former IRS auditor, was convicted for accepting "illegal gratuities" from the Gulf Oil Company. See *Wall Street Journal*, "Ex-IRS Aide Guilty of Letting Gulf Oil Pay for 4 Vacations," Feb. 28, 1977, p. 4. Gulf does not deny the gratuities

but comments that "there is no indication that any benefit to Gulf has been asked or received in connection with these actions." See *Wall Street Journal*, "Retired IRS Agent Indicted over Gratuity Gulf Oil Allegedly Paid," July 19, 1976, p. 2; *Wall Street Journal*, "Initial IRS Probe of Gulf Oil Slush Fund in '74 Was Incomplete, U.S. Aide Charges," Feb. 18, 1977, p. 10; *New York Times*, "Taking Gulf Favors Laid to I.R.S. Agent," Feb. 18, 1977, pp. D-1, D-11; and B. Calame, "Two Gulf Oil Aides Are under Scrutiny over Alleged Gifts to Ex-IRS Supervisor," *Wall Street Journal*, Feb. 10, 1977, p. 19. For details of a similar case, see *Wall Street Journal*, "Jeweler in New York Is Indicted for Gifts to Former IRS Agent," March 4, 1977, p. 3; and *New York Times*, "Head of Van Cleefs Charged with Gifts to I.R.S. Auditor," March 4, 1977, p. A-13.

25. Recent federal examples include the alleged bribe paid to then treasury secretary John Connally in 1971 for help in getting then president Nixon to increase federal milk price supports. See *Los Angeles Times*, "Witness in Connally Trial Gets Lecture, Probation in Milk Fund Bribe Allegations," Aug. 21, 1976, pt. 1, p. 6. A more recent federal example involves senators who changed their votes on the national no-fault auto insurance bill in March 1977 and received $5,000 each from a trial lawyers' political campaign committee. See M. Mintz, "Senators Change Votes, Get Funds: Two Switch on No-Fault Insurance, Receive Gifts from Lawyers' Group," *Los Angeles Times*, Aug. 30, 1976, pt. 1, p. 14. See also *Wall Street Journal*, "Six Are Fined, Jailed in Illinois Bribes Case over Concrete Trucks," Nov. 1, 1976, p. 10. For the medical profession's efforts at influencing legislation through bribery, see M. Seigel, "11 Podiatrists and 2 Crime Figures Indicted in Medicaid Bribery Plot," *New York Times*, Feb. 10, 1977, p. 43.

26. Thus Daniel Moynihan asserted that vote-buying occurs, albeit irregularly, on critical General Assembly resolutions. See K. Teltsch, "Moynihan Cites U.N. Vote-Buying, Says He Knew of Payments in Key Assembly Ballots," *New York Times*, May 30, 1976, p. 10. The American ambassador in Jamaica allegedly solicited $25,000 from the Aluminum Company of America, and apparently paid this money to Jamaican officials in order to gain support for an educational program that would explain to the citizens of Jamaica the advantages of permitting United States

investment in Jamaica. See R. Hershey, "U.S. Envoy Sought Gifts in Jamaica; Evidence Shows Ambassador Asked Alcoa for Money for Political Purposes," *New York Times*, July 16, 1976, p. 1; R. Hershey, "Alcoa Asserts a U.S. Envoy Solicited Payments Abroad," *New York Times*, July 15, 1976, p. 1. A final international example of the use of bribery in attempting to influence general community norms is supplied by the recent investigations of alleged bribes paid by South Korean businessmen, on behalf of the South Korean government, to American congressmen. See N. Horrock, "Inquiry to Korean Influence in U.S. Focuses on a List of 90 in Congress; Big Political Scandal Held Possible; Study Still in Early Stage," *New York Times* Oct. 28, 1976, p. 1; *Time* magazine, "Koreagate on Capitol Hill? Nov. 29, 1976, pp. 14, 19; R. Halloran, "Lobbying by Koreans Apparently Paid Off: 60 Congressmen Voting against Legislation Opposed by Seoul Got Some Form of Favor," *New York Times*, Dec. 6, 1976, p. 15; M. Tharp, "Far East Flap: Scandals Strain Links of South Korea, U.S.; Tension Worries Japan; Charges of Bribery, Bugging Could Undercut Alliance, Political Observers Fear; Business Ties Hold Firm," *Wall Street Journal*, Jan. 10, 1977, pp. 1, 10; and R. Halloran, "U.S. Envoy Said to Have Protested to Seoul on Lobby in Washington," *New York Times*, Feb. 3, 1977, p. 12. But see A. Marro, "Korea Lobby Is Reported Focusing on Two Ex-Congressmen," *New York Times*, March 28, 1977, pp. 1, 23; and *New York Times*, "Korean Watergate or Washout?" an editorial, March 29, 1977, p. 30.

27. In general, see *Time* magazine, "The Lockheed Mystery (*contd.*)," Sept. 13, 1976, pp. 31-32. More recently, see R. Halloran, "Lockheed Ex-Official Says Initiative in Bribe Cases Came from Japanese," *New York Times*, Dec. 20, 1976, p. A-8; M. Tharp, "Tanaka's Trial in Lockheed Payoff Case to Open Today before 3 Judges in Japan," *Wall Street Journal*, Jan. 27, 1977, p. 15; and *Wall Street Journal*, "Italian Panel Indicts Ex-Defense Officials in Lockheed Scandal," Jan. 31, 1977, p. 5. Another example is Northrop Corporation's bribe of $450,000 to two Saudi Arabian generals in 1972 and 1973 in order to secure aircraft contracts. See H. Watkins, "Effects of Aerospace Payoffs," *Los Angeles Times*, Feb. 15, 1976, pt. 6, pp. 1,4; and Nehemkis, "Business Payoffs," pp. 14-15. Other examples include Honeywell Bull and the stevedoring case men-

tioned in chapter 2. See C. Farnsworth, "Honeywell Bull: Episodes in Swiss Finance; After Being Defrauded, a Question of Bribes," *New York Times,* April 25, 1976, sec. F, p. 3; and R. Tomasson, "Stevedore Cited in $100,000 Bribe, Head of 5 Concerns Accused by Waterfront Commission," *New York Times,* May 10, 1976, p. 48. Many of the multinational corporate bribes disclosed during the past three years appear to be this form of variance bribe. See also the following articles for details of disclosures of further corporate payoffs: S. Hersh, "Hughes Aircraft Faces Allegations That It used Bribery in Indonesia," *New York Times,* Feb. 4, 1977, pp. 1, 14; D. Andelman, "Indonesia Opens Inquiry on Charge of Huge Payoffs in Satellite Project," *New York Times,* Feb. 4, 1977, p. A-1; *Wall Street Journal,* "SEC Complaint Says General Telephone Made a Questionable Payment in Iran," Jan. 28, 1977, pp. 2, 22; *Wall Street Journal,* "GTE Narrows List of South American Countries in Payoff," Feb. 8, 1977, p. 46; *Wall Street Journal,* "False Reporting Laid to American Hospital Supply; SEC Accuses Firm of Trying to Cover Up $4.6 Million of Saudi Arabia Payoffs," Dec. 30, 1977, p. 16; and *Wall Street Journal,* "Uniroyal Enjoined from Future Illegal Overseas Payments," Jan. 28, 1977, p. 2. This form of variance bribery has been exposed in the beer industry, in methods for awarding contracts and distributorships. The brewers were the first domestic industry to be investigated by the Securities and Exchange Commission; others may follow. See F. Klein, "Brewing Scandal: Beer Firms Are Target As Agencies Extend Bribery Probes to U.S.," *Wall Street Journal,* June 10, 1976, pp. 1, 22; R. Hershey, "S.E.C. Bribery Suit Names Emersons: Charge Is First Domestic One of Its Kind over Corporate Payments," *New York Times,* May 12, 1976, pp. 57, 69. See also E. Morgenthaler, "Bribery Build-up: How a Fraud Scheme & Steel Mill Arose Together in Indiana," *Wall Street Journal,* June 8, 1976, pp. 1, 16.

A statement by a member of the commercial fraternity distinguishing sharply between transaction bribes and variance bribes was made by a Budd Company spokesman in that company's formal disclosure of its practices in the United States and abroad. The spokesman said that payments were made "to induce them (officials) to expedite the performance of their routine duties" [transaction bribery] and "to obtain commercial advantages or to meet contractual obligations in a manner prohibited by local law [variance bribery]." See *Wall Street Journal,* "Budd Co. Discloses 'Improper Payments' in U.S. and Abroad," Nov. 8, 1976, p. 16.

28. The activities of virtually all oil companies in Italy are the best documented international case of this type of variance bribe. See in general G. Hodgson, "The Secret Power, Buying Italian Favours: The Role of BP and Shell," *Sunday Times* (London), April 11, 1976, p. 6; G. Hodgson, "Pay-off for the Oil Companies' Handouts: £500 Million," Sunday *Times* (London), April 18, 1976, p. 6. Other companies involved in this form of bribery include Gulf Oil in Korea, United Brands in Honduras, ITT in Chile and, of course, Exxon and Mobil Oil in Italy. For recent revelations on the ITT-Chile case, see *Los Angeles Times,* "500,000 Offer to Aid Allende Opponent Told," Dec. 25, 1976, pt. I, p. 10; G. Hovey, "Former U.S. Ambassador to Chile Charges Officials Lied on U.S. Role," *New York Times,* Jan. 12, 1977, p. A-9; and *Wall Street Journal,* "The Korry Case," Jan. 12, 1977, p. 14. For good coverage of these cases, see *Economist,* Intelligence Unit, "Bribery, Corruption, or Necessary Fees and Charges?" *Multinational Business,* no. 3 (1975), pp. 1–17; C. Flannery, "Multinational 'Payoffs' Abroad: International Repercussions and Domestic Liabilities," *Brooklyn Journal of International Law* 2:1 (1976), pp. 111–13; Nehemkis, "Business Payoffs," pp. 9–15. Nehemkis suggests that this form of corporate variance bribe does not elicit any attention in the United States because it is institutionalized domestically through lobbying. As we saw in chapter 2, transnational bribery designed to influence the creation of a specific community's or nation's general norms or legislation is a technique used by many agencies. See D. Binder, "More Heads of State Reported to Have Received C.I.A. Payments," *New York Times,* Feb. 19, 1977, p. 9; E. Behr, "CIA Reportedly Gave Israelis Millions While It Was Paying Jordan's Hussein," *Wall Street Journal,* Feb. 22, 1977, p. 2; and *Time* magazine, "Cutting Off the King's Dole," Feb. 28, 1977, p. 13.

29. In communities, organizations, or arenas where bribery is an accepted instrument of legislation, this characterization of bribery (that is, as a suspending of legislative norms) is inaccurate. Certainly bribery in the legislative process cannot imply a suspension of a norm if bribery itself, while not being a routine technique, is an accepted norm of legislative behavior.

30. We may hypothesize that any variance system in which effective elites receive rewards or otherwise secure gains will tend to institutionalize itself and routinize procedures as its workload increases. Over time, the variance character will become familiar and even authoritative. In the United States, for example, foreign states impleaded by our citizens for violations of private rights regularly turned to the Department of State and asked that "Suggestions of Immunity" be issued to the court seised of the case. These requests for variances increased in volume until the department found it necessary to develop an internal quasi-judicial procedure to respond to these claims for sovereign immunity.

31. P.A.Z. Banks, "Liberia: A Duality in the Law" (student paper, Yale Law School, 1975).

32. See J. Douglas, "Boss Tweed's Revenge," *Wall Street Journal,* June 30, 1976, p. 16. See also Key, "Techniques of Political Graft," pp. 51–52; Bayley, "The Effects of Corruption," p. 730. See in general J. Gardiner & D. Olson, *Theft of the City* (1974); A. Callow, *The City Boss in America* (1976); and L. Hershkowitz, *Tweed's New York* (1977).

33. A recent example of this phenomenon involves the Israeli government and the ruling Labor Party. For the Yadlin case, see *New York Times,* "Israeli Once Nominated for High Banking Position Is Indicted in Bribery," Dec. 14, 1976, p. 6; *New York Times,* "A Guilty Plea Shakes Israel's Ruling Party," Feb. 15, 1977, pp. 1, 4; *Wall Street Journal,* "Israeli Politician Discloses '73 Kickbacks to Labor Party, Implicates Rabin Aides," Feb. 15, 1977, p. 18; W. Farrell, "Israeli Labor Party Ponders Its Future; Disclosures on Kickback Money Add to Doubt about Outlook for Ruling Political Group," *New York Times,* Feb. 16, 1977, p. A-6; and W. Farrell, "Likud Bid to Check Israeli Labor Party's Funds Provokes Angry Debate and Shouts of Thieves!" *New York Times,* Feb. 17, 1977, p. 3. For the Ofer case, see *Time* magazine, "Suicide, Scandal and Political Chaos," Jan. 17, 1977, pp. 28, 29. For a rundown of a variety of Israeli government scandals, see p. 29 of this article. In addition, on the Ofer affair, see *New York Times,* "Week after Suicide Israel Halts Inquiry," Jan. 10, 1977, p. 8; and *Time* magazine, "Rabin on the Razor's Edge," March 7, 1977, pp. 32, 37.

34. The McCloy report on Gulf's bribe activities indicates that Western

bribers who entered into these arrangements abroad seemed to assume that bribe fees were either single payments or, if annual, were at a fixed price. In Korea, at least, it became clear that, from the bribe receiver's standpoint, the agreement regarding the bribe did not deal with the amount so much as with the commitment to continue to pay. Subsequent bribe requests might take account of factors such as inflation and windfall gains from the enterprise that could be "shared" through higher bribes. See, generally, J. McCloy, *The Great Gulf Oil Spill* (1976).

35. Agents skim in both national and transnational contexts. For skimming in regard to bank loans, see *Wall Street Journal,* "Two Former Aides of American City Bank Are Indicted," Dec. 28, 1976, p. 4; and *New York Times,* "Four Charged with Fraud in S.B.A. Loans by Banks," Jan. 12, 1977, p. D-3. For one case, among many, of transnational skimming, see R. Hershey, "$1.3 Million in Questionable Fees Cited by T.W.A. and Subsidiaries," *New York Times,* Feb. 9, 1977, p. D-1.

36. According to the *New York Times,* a Business International Report, "Questionable Corporate Payments Abroad," makes clear that some countries have unwritten codes stating which persons are "entitled" to receive irregular payments and setting out the proper amounts. If a "qualified" recipient requests too much, he risks a trip to jail. See A. Crittenden, "Business Bribery Abroad: A Deeply Etched Pattern," *New York Times,* Dec. 20, 1976, pp. D-1, D-3.

37. H.D. Lasswell & A. Kaplan, *Power and Society: A Framework for Political Inquiry* (1950).

38. Thus a legitimated variance bribe arrangement leads Russell Baker to the conclusion that legalization of bribery is a "sensible solution to a nasty problem." See R. Baker, "Passing the Buck," *New York Times,* March 30, 1976, p. 31.

39. Key, "Techniques of Political Graft," pp. 399–400.

40. See also M. Tolchin & S. Tolchin, *To the Victor: Political Patronage from the Clubhouse to the White House* (1971), p. 9.

41. See in this regard M. Goodman, "Does Political Corruption Really Help Economic Development?: Yucatan, Mexico," *Polity* 7:2 (Winter 1974), p. 143.

42. Ambrose Lindhorst, a Cincinnati lawyer, who spent twenty years

in local politics, warns prospective one-time bribers that once payoffs are initially made to policemen, building inspectors, and others, at "the curbstone level," there will be trouble. Once started, the practice never ends. Another veteran political worker, from Illinois, warns businessmen on state-level campaign contributions: "Stay away from anything that smacks of a trade-off. Do it once, and you'll do it forever, and it will get more costly." See *Business Week,* "Stiffer Rules for Business Ethics," March 30, 1974, p. 90.

In general, transnational bribers must be aware that investments secured by bribery are thereby made more subject to the caprice of a host government. If a political party in power is paid off, another party coming to power is likely to discover the arrangement and either up the ante or expropriate the holdings. Pertinent here are Gulf's experience in Bolivia—see J. McCloy, *The Great Gulf Oil Spill* (1976)—and Occidental Petroleum Company's experience in Venezuela—see *Wall Street Journal,* "Venezuelan Panel Assails Occidental, Urges No Compensation for Its Holdings," June 4, 1976, p. 7.

43. The relationship may become isonomic, that is, the briber may also have "captured" the official he has corrupted. As we will see, this really involves a distinct species of bribery, "the outright purchase."

44. See, generally, M. Zonis, *The Political Elite of Iran* (1971), pp. 101–103, 66–69, 305–306.

45. R. West, *The New Meaning of Treason* (1964). Students of the Soviet economy have suggested that a comparable function is performed by the USSR's highly structured market system and the centrally imposed *plan* or quota for each enterprise. It is impossible to fulfil the plan without committing severely sanctioned "economic crimes." Violations are detected by the control apparatus of the party that reaches into the factory itself and hence are accomplished with the knowledge and tacit collaboration of the local party watchdog. One consequence is that there is always fear and anxiety of exposure and punishment in the politically relevant managerial class, a fear that is periodically reinforced by well-publicized trials for economic crimes against the Soviet state. Anxiety-management results in submission. Professor Michael Libonati

remarks that "the system is less costly in terms of bodies than Stalinist purges, but no less effective."

46. See, in relation to the concentration of power through variance bribery, Key, "Techniques of Political Graft," pp. 50-52; and J. Scott, *Comparative Political Corruption* (1972), p. ix. Key's essay also deals with the use of bribery as a technique for retaining a position of power; see page 52.

47. But the chances of severe sanctioning for any public official for these infractions appear extremely low; see chapter 2. As *Newsweek* put it, "Like most other white-collar criminals, Congressmen spend little time behind bars." When a public official actually spends time in prison it does not, it seems, necessarily damage his public stature. But few congressmen have handled a prison sentence with the "flair of the late Rep. James Michael Curley of Massachusetts. Convicted on mail fraud charges, Curley spent six months in jail and had five brass bands waiting outside to trumpet his release in 1947. He then served out his fourth stint as Mayor of Boston—to which post he had been overwhelmingly elected while under indictment." See *Newsweek*, "Capitol Capers," June 14, 1976, p. 22. More recent examples of judicial deference to the operational codes of public officials are found in the Cunningham and Saypol cases. See D. Kleiman, "Keenan Will Appeal in Cunningham Case; Special Prosecutor Will Petition Court to Rescind the Dismissal of Indictment for Bribery," *New York Times,* Jan. 12, 1977, p. B-2; and idem, "Saypol Indictment Is Dismissed; Prosecutor Won't Appeal Ruling," *New York Times,* Jan. 18, 1977, p. 52.

48. See chapter 2 for examples of conflicting interests in the United States government. In particular, see A. Kneier, *Serving Two Masters: A Common Cause Study of Conflicts of Interest in the Executive Branch* (1976); and L. Reed, *Military Maneuvers: An Analysis of the Interchange of Personnel between Defense Contractors and the Department of Defense,* Council on Economic Priorities, New York (1975). See also L. Kohlmeier, "When Regulators Enlist with the Regulated," *New York Times,* Aug. 1, 1976, sec. 3, pp. 1, 2; W. Green, "Unlikely Alliance: Justice Agency, Law Firms Team Up to Oppose Lawyers' Ethics Plan on Regulatory Conflicts," *Wall Street Journal,* Aug. 11, 1976, p. 30; J. Finney, "Aid

to Contractor by Currie Reported: Pentagon Official Cooperated on Missile Plan with Rockwell, Congressional Unit Says," *New York Times,* Oct. 15, 1976, p. A-9; N. Horrock, "Inquiry on Korean Influence in the U.S. Focuses on a List of 90 in Congress; Big Political Scandal Held Possible; Study Still in Early Stage," *New York Times,* Oct. 28, 1976, pp. 1, 12. Early in his administration, President Carter focused further attention on the issue of conflict of interests. For Carter's code of ethics, designed for his cabinet and top 2,000 political appointees, see *Congressional Quarterly Weekly Report* 35:2 (Jan. 8, 1977), pp. 52–53; *Los Angeles Times,* "Texts of Carter's Ethics and Conflict Rules," Jan. 5, 1977, pt. 2, p. 8; *Los Angeles Times* editorial, "Ethics: Breaking Fresh Ground," Jan. 5, 1977, pt. 2, p. 6; and D. Burnham, "G.A.O. Asks New Rules and Panel to Check on Conflicts of Interest," *New York Times,* March 1, 1977, p. 29.

49. The evaluation of the functional condition called conflict of interest in the United States may vary with culture and sector. One journalist noted that "the concept of conflict of interest for those holding positions in both government and business does not exist in France." See F. Lewis, "Business-Political Scandals Are Disillusioning French," *New York Times,* Jan. 10, 1977, p. 8.

50. P. Agee, *Inside the Company: CIA Diary* (1975). For details of a specific case involving similar techniques of outright purchase bribery, see R. Lindsey, "Alleged Soviet Spy Testifies He Was Blackmailed after Telling a Friend of C.I.A. 'Deception' of Australia," *New York Times,* April 27, 1977, p. A-16.

51. See D. Bell, "Crime and Mobility among Italian-Americans," in A.J. Heidenheimer, ed., *Political Corruption* (1970), pp. 159–66; H. Ford, "Municipal Corruption," *Political Science Quarterly* 19 (1904), pp. 673–86; J.Q. Wilson, "Corruption: The Shame of the States," 2 *Public Interest* (1966), pp. 28–38; A. Rogow & H.D. Lasswell, *Power, Corruption, and Rectitude* (1963), pp. 44–45; and Key, "Techniques of Political Graft," pp. 46–53.

52. For recent espionage cases, which were curtailed as a result of their disclosure, see *Los Angeles Times,* "Egypt Unmasks Double Agent Used in Israel," Dec. 25, 1976, pt. 1, p. 4; *Los Angeles Times,* "FBI Arrests Russian Emigrant as Spy," Jan. 8, 1977, pt. 1, p. 5; *Los Angeles Times,* "Ex-CIA Aide Accused of Bid to Sell Data to

Russia," Dec. 23, 1976, pt. 1, p. 12; *Los Angeles Times,* "CIA Data Seized in Arrest Described," Dec. 30, 1976, pt. 1, p. 23; *Time* magazine, "An Offer the Soviets Refused," Jan. 3, 1977, p. 53; and *Time* magazine, "From Russia with Lovers," Feb. 28, 1977, p. 32.

53. M. Copeland, *Without Cloak or Dagger: The Truth about the New Espionage* (1974), pp. 154–59.

54. P. Knightley, *The First Casualty: From the Crimea to Vietnam; The War Correspondent as Hero, Propagandist, and Myth Maker* (1975), p. 175.

55. Agee, *Inside the Company*; Key, "Techniques of Political Graft," p. 47.

56. The revelations of irregular activities between the South Korean government and certain United States congressmen and officials may bring to light recent examples of the old and "more subtle techniques of entrapment." See *Time* magazine, "Seoul Brother," Nov. 8, 1976, p. 27.

57. In the case of the United States government and the entire graphic arts industry in Washington, D.C., money equivalents ranged from lunches, dinners and Christmas presents to home furnishings, electronic sound-reproducing equipment, and lawn mowers. Of course there were large cash payments, and sex and whisky played their parts as well. See T. Robinson, "Graphic Arts Firms under Payoff Probe," *Washington Post,* Feb. 27, 1976, p. A-1.

58. See in general L. Kohlmeier, "When Regulators Enlist with the Regulated," *New York Times,* Aug. 1, 1976, sec. 3, pp. 1, 2; W. Green, "Unlikely Alliance: Justice Agency, Law Firms Team Up to Oppose Lawyers' Ethics Plan on Regulatory Conflicts," *Wall Street Journal,* Aug. 11, 1976, p. 30; and the saga of Dr. Malcolm Currie of the Pentagon discussed in chapter 2. See also J. Finney, "Rumsfeld Clears Pentagon Aide of Conflict of Interest in Missile Program; Eagleton Charges a 'Whitewash,' " *New York Times,* June 9, 1976, p. 9; J. Finney, "Aid to Contractor by Currie Reported; Pentagon Official Cooperated on Missile Plan with Rockwell, Congressional Unit Says," *New York Times,* Oct. 15, 1976, p. A-9; *Los Angeles Times,* "Official Resigns Defense Position," Jan. 6, 1977, pt. I, p. 10; and W. Rawls, "Ex-Pentagon Aide Joins Hughes Aircraft to Oversee Missile He Promoted," *New York Times,* Feb. 15, 1977,

p. 53. See also D. Burnham, "Ex-U.S. Controller Joins Bank Company; Took a Post with Concern That Owns Chicago First National Soon after Leaving Office," *New York Times,* Nov. 28, 1976, p. 27; B. Wolfe, "Corruption in Government Regulation, the Judge Who Made Oil Companies Richer," *New Haven Advocate,* Dec. 1, 1976, pp. 12, 13.

59. For a 1976 example of patronage in American machine politics, see M. Schumach, "Tammany Lives On in a Queens Club," *New York Times,* June 8, 1976, p. 35. For a classic discussion of patronage politics, see J. Douglas, "Boss Tweed's Revenge," *Wall Street Journal,* June 30, 1976, p. 16.

60. C. Rossiter, *Conservatism in America* (1962); see also L. Hershkowitz, *Tweed's New York: Another Look* (1977); and R. Butler & J. Driscoll, *Dock Walloper: The Story of "Big Dick" Butler* (1933).

61. Students of bribery have observed that machines tend to be mildly inflationary and that they flourish in economies in states of expansion. A concurrent condition may be the social changes and disintegrations of traditional loyalty units that may attend such expansion. See also J.C. Scott, "Corruption, Machine Politics, and Political Change," pp. 1154–59.

62. For a reference to this phenomenon, see S. Raab, "Corruption Charges against New York Police Decline," *New York Times,* Jan. 14, 1977, p. B-3.

63. For a case where a deputy inspector is suspected of being the "small fry," see L. Maitland, "Inspector Indicted in Inquiry on Police; Jury Studying Bribery in Harlem Cites McMahon for Perjury," *New York Times,* Feb. 23, 1977, pp. 1, 59; and idem, "Second Deputy Inspector Indicted by Jury Studying Bribery of Police," *New York Times,* March 9, 1977, p. B-2.

Chapter 4: **Campaigns against Bribery**

1. E.C. Banfield, *The Moral Basis of a Backward Society* (1958).

2. K. Horney, *The Neurotic Personality of Our Time* (1937).

3. See C. Becker, *Freedom and Responsibility in the American Way*

of Life (1944), pp. 11, 12, 15; and R.H. Gabriel, *American Values: Continuity and Change* (1974); pp. 12, 32.

4. R. Hofstadter, *Anti-Intellectualism in American Life* (1963); and S. Mandelbaum, *The Social Setting of Intolerance: The Know-Nothings, the Red Scare, and McCarthyism* (1964).

5. See M. Weber, *Max Weber on Charisma and Institution Building,* ed. S.N. Eisenstadt (1968). But cf. R. Tucker, "The Theory of Charismatic Leadership" *Daedalus* (1968), p. 731.

6. See chapter 3, "Variance Bribes," on the institutionalization of variance bribe systems.

7. R. Baker, "Passing the Buck," *New York Times,* March 30, 1976, p. 31.

8. See J. Lambert, *Latin America: Social Structures and Political Institutions,* trans. H. Katel (1968), pp. 140-42. Red tape seems to appear increasingly in every society. A Brazilian businessman explains it succinctly: "Corruption is directly related to state control—you need paper, stamps, documents and seals for everything you do so there is more temptation and more opportunity to take short-cuts." See E. McDowell, "In Brazil, 'Mordomia' Is Rampant," *Wall Street Journal,* Nov. 9, 1976, p. 24. See also V.O. Key, "Techniques of Political Graft," in A.J. Heidenheimer, ed. *Political Corruption* (1970), p. 52.

9. A. de Tocqueville, *Democracy in America,* ed. J.P. Mayer & M. Lerner (1965). See especially vol. 2, pt. 1: "Influence of Democracy on the Intellectual Movements in the United States," and in particular chapter 8, pp. 419-20, "How Equality Suggests to the Americans the Idea of the Indefinite Perfectibility of Man." See also M. Mintz & J. Cohen, *Power Inc.* (1976).

10. For an example of this phenomenon in reference to the recent disclosures of transnational corporate bribery, see *Business International,* "The Pattern of Reaction," March 26, 1976, p. 99.

11. D. Bell, *The End of Ideology: On the Exhaustion of Political Ideas in the Fifties* (1960), p. 128.

12. J.N. Shklar, *Legalism: An Essay on Law, Morals and Politics* (1964), pp. 17-18.

13. J. Eisenstein, *Politics and the Legal Process* (1973), p. 348.

14. See, for example, W.W. Jaeger, *Paidea: The Ideals of Greek Culture,* vol. 1 (1945), pp. 353 ff.

15. See chapter 1.

16. R. Dahrendorf, *Class and Class Conflict in Industrial Society* (1959).

17. R.M. Hills, "Doing Business Abroad: The Disclosure Dilemma," *Yale Law Report* (Fall 1976), pp. 6–7. For a similar perspective, see L.N. Cutler, "The Payoff Muddle and How It Grew," *Trialogue* (Summer 1976) no. 11, published by the Trilateral Commission. In contrast to other contemporaneous statements, these must be considered comparatively militant. One former SEC official criticized the SEC itself for trying to turn the investigations of corporate bribery into a crusade. In response to the SEC's extensive probing into corporate affairs, former SEC commissioner A.A. Sommer said, "The SEC doesn't have a mandate to police the morality of American Corporations abroad and when it seeks to become a policeman of the world . . . its credibility is in danger." Sommer asserted that the SEC was "engaging in an orgy of self-flagellation [*sic*] of companies." He mentioned as one such instance a multimillion-dollar corporation that reported a $6,000 payment: such disclosures create "the notion in the minds of people that companies are without moral standards and that's an unfair charge." See R.J. Cole, "3 Assail Agencies on Payoff Positions," *New York Times,* April 10, 1976, pp. 36, 37 (quotes are from p. 37). Others, of course, feel that the SEC is not doing enough. See R. Hersey, "S.E.C. Criticized on Payment Data; Panel in House Discloses Disbursements by DuPont, Celanese & Wrigley; Voluntary Plan Scored, Shortcoming Cited," *New York Times,* May 25, 1976, pp. 47, 55; B. Schoor, "Shady Gray Areas: SEC's Fuzziness on What Illicit Dealings Should Be Reported Limits Disclosure," *Wall Street Journal,* March 29, 1976, p. 24; *Wall Street Journal,* "Flaws in SEC Bribe-Disclosure Program Are 'Serious,' Congressional Study Finds," May 21, 1976, p. 3.

18. The legislative proposals to date concerning corporate bribery have not preempted congressional scrutiny of corporate behavior. See Senate Bills S. 3741 (Richardson and Ford administration) and S. 3664 (Proxmire Bill). See also R. Nader, "Curbing Corporate

Bribery," *Washington Post,* June 13, 1976, pp. C-1, C-3.

19. See the epilogue for a discussion of *lex imperfecta* and *lex simulata* as they pertain to legislation designed to "regulate" transnational corporate conduct. In reference to the national bills sponsored by then president Ford and Senator Proxmire, see *Time* magazine, "The Double Damn," June 28, 1976, p. 58. Concerning business reaction to the International Code of Conduct for Transnational Commerce promulgated by the Organization for Economic Cooperation and Development, see *Business Week,* "World Roundup: Multinationals," June 14, 1976, p. 43.

20. C. Elias, *Fleecing the Lambs* (1971), p. 210.

21. See W.M. Reisman, "Response to an Insider's Coup d'Etat," *Nation,* Aug. 13, 1973, p. 102.

22. S. Ranulf, *Moral Indignation and Middle Class Psychology* (1938), reprint (1964). A similar hypothesis, which focuses on the *ineffectiveness* of white-collar crime, is suggested by V. Aubert, "White-Collar Crime and Social Structure," *American Journal of Sociology* 57 (1962), pp. 263, 269. In assuming that an ineffective law satisfies both those who demanded it and those who are subject to it Aubert comes close to earlier theories of Thurmond Arnold.

23. Ranulf, *Moral Indignation,* pp. ix, xii. Interestingly, V.O. Key has suggested that upper-class formations in decline, in addition to invoking moral legislation for maintaining social control, may resort to bribery as "a means of retaining a privileged position which would otherwise have been lost earlier." See Key, "Techniques of Political Graft," p. 52.

24. During the past ten years, opinion surveys indicate a steady decline among Americans in their confidence in leadership roles and institutions. See *Current Opinion,* "Less Confidence in Leadership," May 1976, p. 42; *Current Opinion,* "Americans Consider Hays Case Typical of Leaders," Aug. 1976, p. 88; *Current Opinion,* "Ratings of Ethical Standards for Several Occupations," Sept. 1976, p. 90; and *Current Opinion,* "Doctors Highest for Ethical Standards," Nov. 1976, p. 117. See also *Business Week,* "The Troubled Professions," Aug. 16, 1976, pp. 126–38.

25. See R.E. Roberts & R.M. Kloss, *Social Movements: Between the Balcony and the Barricade* (1974), p. 178.

26. Ibid., pp. 154–55. On the substantial literature regarding social movements, see, generally, R. Turner & L.M. Killian, *Collective Behavior* (1957); J.R. Gusfield, *Protest, Reform and Revolt: A Reader in Social Movements* (1970); R. Heberle, *Social Movements: An Introduction to Political Sociology* (1951), esp. pp. 307–308; B. McLaughlin, ed., *Studies in Social Movements: A Social Psychological Perspective* (1969); and W.B. Cameron, *Modern Social Movements: A Sociological Outline* (1966).

27. See in this regard Roberts & Kloss, *Social Movements*, pp. 382–84.

28. Regarding the campaign focusing on transnational commercial practices, see C. Eklund, "Corporate Social Responsibility," *Vital Speeches*, Jan. 1, 1977, p. 168; G. Gore, "Another Kind of Oil Shortage: Individual Responsibility," *Vital Speeches*, March 1, 1977, pp. 292–94; D. Linowes, "International Business and Morality, Integrity and Ethics," *Vital Speeches*, May 15, 1977, pp. 475–78; J. Greene, "Ethics Not Customs: Corporate Misconduct Abroad," *Vital Speeches*, Oct. 15, 1975, pp. 25–27; T. Murphy, "The Corporation and Public Opinion: Economic Freedom or Government Control," *Vital Speeches*, Nov. 1, 1976, pp. 55–58; T. Phelps, "Can We Afford to Be Honest? Christ Was the Greatest Economist," *Vital Speeches*, Oct. 15, 1976, pp. 2–4; I. Shapiro, "The Future Role of Business in Society: Personal Integrity and Accountability of the Individual," *Vital Speeches*, Oct. 15, 1976, pp. 16–19. Concerning congressional activity, see M. Tolchin, "Senate to Consider 'Tough' Ethics Code; Work Restrictions and Disclosures Would Go Beyond the Provisions Enacted Recently by the House," *New York Times*, March 14, 1977, p. 19; idem, "Senate Votes Limit of $8,625 a Member on Outside Earnings," *New York Times*, March 23, 1977, pp. A-1, A-19; idem, "House Debates Plan for New Ethics Rule to Restore Prestige," *New York Times*, March 3, 1977, pp. 1, 13.

29. See Turner & Killian, *Collective Behavior*, pp. 502–504.

30. H.D. Lasswell & A. Kaplan, *Power and Society: A Framework for Political Inquiry* (1950).

31. See Turner & Killian, *Collective Behavior*, pp. 502–504.

32. See Roberts & Kloss, *Social Movements*, pp. 173–81.

33. See, generally, H.D. Duncan, *Communication and Social Order*

(1962); D. Bell, *Power, Influence and Authority: An Essay in Political Linguistics* (1975); and in particular Turner & Killian, *Collective Behavior*, pp. 276–303.

34. See, for example, J. Ortega y Gasset, *The Revolt of the Masses* (1932); and P. Selznick, "Institutional Vulnerability in Mass Society," *American Journal of Sociology* 56 (Jan. 1951), pp. 320–31.

35. See Turner & Killian, *Collective Behavior*, pp. 165–75.

36. In this regard, see S. Kass, "What Should We Do about Lawyers?" *Business and Society Review* 20 (Winter 1976–77), p. 14.

37. Milton Handler, an antitrust specialist recently retired from the Columbia University Law School, says, "I believe recent antitrust developments may go a long way in solving the country's unemployment problems—particularly for lawyers." See T. Schellhardt, "Rivals' Revenge: More Firms Are Filing Antitrust Lawsuits against Competitors; Spurred by Recession & Hope of Big Awards, Plaintiffs Charge Trade Restraint; Campbell & Heinz in a Stew," *Wall Street Journal*, Dec. 29, 1976, pp. 1, 17. Concerning the Gulf Oil shareholder suit, see also Kass, "What Should We Do about Lawyers?" p. 12. For consideration of this phenomenon in general, see *Time* magazine, "Antitrust Trial by Congress," May 23, 1977, p. 71; and *Time* magazine, "Those Cases That Go On and On," June 27, 1977, pp. 40–41, 48. Regarding the current antibribery campaign, see R. Phalon, "Management, S.E.C. Crackdown a Boon for Insurers," *New York Times*, June 4, 1976, pp. D-1, D-9.

38. See C.R. Fish, *The Civil Service and the Patronage* (1905), pp. 209–45. But see D. Shuit, "Civil Service Promotions: Knotty Game; County Merit System Is Increasingly Being Challenged As a Sham," *Los Angeles Times*, July 23, 1976, pp. 1, 25, 26.

39. E. Turner, *The Shocking History of Advertising* (1953), pp. 176–77.

Chapter 5: Moralizing Bribery

1. J. Bentham, *Introduction to the Principles of Morals and Legislation* (1879).

2. J. Austin, *The Province of Jurisprudence Determined* (1832), reprint of 1861 edition in 3 vols. (1971); see especially lecture I.

3. M. Tolchin & S. Tolchin, *To the Victor: Political Patronage from the Clubhouse to the White House* (1971), p. 9.

4. But see E. Burke, *Thoughts on the Cause of the Present Discontents* (1770), in *Works,* vol. 1, p. 372.

5. R. Rovere, "Letter from Washington," *New Yorker,* March 3, 1977, p. 113. One rubber-company vice-president: "Whatever your moral viewpoint may be, the fact is that if you are going to do business in those countries and remain competitive, some such payments must be made." See M. Jensen, "Many U.S. Executives Reported in Favor of Overseas Bribes," *New York Times,* Feb. 13, 1976, sec. C, pp. 45, 49 (quote is from p. 49). In contrast, one staff member of the Senate's Subcommittee on Multinational Corporation thinks the leaders of the United States aerospace industry "may have been had." He says, "They [aerospace industry leaders] go over to some country and the first thing they're told by some hustler is that they've got to make payoffs. So right away they give in." He argues that in many cases the United States manufacturer has the superior aircraft, so that "influence buying" is not necessary. See H. Watkins, "Effects of Aerospace Payoffs; U.S. Firms Add Up the Balance Sheet," *Los Angeles Times,* Feb. 15, 1976, pp. 1, 4 (quote is from p. 1). Eugene E. Jennings, a management consultant and professor at Michigan State University's graduate school of business, contends that "a lot of the payments were unnecessary and reflected a lack of confidence in our ability to compete." See V. Pappas, "Payoff Aftermath: Crackdown on Bribery Hasn't Damaged Sales, Big Companies Report; Some Tell of Slight Impact, and Some Believe Losses May Show Up in Future," *Wall Street Journal,* Feb. 18, 1977, pp. 1, 18. Still other executives claim that many reports of bribes being solicited by foreign officials may actually only be excuses fabricated by salesmen who failed to make a sale. See H. Lawson, "Boeing Ex-Salesmen Recall Jobs' Pressures & Foreign Intrigues," *Wall Street Journal,* May 7, 1976, pp. 1, 23.

6. G. Simmel, *The Sociology of Georg Simmel,* ed. K. H. Wolff (1950), p. 226.

7. H. Gerth & C. W. Mills, *Character and Social Structure: The*

Psychology of Social Institutions (1953), p. 123.

8. For a thoughtful examination of the causes for violation of economic regulation laws, see R. E. Lane, *The Regulation of Businessmen: Social Conditions of Government Economic Control* (1954), chap. 5, passim.

9. H. V. Ball, "Social Structure and Rent Control Violations," *American Journal of Sociology* 65 (1960), pp. 598, 604.

10. H. V. Ball & L. M. Friedman, "Criminal Sanctions in Enforcement of Economic Legislation," *Stanford Law Review* 17 (1965), p. 302.

11. E. H. Sutherland, *White Collar Crime* (1949), p. 234.

12. See H. D. Lasswell, "Bribery," *Encyclopaedia of the Social Sciences* (1931), vol. 2, pp. 691–92. An obvious parallel here is the predilection of certain personalities or cultural types to resort to violence as a strategic device, even when their objective could be secured by more persuasive means. Torturers, for example, have access to an armamentarium of modern drugs for a most effective and painless extraction of information; the true thug invariably opts for the good old-fashioned means.

13. See, for example, R. C. Dwivedi, "Bureaucratic Corruption in Developing Countries," *Asian Survey* 7 (1967), p. 245; R. J. Braibanti, "Reflections on Bureaucratic Corruption," *Public Administration* 40 (1962), p. 357; and see in particular M. Young & P. Willmott, *Family and Kinship in East London* (1957), Pelican ed. (1966), pp. 41–42.

14. The element of assertion of autonomy against the demand for self-subordination to some larger group is operating even when the bribe seems to be purely economically motivated. Even "picking up a little extra change" in violation of the norms is such an assertion.

15. R. D. Laing, *The Divided Self: An Existential Study in Sanity and Madness* (1960).

16. An intriguing *New York Times* editorial, "To Bribe or Not to Bribe," discusses the appropriateness of clandestine Central Intelligence Agency payments made abroad. It concludes, "uneasily and with qualifications," that certain payments may be required and may require secrecy in order to be effective. The president should

have the discretion to make such determinations. See *New York Times,* "To Bribe or Not to Bribe," Feb. 23, 1977, p. A-28. See also B. Gwertzman, "Vance Supports C.I.A. Payments as 'Appropriate'; Hussein Says Money Was for Intelligence," *New York Times,* Feb. 18, 1977, pp. 1, 7.

17. J. Rawls, *A Theory of Justice* (1971), pp. 363 ff.; J. Childress, *Civil Disobedience and Political Obligation* (1971); and M. Walzer, *Obligations: Essays on Disobedience, War and Citizenship* (1970).

18. See in this regard Lenin's interesting comments on Communist morality in G. Hampsch, *The Theory of Communism* (1965), p. 113.

19. The objective of bribery is thus a key factor in determining lawfulness. I would speculate that bribery on behalf of an organization would be deemed less odious, by members of another organization, than bribery for personal gain. *Raison d'etat* is only a part of a more general species we might call *raison d'organisation*; if you accept one, it becomes comparatively harder to deny the other. Consider the aftermath of the ITT payments in Chile. In 1978 the *Wall Street Journal* reported that high officials of ITT who had lied about corporate payments in Chile to secure the overthrow of Allende would be permitted to plead guilty to misdemeanors and could expect very mild sentences. See J. Landauer, *Wall Street Journal,* March 21, 1978, p. 2. Would they have been permitted to plead thus if they had pocketed the bribes or undertaken the bribery not for their company but for themselves? Of course, if the executives were acting as agents of or with the connivance of parts of the United States government, there would be a strong interest in settling the case as quickly and as quietly as possible.

20. H. Kelsen, *General Theory of Law and State* (1945).

21. See chapter 1.

22. For discussion of the use of bribery for achieving the demands of a traditional or exclusive community located within a larger, and most likely, modern inclusive political community, see Lasswell, "Bribery," p. 691; D. Bayley, "The Effects of Corruption in a Developing Nation," *Western Political Quarterly* 19:4 (Dec. 1966), pp. 731–32; J.C. Scott, "Corruption, Machine Politics, and Political Change," *American Political Science Review* 63:4 (1969), pp.

1142–59.

23. J.S. Nye, "Corruption and Political Development: A Cost-Benefit Analysis," *American Political Science Review* 61:2 (1967), pp. 417–27.

24. Young & Willmott, *Family and Kinship in East London* (1957).

25. W.F. Wertheim, *Indonesian Society in Transition* (1956), p. 86.

26. The *locus classicus* of multiple loyalties and bribery is Matthew Feldman's, the president of New Jersey State Senate. While pleading guilty to charges of commercial bribery, Feldman claimed that his "public" record remained unblemished: "It was Matty Feldman the businessman, who did it [paid the bribe], not Matty Feldman the state senator." Alas, the judge, unable to appreciate the complexities of the modern personality, replied, "You can't operate as president of the state senate by day and by night slip into a terminal at Newark Airport and violate the laws you were sworn to uphold." See *Wall Street Journal*, "New Jersey State Aide Draws Maximum Fine for Commercial Bribe," Dec. 16, 1976, p. 24. For further details, see W. Waggoner, "Jersey Legislator Concedes Bribery," *New York Times*, Nov. 30, 1976, pp. 1, 43; and *Wall Street Journal*, "New Jersey Senate's President Admits Paying $6,400 Bribes," Nov. 30, p. 23.

27. E.A. Ross, *Sin and Society: An Analysis of Latter Day Iniquity* (1907), pp. 55–56.

28. In the Italo-Ethiopian campaign, as mentioned earlier, Evelyn Waugh "secretly employed an Abyssinian called Wazir Ali Bey, until, so he said, he found that Ali Bey was also secretly employed by nearly every other correspondent in the capital." See P. Knightley, *The First Casualty: From Crimea to Vietnam; The War Correspondent as Hero, Propagandist and Myth Maker* (1975), p. 175.

29. See M. Weber, *Max Weber on Charisma and Institution Building*, ed. S.N. Eisenstadt (1968).

30. See, generally, E.J. Hobsbawm, *Bandits* (1969). See also Bernard Lewis's interesting study of the assassins. "In the atomized and insecure society of the later Caliphates, men sought comfort and assurance in new and stronger forms of associations." See B. Lewis, *The Assassins: A Radical Sect in Islam* (1968), p. 128.

31. For discussion of the social functions of this discrete identification

process, see W.M. Reisman, "Responses to Crimes of Discrimination and Genocide: An Appraisal of the Convention on the Elimination of Racial Discrimination," *Denver Journal of International Law and Policy* (1971), pp. 29, 42.

32. For further discussion of this point, see G. Myrdal, *Asian Drama* (1968), vol. 2, pp. 937-58; A. Rogow & H.D. Lasswell, *Power, Corruption, and Rectitude* (1963), pp. 132-34; S. Rajaratnam, "Bureaucracy versus Kleptocracy," in A.J. Heidenheimer, ed., *Political Corruption* (1970), pp. 546-48; G. Myrdal, "Corruption: Its Causes and Effects," in ibid., pp. 540-45; and Bayley, "The Effects of Corruption," pp. 725-27.

33. For what may be the most remarkable and detailed discussion of such a society, see E.C. Banfield, *The Moral Basis of a Backward Society* (1958). Some countries stereotyped as having distinctively bribal societies by Americans include Mexico, Brazil, and Italy. In Mexico, bribery and other forms of corruption abound, it has been suggested, because "the two principal watchdogs of public morality—the judiciary and the press—are themselves part of the same system of values." See A. Riding, "Corruption Again Election Issue in Mexico," *New York Times*, June 29, 1976, sec. C, p. 2. In Italy, according to the London Sunday *Times*, "Italian society works on the exchange of favours." See G. Hodgson, "Secret Power, Buying Italian Favours: The Role of BP and Shell," Sunday *Times* (London), April 11, 1976, p. 6. In Brazil, notice was served in 1964 that corruption would not be tolerated. It's now, according to a São Paulo businessman, "business as usual, and corruption exists at almost every level." See E. McDowell, "In Brazil, 'Mordomia' Is Rampant," *Wall Street Journal*, Nov. 9, 1976, p. 24. McDowell opined that the Brazilian condition is not all that different from the "virus known in the United States as Potomac fever. Indeed, the analogy to the U.S. is not unapt, in view of influence peddling, scandal and corruption from Washington to state house to city hall." On influence peddling and patronage in the United States, see Tolchin & Tolchin, *To the Victor*.

   From January 1975 through the summer of 1976, ships laden with cement had paralyzed Nigeria's ports. Under General Gowon's government, officials ordered 20 million tons of cement—16 million tons by the Ministry of Defense alone—to be delivered in twelve months. At this rate the ships would have had to have been unloaded at a rate twice the unloading capacity of all of Nigeria's ports combined. As the ships lined up along the Lagos coastline, the cement, resting in the moisture-ridden hulls, may have lost its binding quality. Some officials speculate that the bad cement has been mixed with the good and one building made with the cement has already collapsed. Says one official, "In two or three years we may be seeing buildings collapsing all over Nigeria." The new government appointed a tribunal to investigate the scandal "but it seems to have made little progress in untangling a web of kickbacks and bribes involving Government officials, foreign shipowners, corrupt purchasing agents, unscrupulous middlemen, phony corporations, dubious letters of credit and Swiss bank accounts." The cement scandal appears to have been a major reason for the coup that overthrew the regime of General Gowon in February 1975. See J. Darnton, "Nigerians Fear New Revelations in Cement Scandal," *New York Times,* June 28, 1976, p. 6.

34. Banfield, *The Moral Basis.*

35. As reported to me by an international trader with dealings in Iran.

36. A curious exception to this practice is §162(c) of the Internal Revenue Code. See chapter 1.

37. Ross, *Sin and Society,* p. 106.

38. Ibid., 107–108.

39. Gerth & Mills, *Character and Social Structure,* p. 123.

40. The role and activities of the specific group of boundary mediators known as sales agents is often associated with the problem of transnational corporate payoffs. See in this regard United Nations Economic and Social Council, Report of the Secretariat, "Corrupt Practices, Particularly Illicit Payments in International Commercial Transactions: Concepts and Issues Related to the Formulation of an International Agreement," E/AC.64/3, Jan. 20, 1977, pp. 9–11. Many multinational companies have sales agents in order to facilitate the promotion and sales of their merchandise. Agents are usually natives of the country where the sales are sought and are hired, as with the domestic middleman, because of knowledge of the product and familiarity with public officials or private businessmen who would or could be interested in purchasing the multina-

tional's wares. A sales agent can legitimately receive an extremely large sales commission if his assistance was important in obtaining the sales. Trans World Airlines paid $20.1 million in commissions to one sales agent in connection with its sales in 1975 to Iran of nine used Boeing 747s. It was the highest commission rate ever, about 11 percent, for a used-aircraft sale. "The airline didn't believe anything improper, illegal or unusual—other than the amounts—was involved." See T. Fandell, "TWA Paid Agent $20.1 Million Fee in Iran Transaction," *Wall Street Journal,* March 31, 1976, p. 12. To put this figure in perspective, remember that Lockheed Aircraft Corporation paid a total of $24 million in overseas bribes and that the serious commotion over the Lockheed payments in Japan revolves around the trifling sum of $12.6 million. See *Time* magazine, "The Lockheed Mystery (*contd.*)," Sept. 13, 1976, pp. 31–32.

The magnitude of such commissions has prompted some multi-national corporate executives to refer to them as "extraordinary payments." No one, according to some executives who retain them, knows exactly how an agent helps obtain a contract, or what he does with the commission. Some multinational companies "may suspect that their agents or distributors are making unusual or illegal payments, but feel they can do little or nothing about it because the middlemen are independent entrepreneurs and not company employees." See J. Basche, "Unusual Foreign Payments: A Survey of the Policies and Practices of U.S. Companies," The Conference Board, *Conference Board Report* no. 682, p. 14. Adds J.E. Prince, senior vice-president and secretary of Boeing Company, "Boeing cannot police the morality of the foreign businessmen or officials whom it hires as consultants or representatives.... They're independent contractors, and we don't stick our noses into what they do." See V. Pappas, "Payoff Aftermath; Crackdown on Bribery Hasn't Damaged Sales, Big Companies Report," *Wall Street Journal,* Feb. 28, 1977, pp. 1, 18. At its most polite, there can be an innuendo of bribery in many of these transactions. Some have voiced skepticism about these protestations of innocence and ignorance. "It is blinking at reality to suppose that sophisticated aerospace managements are not aware that some portion of the fees paid to agents is used for payoffs to government officials to secure favorable decisions on government procurement of aircraft and military hardware." See P. Nehemkis, "Business Payoffs Abroad: Rhetoric and Reality," *California Management Review* 18 (Winter 1975), p. 15.

Boundary mediators are not an exclusively foreign commodity. In a lengthy four-part news report—*New York Times,* "The Contrasting Lives of Sidney Korshak," June 27, 1976, pp. 1, 20; *New York Times,* "Korshak's Power Rooted in Ties to Labor Leaders," June 28, 1976, pp. 1, 20; *New York Times,* "Major Corporations Seek Korshak's Labor Advice," June 29, 1976, pp. 1, 16; and *New York Times,* "Korshak Again the Target of a Federal Investigation," June 30, 1976, pp. 1, 14—Seymour Hersh attempted to chronicle the story of Sidney Korshak, a lawyer with close connections to both big business and big labor, who is apparently legendary among legitimate businessmen. Rarely does anyone ask Sidney Korshak how he gets results. In a review of the Hersh series, Frank Lalli of *New West* magazine asked a crucial unanswered question: why is it that businessmen seek out a man like Korshak? If there were no Sidney Korshak, would many legitimate businessmen "want to create such a man—a man who gets things done, one way or another?" See F. Lalli, "The Korshak Series: Firecrackers, Not Dynamite," Aug. 2, 1976, p. 29.

On the use of sales agents in transnational contexts, see H. Lawson & A.R. Immel, "Using Agent with Family Ties to Buyer, Boeing Sold 11 Jets to Pakistan Airlines," *Wall Street Journal,* June 15, 1976, p. 2. Sales agents can prove a handicap at times. See C. Farnsworth, "Honeywell Bull: Episodes in Swiss Finance; After Being Defrauded, a Question of Bribes," *New York Times,* April 25, 1976, sec. F, p. 3; W. Carley, "Loose Reins, How Exxon Missed Red Flags That Signaled Secret Money Deals in Its Italian Subsidiary," *Wall Street Journal,* May 24, 1976, p. 30; and *Economist,* Intelligence Unit, "Bribery, Corruption, or Necessary Fees and Charges?" *Multinational Business,* no. 3 (1975), pp. 5–6.

41. The trick is "know-who." In Brazil it is reportedly easy to avoid paying income tax. According to one "well-placed" accountant, it is "easy to evade if you know the right people." Some Brazilians have begun to complain that the talent necessary to skirt the law successfully depends less on know-how and more on "know-who." See E. McDowell, "In Brazil, 'Mordomia' Is Rampant," p. 24. In transnational corporate sales, "know-who" is just as important.

42. L. Clark, "Innocents Abroad? How a Multinational Avoids Paying Bribes Overseas—Probably," *Wall Street Journal*, April 14, 1976, pp. 1, 22 (quote is from p. 22).

43. R. Butler & J. Driscoll, *Dock Walloper: The Story of "Big Dick" Butler* (1933), pp. 129–30. (Italics in original.)

44. The following account is based on an article written by Anthony Lukas for the *New York Times Magazine*. *New York Times, New York Times Magazine*, "The Hughes Connection: What Were the Watergate Burglars Looking For?" Jan. 4, 1976, sec. 6, pp. 8–9, 25–33; and Lukas's book, *Nightmare: The Underside of the Nixon Years* (1976), pp. 112–15. The main focus of the articles is the author's hypothesis that the Watergate burglary had a specific motive: to find out how much Nixon's enemies knew about the Hughes-Rebozo-Nixon relationship and what plans were being made to use it against Nixon in the 1972 election. Although the overall article makes intriguing and speculative reading, our emphasis here is on the methods used by Hughes and his associates to obtain his goals by bribing Nixon.

45. G.P. Verbit, *International Monetary Reform and the Developing Countries: The Rule of Law Problem* (1975), pp. 21–24.

46. See, for example, J.E. Carlin, *Lawyers on Their Own: A Study of Individual Practitioners in Chicago* (1962); and idem, *Lawyers' Ethics: A Survey of the New York City Bar* (1966), pp. 47–52.

47. J. Davidow, "Recent Developments in International Antitrust," *International Law Perspective* 2:11 (1976), a speech delivered on Nov. 4, 1976.

48. Carlin, *Lawyers on Their Own*, p. 208.

49. Ibid, p. 209.

50. W. Carley, "Bribery (*cont.*): Despite Early Gains, Anti-Payoff Campaign Is Beginning to Sputter," *Wall Street Journal*, July 9, 1976, pp. 1, 17 (quote is from p. 1).

51. For a collection of intriguing essays regarding social order, hierarchy, and authority, see H. Duncan, *Communication and Social Order* (1962), pp. 253–346.

52. A recent case in point may be the bribes paid by Tongsun Park to members of the United States Congress. If Mr. Park, as has been surmised, made these payments on behalf of the South Korean

government, it would be bizarre to construe his behavior (in contrast to that of those congressmen who accepted the money) as violating the goals of the organization (that is, the South Korean government) he was representing and to which he allegedly paid primary loyalty. See, generally, *Time* magazine, "South Korea, Spooking Capitol Hill," Nov. 15, 1976, p. 66; *New York Times,* "Koreans and Americans in Seoul Doubt Park Didn't Know of Gifts," Nov. 8, 1976, p. 3; *New York Times,* "Korean Chief Linked to Illegal Lobbying; Intelligence Sources Tell of Effort to Sway Congress," Nov. 9, 1976, pp. 1, 22.

53. H.D. Thoreau, "On the Duty of Civil Disobedience."

54. R. Dahrendorf, *Class and Class Conflict in Industrial Society* (1959).

55. B. Nelson, *The Idea of Usury: From Tribal Brotherhood to Universal Otherhood,* 2d ed. (1969).

Epilogue: The Current Bribery Campaign

1. Recent revelations regarding CIA payments and subsequent official response to these revelations seem to support this thesis. See B. Gwertzman, "Vance Supports C.I.A. Payments as 'Appropriate,' Hussein Says Money Was for Intelligence," *New York Times,* Feb. 28, 1977, pp. 1, 7; E. Behr, "CIA Reportedly Gave Israelis Millions While It Was Paying Jordan's Hussein," *Wall Street Journal,* Feb. 22, 1977, p. 2; D. Binder, "More Heads of State Reported to Have Received C.I.A. Payments," *New York Times,* Feb. 19, 1977, p. 9; C. Mohr, "U.S. Tries to Minimize the Impact of Report on C.I.A. Aid to Hussein," *New York Times,* Feb. 19, 1977, pp. 1, 9; A. Marro, "C.I.A. Money Flowed, but U.S. Aides Insist It Was for Intelligence," *New York Times,* March 1, 1977, p. 8; *New York Times* editorial, "To Bribe or Not to Bribe," Feb. 23, 1977, p. A-28; and *New York Times,* "O'Neill Moves to Curb Access to Secret Data," Feb. 24, 1977, p. 29.

2. A. Marro, "C.I.A. Money Flowed, but U.S. Aides Insist It Was for Intelligence," *New York Times,* March 1, 1977, p. 8.

3. Yet interelite exchanges and collaborations as well as conflicts are also present. James Akins, former United States ambassador to

Saudi Arabia, testified that the CIA and State Department had not infrequently acted directly or indirectly through multinational corporate cash channels in order to help secure United States government interests. See chapter 2. The Church committee ignored these allegations of government dealing and focused primarily on what may be euphemistically called transnational commercial or corporate bribery and questionable practice. See J. Landauer, "CIA May Have Encouraged Firms to Pay Foreign Political Figures, Probe Shows," *Wall Street Journal,* March 1, 1977, p. 2. See also P. Drucker, "The Rise of Production Sharing," *Wall Street Journal,* March 15, 1977, p. 22; and, in general, see *Economist,* "Controlling the Multinationals," Jan. 24, 1976, pp. 68-69.

4. See, for example, 15 U.S.C. §62.

5. See H. Weinstein, "Stockholders versus Payoffs: Lawsuits Grow in Number and Scope, Aiming for Reforms As Well As Money," *New York Times,* March 14, 1976, sec. III, pp. 1, 7. See also *Wall Street Journal,* "Gulf Oil Holders File Objections to Accord on Slush-Fund Suits," Nov. 12, 1976, p. 24; P. Roche, "Taking Management to Task: Activist Shareholders Are Pushing Drive for More Disclosures about Firms' Ethics," *Wall Street Journal,* April 5, 1976, p. 26; and R. Lindsey, "Investors' Lawyer-Sleuth," *New York Times,* March 21, 1976, sec. 3, p. 9.

6. *Wall Street Journal,* "Labor Letter: A Special News Report on People and Their Jobs in Offices, Fields and Factories," April 6, 1976, p. 1.

7. For specific cases regarding this point, see V. Pappas, "Payoff Aftermath: Crackdown on Bribery Hasn't Damaged Sales, Big Companies Report; Some Tell of Slight Impact, and Some Believe Losses May Show Up in Future," *Wall Street Journal,* Feb. 28, 1977, pp. 1, 18; B. Calame, "After the Fall: At Gulf Oil Nowadays, a 'Questionable' Deal Is One to Be Shunned, or So Officials Say As They Try to Repair Concern's Scandal-Damaged Image," *Wall Street Journal,* Jan. 25, 1977, pp. 1, 37; J. Williams, "Gulf & Western Holders Assail Activities of Company Abroad in Raucous Meeting," *Wall Street Journal,* Dec. 15, 1976, p. 14; and *Wall Street Journal,* "Lockheed Air Says 'Financial Viability' Has Improved Sharply," Feb. 7, 1977, p. 28. A study, commissioned by

the SEC to examine the impact of disclosures on the stock market, not available at this writing, was to be presented in December 1976. See F. Andrews, "Management, Wall St. Winks at Bribery Cases," *New York Times,* Nov. 12, 1976, p. D-5.

8. R. Mills, "Doing Business Abroad," *Yale Law Report* (Fall 1976), p. 4.

9. R. Lindsey, "Northrop Shareholders Focus on Rising Profit Not on Bribes," *New York Times,* May 12, 1976, pp. 1, 69. See also R. Cooper, "High Flyer: Clearing Payoff Storm, Northrop Chief Keeps Firm Hand on Controls; Tom Jones Can Still Boast Firm Delivers on Time, Within Contract Costs; 'We Considered Firing Him,' " *Wall Street Journal,* Dec. 15, 1976, pp. 1, 31.

10. R. Witkin, "Canada Will Buy Lockheed Planes: $697 Million Deal Is Signed after Months of Repeatedly Jeopardized Talks; Chairman Is Jubilant; Haak Views Transaction As a Vote of Confidence from Major Country," *New York Times,* July 22, 1976, pp. 43, 52.

11. For summaries and brief appraisals of these four modalities, see R. Cohen, "Corporate Bribery: Something Is Wrong, but What Can Be Done about It?" *National Journal,* May 15, 1976, pp. 658–63; and R. Barovick, "The SEC Unleashes a Foreign Payoffs Storm," *Business and Society Review* 19 (Fall 1976), pp. 48–53.

12. But according to the *Wall Street Journal,* a general prohibition against transnational commercial bribery is not likely. Too many foreign governments are explicitly uninterested in such a prohibition. See J. Landauer, "Proposed Treaty against Business Bribes Gets Poor Reception Overseas, U.S. Finds," *Wall Street Journal,* March 28, 1977, p. 11.

13. Statement of Mark B. Feldman, Department of State, Nov. 15, 1976, reprinted in *Department of State Bulletin,* Dec. 6, 1976.

14. UNGA Res. 3514, Dec. 1975.

15. Department of State, "International Investment and Multinational Enterprises," OECD Declaration 7 (1976), p. 14.

16. See R. Cohen, "Corporate Bribery: Something's Wrong, but What Can Be Done about It?" *National Journal,* May 15, 1976, pp. 662–63. The author speculates on the tradeoffs that could accompany a GATT-sponsored code of commercial practices: If the U.S. government pursues its plan to get a GATT proposal on bribery, it

will have to yield on other vitally important trade matters." Ibid., p. 663.

17. *United Nations Monthly Chronicle* 14:2 (Feb. 1977), p. 24; *United Nations Monthly Chronicle* 13:11 (Dec. 1976), p. 54; and *United Nations Monthly Chronicle,* 13:8 (Aug.–Sept. 1976), pp. 34, 38. For details of some of the working group's activity, see the following United Nations Reports; United Nations Economic and Social Council, Report of the Secretariat, "Transnational Corporations: Views and Proposals of States on a Code of Conduct," E/C.10/19, Dec. 30, 1976; United Nations Economic and Social Council, Report of the Secretariat, "Transnational Corporations: Views and Proposals of States on a Code of Conduct," E/C.10/19/Add., March 22, 1977; and United Nations Economic and Social Council, Report of the Secretariat, "Transnational Corporations: Views and Proposals of Non-Governmental Interests on a Code of Conduct," E/C.10/20, Dec. 30, 1976. For general background, see *New York Times,* "Anti-Bribe Unit Planned by U.N.; Economic and Social Council Seeks Accord to Prevent Multinational Corruption," Aug. 5, 1976, pp. 43, 48.

18. See note 2 to chapter 3. See also United Nations Economic and Social Council, Report of the Secretariat, "Transnational Corporations: Material Relevant to the Formulation of a Code of Conduct," E/C.10/18, Dec. 10, 1976.

19. See W. Kennedy, Statement before the Subcommittee on Consumer Protection and Finance Committee on Interstate and Foreign Commerce, House of Representatives, Sept. 22, 1976, p. 4.

20. Letter from the Federal Trade Commission, May 15, 1918, 66th Cong., 2d sess., Senate, Doc. 258, p. 8.

21. 15 United States Code §1, 2; §§12–27; §45. Not all payments that the current campaign has stigmatized as bribes are unlawful under these acts. It has been held that payments by a seller to a state official to influence state purchases of its products were not the type of misconduct prohibited by §§1 and 2 of the Sherman Act. See *Sterling Nelson & Sons* v. *Ranger Inc.* (D.C. Idaho), 235 F. Supp. 393 (1964). See also *Eastern Railroad Presidents Conference* v. *Noerr Motor Freight Inc.,* 365 U.S. 127. But given the density of legislation, bribes that manage to evade one strand are likely to run afoul of another. The fraud and antiracketeering laws

seem particularly sweeping. See 18 United States Code §1952.

22. 18 United States Code §1952.

23. See, generally, Commercial Clearing House, *Trade Regulation Reporter,* vol. 1, paras. 4010–75, 1640, and especially 7903 (on bribery and payola).

24. See, generally, E.W. Kintner, *An Antitrust Primer,* 2d ed. (1973), pp. 159 ff.

25. Internal Revenue Code, §162(c)(1). See in addition D. Alexander, commissioner of internal revenue, Statement before the International Economic Policy Subcommittee on the House Committee on International Relations, July 17, 1975. For IRS activity regarding transnational corporate practices, see *New York Times,* "I.R.S. to Require Companies to Answer 11 Bribe Questions; Refusal to Reply to Bring Summons," April 8, 1976, pp. 55, 60; *Wall Street Journal,* "IRS Discloses Some of Questions Asked in Payoff Inquiry; Officials at 1,200 Large Firms Queried on Participation, Existence of Hidden Fund," April 8, 1976, p. 6; and T. Schellhardt, "IRS Account: Many Big Corporations Face Tax-Fraud Cases in Slush Fund Audits; Agency Sees Signs of Funds for Funneling Kickbacks at About 300 Companies; Some Suspect Being Targets," *Wall Street Journal,* Dec. 10, 1976, pp. 1, 21.

26. See *Blackmer* v. *U.S.,* 284 U.S. 421 (1932). For reviews of this phenomenon in regard to transnational commerce, see R. Hershey, "S.E.C. to Seek Rise in Subpoena Power on Inquiries Abroad; Could Act through Courts, Agency Is Often Blocked in Hunting Information in Investigations That Lead Overseas," *New York Times,* Feb. 28, 1977, p. 39; and *Wall Street Journal,* "Court Expands SEC Powers to Challenge Certain Transnational Stock Schemes," Jan. 21, 1977, p. 4. Regarding Teapot Dome, see in general M.E. Ravage, *The Story of Teapot Dome* (1924).

27. See House Resolution 15149 and Senate Bill 3741.

28. Pub. L. No. 94-329, 90 Stat. 729 (1976) §604 (to be codified in 22 United States Code §2779(a,b,c,); and ibid., §607 (to be codified in 22 United States Code §2394a).

29. Tax Reform Act of 1976, Pub. L. No. 94-455, 90 Stat. 1520, §1065 (to be codified in Internal Revenue Code §999). See in addition *New York Times,* "I.R.S. to Require Companies to

Answer 11 Bribe Questions; Refusal to Reply to Bring Summons," April 8, 1976, p. 55.

30. See "Foreign Bribes and the Securities Acts' Disclosure Requirements," *Michigan Law Review* 74:6 (May 1976), pp. 1222–42. For a discussion of possible unintended consequences of disclosure, see W. Bennis, "Have We Gone Overboard on 'The Right to Know'?" *Saturday Review,* March 6, 1976, pp. 18–21.

31. See Senate Bill 3664. For brief discussion of the bill, see R. Hershey, "Blumenthal Sees No Use in Stock Bill to Identify Owners, Deals Severe Blow to Senate Plan, Asks Changes in Proposal to Make Foreign Bribery a Crime," *New York Times,* March 17, 1977, p. D-1; *Wall Street Journal,* "Blumenthal Backs Corporate Bribe Ban, Discloses Probe of 8 Multinational Firms," March 17, 1977, p. 2; *Wall Street Journal,* "Senate Unit Clears Bill Outlawing Bribery Abroad and Setting Fines Up to $500,000," April 7, 1977, p. 3; and *Wall Street Journal,* "Senate Approves Bill Making Foreign Bribes by U.S. Firms a Crime," May 6, 1977, p. 12.

32. Statement of Gerald Parsky to House subcommittee, Sept. 21, 1976, p. 13.

33. William Kennedy, in his statement to the House subcommittee, was quite blunt on this point. "The problem in a word was not law, but law enforcement." See Kennedy Statement, Sept. 22, 1976, p. 3. He continued, "it appears that almost all foreign countries have laws against bribery. There were, to put it plainly, failures not only of U.S. law enforcement, but failures of foreign law enforcement as well." Ibid., p. 4.

34. See R. Barovick, "The SEC Unleashes a Foreign Payoffs Storm," *Business and Society Review* 19 (Fall 1976), p. 49 for Securities and Exchange Commission behavior on this issue regarding its investigation of transnational commercial bribery.

35. Foreign Corrupt Practices Act of 1977, Public Law 95-213 [hereinafter FCPA].

36. FCPA §102(3)(A).

37. FCPA, Senate Report (Banking, Housing and Urban Affairs) No. 95-114, May 2, 1977, Senate Report No. 114, 6306, 6309 [hereinafter Senate Report].

38. FCPA §103 amending §30A of the Securities Exchange Act of 1934: §30A(a).

39. FCPA §30A(b).

40. Senate Report, 6316.

41. Ibid.

42. FCPA §103.

43. Senate Report, 6315.

44. Ibid., 6315–16.

45. See in general E.D. Herlihy & T.A. Levine, "Corporate Crisis: The Overseas Payment Problem," *Law and Policy in International Business* 8 (1976), p. 547, for a detailed analysis of the commission's investigative and enforcement actions. See also *Business Week,* "Why the SEC's Enforcer Is in Over His Head," Oct. 11, 1976, pp. 70–76.

46. For reviews of proposed changes regarding the content and filing frequency of Form 8K reports, see R. Stuart, "S.E.C. Is Proposing Disclosure Shifts; Suggestions Would Simplify Procedures and Expand Data Takeovers," *New York Times,* July 15, 1976, p. 49; and *Wall Street Journal,* "SEC Seeks Streamlining of 8K Interim Reports," July 15, 1976, p. 32. For a brief review of disclosure requirements in general, see J. Gillis, "Securities Law and Regulation," *Financial Analysts Journal* (Jan.–Feb. 1976), pp. 8–11, 75–76. For developments regarding disclosure of transnational commercial activity, see *New York Times,* "S.E.C. Proposal Seeks to Inform Holders of Dubious Payments; Disclosure of Any Director or Officers Involved in Payoffs to Be Reported in Proxy Material," Jan. 20, 1977, p. 53; B. Schorr, "SEC's Program for Voluntary Disclosure of Questionable Payments May End Soon," *Wall Street Journal,* March 7, 1977, p. 4; and *Wall Street Journal,* "SEC Proposes Rules to Combat Bribery, Making Lying to Firms' Auditors Illegal," Jan. 20, 1977, p. 3.

47. W. Carley, "Bribery (*cont.*): Despite Early Gains, Anti-Payoff Campaign Is Beginning to Sputter; Companies Demur, Congress Bickers, IRS Backs Off; 'Barn Door Is Fastened,' Forcing Puritanism Abroad?," *Wall Street Journal,* July 9, 1976, p. 1.

48. *Business Week,* "Why the SEC's Enforcer Is in Over His Head,"

Oct. 11, 1976, pp. 70–76 (first quote is from p. 76, second quote is from p. 70). See also *Wall Street Journal,* "SEC Proposes Rules to Combat Bribery, Making Lying to Firm's Auditors Illegal," Jan. 20, 1977, p. 3.

49. For reviews of some of these cases, see M. Weinstein, "Stockholders versus Payoffs: Lawsuits Grow in Number and Scope, Aiming for Reforms As Well As Money," *New York Times,* March 14, 1976, sec. 3, pp. 1, 7; and R. Lindsey, "Investors' Lawyer-Sleuth," *New York Times,* March 21, 1976, sec. 3, p. 9.

50. See P. Roche, "Taking Management to Task, Activist Shareholders Are Pushing Drive for More Disclosure about Firms' Ethics," *Wall Street Journal,* April 5, 1976, p. 26.

51. B. Calame, "Gulf Oil Settlement of Eight Holder Suits on Illegal Payoffs Is Approved by Judge," *Wall Street Journal,* Nov. 19, 1976, p. 10. See also S. Kass, "What Should We Do about Lawyers?" *Business and Society Review* 20 (Winter 1976–77), p. 12. For a brief summary of a similar case, see *Wall Street Journal,* "Occidental Petroleum Suit Filed by Holder Is Dismissed by Judge," March 23, 1977, p. 16.

52. Kintner, *An Antitrust Primer.*

53. In 1975, Illinois and New York enacted such laws; they were joined in 1976 by Maryland, Massachusetts, Ohio, and California. See Title VII of the Civil Rights Act of 1964, 42 United States Code §20000-2(a)(1970); Discrimination by Business Establishments, ch. 366, §§1–2, 1976 Cal. Legis. Serv. 1010 (West) (to be codified in Cal. Civ. Code §§51.5–52, relating to Civil Rights [West]); Restraint of Trade—Discrimination, ch. 1247, §§1–2, 1976 Cal. Legis. Serv. 5426 [West] (to be codified in Cal. Bus. & Prof. Code §§16721–16721.5 [West]); The Illinois Blacklist Trade Law, Ill. Ann. Stat. ch. 29, §§91–96 (Smith-Hurd 1975); Foreign Discriminatory Boycotts, 1976 Md. Laws, ch. 613; Prohibition of Certain Discrimination by Business, ch. 297, §§1–2, 1976 Mass. Adv. Legis. Serv. 371 (West) (to be codified in Mass. Gen. Laws Ann. ch. 151E, §§1–6 [West]); N.Y. Exec. Law §§296.13, 298-a (McKinney 1975); Ohio Rev. Code Ann. §§1129.ii, 1153.05, 1331.01–03, 1331.08, 1331.10.11 (p. 1976). See also Antitrust & Trade Reg. Rep. (BNA) A-21 (June 8, 1976); 4 Trade Reg. Rep. (CCH) para. 32.303 (1976).

54. *Jones* v. *Rath,* 97 S. Ct. 1305 (1977).

55. See M. Weidenbaum, "Business Policy and the Public Welfare: The Excesses of Government Regulations," *Vital Speeches,* March 1, 1977, pp. 317–20; W. Mette & C. Werner, "Stopping Illegal Corporate Payments," *Business Week,* July 26, 1976, p. 19; *Business Week,* "How Companies React to the Ethics Crisis," Feb. 9, 1976, pp. 78–79; and F. Andrews, "Corporate Ethics: Talks with a Trace of 'Robber Baron,'" *New York Times,* April 18, 1977, pp. 49, 52.

56. C. Farnsworth, "U.S. Concerns Ask World Bribe Pact; Multinationals Are Pressing for U.N. Treaty to Provide Compulsory Disclosure; Competition Is Feared; American Companies Seek Support of International Chamber of Commerce," *New York Times,* July 6, 1976, pp. 1, 42.

57. C. Elias, *Fleecing The Lambs* (1971), p. 206.

58. G. Adams & S. Rosenthal, *The Invisible Hand: Questionable Corporate Payments Overseas,* Council on Economic Priorities, (1976), pp. 10–11. Another problem with a strategy of internal housecleaning is that delicts under the new code must be exposed by lower level operators who are themselves subject to penalties for blowing the whistle. See, generally, R. O'Day, "Intimidation Rituals: Reactions to Reform," *Journal of Applied Behavioral Science* 10 (1974), p. 373; and see note 16 to the prologue.

59. *Business Week,* "The Pressure to Compromise Personal Ethics," Jan. 31, 1977, p. 107. See also *Business Week,* "Stiffer Rules for Business Ethics," March 30, 1974, pp. 87–90, for a list of ethical dilemmas confronting businessmen. The discussion includes general guidelines for dealing with these dilemmas. For a general and longitudinal study of business ethics in the United States, see S. Brenner & E. Molander, "Is the Ethics of Business Changing?" *Harvard Business Review* (Jan.–Feb. 1977), pp. 57–71.

60. R. Merton, "Social Structure and Anomie," *American Sociological Review* 3 (1938), p. 672.

61. But see T. Mechling, "The Mythical Ethics of Law, PR, and Accounting," *Business and Society Review* 20 (Winter 1976–77), pp. 6–10; and "Disbarment in the Federal Courts," *Yale Law Journal* 85:7 (June 1976), pp. 975–89.

62. See Senate Report, "The Accounting Establishment," a staff study prepared by the Subcommittee on Reports, Accounting and Management of the Committee on Government Operations, United States Senate, 94th Cong., 2nd sess., Dec. 1976 (known in abbreviation as the Metcalf report). For brief reviews and rebuttals to the report, see *Business Week,* "Should CPAs Be Management Consultants?" April 18, 1977, pp. 70, 73; *Business Week,* "The CPAs Get Another Lashing," Jan. 31, 1977, p. 76; and *Wall Street Journal,* "Accounting Field Is Too Closely Linked with Corporations, Senate Study Finds," Jan. 17, 1977, p. 10. For references to the accounting profession's call for self-reform, see J. Biegler, "Who Shall Set Accounting Standards? The Financial Accounting Standards Board," *Vital Speeches,* March 15, 1977, pp. 347–49; C. Stabler, "Accounting Rule Seeks Breakdown of Firms' Filings; Board Requires Concerns Disclose Audited Figures on All Major Interests," *Wall Street Journal,* Dec. 15, 1976, p. 7; *Wall Street Journal,* "Changes in Auditing to Cut Vulnerability from Clients' Wrongdoing to Be Urged," March 10, 1977, p. 14; *Business International,* International Firms Face New Accounting Rules on Consolidations," July 2, 1976, p. 213; *Wall Street Journal,* "World-Wide Measures for Accounting Issued by International Board," Oct. 7, 1976, p. 3; and *Wall Street Journal,* "Accountants Issue Standards for Dealing with Illegal Actions by Client Companies," Jan. 31, 1977, p. 8.

63. Testimony of American Institute of Certified Public Accountants on H.R. 15481, United States House of Representatives, Sept. 22, 1976.

64. On this issue, in regard to business and accounting, see *Business Week,* "A Cost Criterion for the Regulators," March 14, 1977, pp. 36, 38; M. Weidenbaum, "Business Policy and the Public Welfare: The Excesses of Government Regulation," *Vital Speeches,* March 1, 1977, pp. 317–20; W. Kanaga, "Business and Accounting: Facing the New Vigilantes," *Vital Speeches,* Feb. 15, 1977, pp. 274–78; and *Business Week,* "The Law Closes in on Managers; Personal As Well As Corporate Actions Land Them in Court," May 10, 1976, pp. 110–16.

65. T. Arnold, *The Symbols of Government* (1935), p. 160.

Bibliography

THIS bibliography is divided into several parts: an annotated list of three notable books recently published; a review of eight key works dealing with or relevant to bribery; a special notice of several general bibliographies on white-collar crime; and a list of selected works on bribery, especially the transnational variety.

Recent Publications

Jacoby, Neil H.; Nehemkis, Peter; and Eells, Richard. *Bribery and Extortion in World Business: A Study of Corporate Political Payments Abroad.* New York: Macmillan, 1977. The authors view foreign payments as a business pathology and suggest ways of stopping the practice.

Johnson, John J.; and Douglas, Jack D., eds. *Crime at the Top: Deviance in Business and the Professions.* Philadelphia: J.P. Lippincott, 1978. A collection of essays.

Kugel, Yerachmiel; and Gruenberg, Gladys W. *International Payoffs: Dilemma for Business.* Lexington, Mass.: Lexington Books, 1977. As the title implies, the authors are sensitive to the dilemmas that the international businessman may face and tolerant of the radically different positions that may be taken on the issue. They suggest models for deciding on payments and considerations pertinent to decision and implementation. The book includes a selected bibliography, with a strong emphasis on the literature of business ethics.

Key Works

Carlin, Jerome. *Lawyers' Ethics: A Survey of the New York City Bar.* New York: Russell Sage Foundation, 1966.

Gardiner, John; and Olson, David, eds. *Theft of the City: Readings on Corruption in Urban America.* Bloomington: Indiana University Press, 1974.

Geis, Gilbert; and Meier, Robert F., eds. *White-Collar Crime: Offenses in Business, Politics, and the Professions.* Rev. ed. New York: Free Press, 1977. A revised edition of *White-Collar Criminal: The Offender in Business and the Professions,* a collection of essays edited by Geis and published by Atherton Press in 1968. The essays deal with a wide range of crime but include comparatively little on bribery of the domestic and foreign sort.

Heidenheimer, Arnold J., ed. *Political Corruption: Readings in Comparative Analysis.* New York: Holt, Rinehart & Winston, 1970. An extremely useful collection of essays, distinctive for its organization, the many foreign contributions, and the variety of viewpoints expressed there. A good many of the essays deal with bribery, often in transnational or transcultural contexts.

Scott, James C. *Comparative Political Corruption.* Englewood Cliffs, N.J.: Prentice-Hall, 1972.

Sutherland, Edwin H. *White Collar Crime.* New York: Dryden Press, 1949.

Tolchin, Martin; and Tolchin, Susan. *To the Victor: Political Patronage from the Clubhouse to the White House.* New York: Random House, 1971.

Verbit, Gilbert P. *International Monetary Reform and the Developing Countries: The Rule of Law Problem.* New York: Columbia University Press, 1975.

Special Bibliographies on White-Collar Crime

PF/PC Newsletter. Study Group on Political Finance and Political Corruption of the IPSA (beginning 1977) contains an extensive bibliography of current material in each issue.

Shapiro, Susan. "A Background Paper on White Collar Crime: Considerations of Conceptualization and Future Research." Yale University, February 1976. Prepared for the Law Enforcement Assistance Administration, U.S. Department of Justice, but not yet published; includes an extensive and up-to-date bibliography.

Tompkins, Dorothy C. "White Collar Crime: A Bibliography." University of California, Institute of Government Studies, 1967.

Selected Works on Bribery

Adams, Gordon; and Rosenthal, Sherri Zann. *The Invisible Hand: Questionable Corporate Payments Overseas.* New York: Council on Economic Priorities, 1976.

Alfred, Stephen J. "Corporate Slush Funds: The Deductibility of 'Sensitive' Payments." *Journal of Corporate Taxation* 4 (1977), pp. 130–46.

American Enterprise Institute for Public Policy Research. *Legislative Analyses, Criminalization of Payments to Influence Foreign Governments.* Washington: The Institute, 1977.

Association of the Bar of the City of New York. *Report on Questionable Foreign Payments by Corporations: The Problem and Approaches to a Solution.* New York: Ad Hoc Committee on Foreign Payments, March 14, 1976.

Ball, Harry V.; and Friedman, Lawrence M. "The Use of Criminal Sanctions in the Enforcement of Economic Legislation: A Sociological View." *Stanford Law Review* 17 (Jan. 1965), pp. 197–223.

Banfield, Edward C. "Corruption as a Feature of Governmental Organization." *Journal of Law and Economics* 18 (1975), p. 587.

———. *The Moral Basis of a Backward Society.* New York: Free Press, 1958.

Barovick, Richard L. "The SEC Unleashes a Foreign Payoffs Storm." *Business and Society Review* (Fall 1976), pp. 48–53.

Basche, James R. *Unusual Foreign Payments: A Survey of the Policies and Practices of U.S. Companies.* New York: Conference Board, 1976.

Ben-Dor, G. "Corruption, Institutionalization, and Political Development." *Comparative Political Studies,* April 1974, pp. 63–83.

Bennis, Warren. "Have We Gone Overboard on 'The Right to Know'?" *Saturday Review,* March 6, 1976, pp. 18-21.

Bensman, Joseph; and Gerver, Israel. "Crime and Punishment in the Factory: The Function of Deviancy in Maintaining the Social System." *American Sociological Review* 28 (1963), pp. 588-98.

Berg, L.L.; Hahn, H.; and Schmidhauser, J.R. *Corruption in the American Political System.* Morristown, N.J.: General Learning Press, 1976.

Beuston, George J. "The Effectiveness and Effects of the SEC's Accounting Disclosure Requirements." In *Economic Policy and the Regulation of Corporate Securities,* edited by H. Manne. Washington: American Enterprise Institute for Public Policy Research, 1969.

Blumberg, Phillip I. "Corporate Responsibility and the Employee's Duty of Loyalty and Obedience: A Preliminary Inquiry." *Oklahoma Law Review* 24 (1971), pp. 279-318.

Brenner, Steven N.; and Molander, Earl A. "Bribes, Kickbacks, and Political Contributions in Foreign Countries: The Nature and Scope of the Securities and Exchange Commission's Power to Regulate and Control American Corporate Behavior." *Wisconsin Law Review* (1976), pp. 1231-63.

———. "Is the Ethics of Business Changing?" *Harvard Business Review,* Jan.-Feb. 1977, pp. 57-71.

Brooks, John. "Annals of Business: Funds Gray and Black." *New Yorker,* Aug. 9, 1976, pp. 28-44.

Brooks, Robert C. *Corruption in American Politics and Life.* New York: Dodd, Mead, 1910.

Bureau of National Affairs. "White-Collar Justice: A BNA Special Report on White-Collar Crime." *United States Law Week* 44 (April 13, 1976), pt. 2.

Business International Corporation. *Questionable Corporate Payments Abroad: Patterns, Policies, Solutions: Executive Summary.* New York: Business International Corporation, 1976.

Callow, Alexander, ed. *The City Boss in America: An Interpretive Reader.* New York: Oxford University Press, 1976.

Chambliss, William J. "Vice, Corruption, Bureaucracy, and Power." *Wisconsin Law Review* 4 (1971), pp. 1150-73.

Chernick, Charles M. "Disclosure of Corporate Payments Abroad and the Concept of Materiality." *Hofstra Law Review* 4 (Spring 1976), pp. 729-58.

Chu, Morgan; and Magraw, Daniel. "The Deductibility of Questionable Foreign Payments." *Yale Law Journal* 87 (1978), pp. 1091-124.

Clarke, Thurston; and Tigue, John J., Jr. *Dirty Money, Swiss Banks, The Mafia, Money Laundering, and White Collar Crime.* New York: Simon & Schuster, 1975.

Coffee, John C. "Beyond the Shut-Eyed Sentry: Toward a Theoretical View of Corporate Misconduct and an Effective Legal Response." *Virginia Law Review* 63 (1977), pp. 1099-278.

Cressey, Donald R. *Other People's Money: A Study in the Social Psychology of Embezzlement.* New York: Free Press, 1953.

Cutler, Lloyd N. "Watergate International Style." *Foreign Policy* 24 (Fall 1976), pp. 160-71.

"Deductibility of Overseas Commercial Bribes." *Columbia Journal of Law and Social Problems* 13 (1977), pp. 235-55.

Denys, L.; et al. "Bribes as Deductible Business Expenses." *European Taxation* 16 (Nov. 1976), pp. 370-81.

"Disclosure of Payments to Foreign Government Officials under the Securities Acts." *Harvard Law Review* 89 (1976), pp. 1848-70.

Dwivedi, R. C. "Bureaucratic Corruption in Developing Countries." *Asian Survey* 7 (1965), p. 245.

Economist, Intelligence Unit. "Bribery, Corruption, or Necessary Fees and Charges?" *Multinational Business,* no. 3 (1975), pp. 1-17.

———. "Bribes and Payoffs: The U.S. Government Takes Control." *Multinational Business,* no. 1 (1976), pp. 40-42.

———. "Bribes: More on the Unacceptable Face." *Multinational Business,* no. 2 (1975), pp. 37-39.

———. "The Cautionary Tale of Gulf Oil." *Multinational Business,* no. 1 (1976), pp. 43-44.

———. "Controlling the Multinationals: Is it Necessary?" *Multinational Business,* no. 1 (1972), pp. 23-35.

———. "Financial Disclosure in Europe: Differences in Accountancy Plague Harmonisation Efforts." *Multinational Business,* no. 2 (1972), pp. 35-43.

———. "The Go-Betweens, Government Relations, otherwise Known as Lobbying." *Multinational Business,* no. 3 (1972), pp. 15–29.

———. "Multinational Companies under International Scrutiny, UN Study Group Presages New Institutions to Monitor Foreign Investment." *Multinational Business,* no. 4 (1973), pp. 12–19.

———. "Parent Companies' Control of Subsidiaries, Evidence from the UK." *Multinational Business,* no. 1 (1974), pp 11–22.

———. "What Is the Case against Multinationals? Recent Criticism Examined." *Multinational Business,* no. 1 (1975), pp. 1–12.

Elias, Christopher. *Fleecing the Lambs.* Chicago: Henry Regnery, 1971.

Farberman, Harvey A. "A Criminogenic Market Structure: The Automobile Industry." *Sociological Quarterly* 16 (Autumn 1975), pp. 438–57.

"Federal Income Taxation: Public Policy and the Deductibility of Kickbacks Under § 162(c)(2)." *Ohio State Law Journal* 35 (1974), pp. 686–714.

Fish, Carl R. *The Civil Service and the Patronage.* New York: Longmans, Green, 1905.

Flannery, Anne C. "Multinational 'Payoffs' Abroad: International Repercussions and Domestic Liabilities." *Brooklyn Journal of International Law* 2 (1976), pp. 108–38.

"Foreign Bribes and the Securities Acts' Disclosure Requirements." *Michigan Law Review* 74 (May 1976), pp. 1222–42.

Fuller, John G. *The Gentlemen Conspirators: The Story of Price-Fixers in the Electrical Industry.* New York: Grove Press, 1962.

Gabriel, Peter P. "A Case for Honesty in World Business." *Fortune,* Dec. 1977, p. 49.

Gardiner, John. *Traffic and the Police: Variations in Law Enforcement Policy.* Cambridge, Mass.: Harvard University Press, 1969.

Gibney, Frank. *The Operators.* New York: Harper & Row, 1960.

Gillis, John G. "Securities Law and Regulation." *Financial Analyst Journal,* January–February 1976, pp. 8–11, 75–76.

Goodman, Margaret. "Does Political Corruption Really Help Economic Development?: Yucatan, Mexico." *Polity* 7 (Winter 1974), pp. 143–62.

Goodman, Walter. *All Honorable Men: Corruption and Compromise in*

American Life. Boston: Little, Brown, 1963.

Greene, James R. "Ethics Not Customs, Corporate Misconduct Abroad." *Vital Speeches,* Oct. 15, 1975, pp. 25–27.

Grienenberger, Warren F. "Emerging Disclosure Requirements: Environmentally and Socially Significant Matters." *Business Lawyer* 31 (1976), p. 1423.

Griffith, Thomas. "Business Morality Can Pay." *Los Angeles Times,* Aug. 24, 1975, pt. 8, pp. 1, 4.

Guzzardi, Walter, Jr. "An Unscandalized View of those 'Bribes' Abroad." *Fortune,* July 1976, pp. 118–21, 178, 180, 182.

Gwertzman, Milton S. "Is Bribery Defensible?" *New York Times,* Oct. 5, 1975, *New York Times Magazine,* pp. 12, 24–27.

Hager, L.M. "Bureaucratic Corruption in India: Legal Control of Maladministration." *Comparative Political Studies,* July 1973, pp. 197–219.

Hazard, John N. "Soviet Socialism and Embezzlement." *Washington Law Review* 26 (Nov. 1951), pp. 301–20.

Henderson, G.D.; and Sommer, A.A., Jr. "Sensitive Corporate Payments: The SEC's Voluntary Disclosure Program." *Institute of Securities Regulation* 8 (1977), pp. 423–51.

Herlihy, Edward D.; and Levine, T.A. "Corporate Crisis: The Overseas Payment Problem." *Law and Policy in International Business* 8 (1976), pp. 547–629.

Hermann, D.H.J. "Criminal Prosecution of United States Multinational Corporations." *Loyola University Law Journal* (Chicago) 8 (Spring 1977), pp. 465–98.

Hershkowitz, Leo. *Tweed's New York: Another Look.* Garden City, N.Y.: Anchor Press, 1977.

Hills, Roderick M. "Doing Business Abroad: The Disclosure Dilemma." In *Yale Law Report* (Fall 1976), edited by Julia E. Merkt, pp. 4–9.

Huntington, S. *Political Order in Changing Societies.* New Haven: Yale University Press, 1968, pp. 59–71.

Iga, M.; and Auerbach, M. "Political Corruption and Social Structure in Japan." *Asian Survey* (1977), pp. 556–64.

Jabbra, J. "Bureaucratic Corruption in the Third World: Causes and Remedy." *Journal of Public Administration* (1976), pp. 673–91.

James, Leslie. "Bribery and Corruption in Commerce." *International and Comparative Law Quarterly* 11 (July 1962), pp. 880–86.

Johnson, O.P.G. "An Economic Analysis of Corrupt Government, with Special Application to Less Developed Countries." *Kyklos* 28 (1975), pp. 47–61.

Kadish, Sanford H. "Some Observations on the Use of Criminal Sanctions in Enforcing Economic Regulations." *University of Chicago Law Review* 30 (1963), pp. 423–49.

Katz, Jack. "Cover-up and Collective Integrity: On the Natural Antagonisms of Authority Internal and External to Organizations." *Social Problems* 25 (1977), pp. 3–17.

Key, Vladimir O. "The Techniques of Political Graft in the United States." Ph.D. dissertation, University of Chicago, 1934.

Kneier, Andrew. *Serving Two Masters: A Common Cause Study of Conflicts of Interest in the Executive Branch.* Washington: Common Cause, 1976.

Kramer, John M. "Political Corruption in the U.S.S.R." *Western Political Quarterly* 30 (1977), pp. 213–24.

Kriesberg, Simeon M. "Decisionmaking Models and the Control of Corporate Crime." *Yale Law Journal* 85 (July 1976), pp. 1091–129.

Kugel, Yerachmiel; and Gruenberg, Gladys. "International Payoffs: Where We Are and How We Got There." *Challenge,* Sept.-Oct. 1976, pp. 13–20.

Lane, Robert E. *The Regulation of Business: Social Conditions of Government Economic Control.* New Haven: Yale University Press, 1954.

Lasswell, Harold D. "Bribery." In *Encyclopaedia of the Social Sciences,* edited by Edwin R.A. Seligman and Alvin Johnson, vol. 2, pp. 690–92. New York: Macmillan, 1930.

———. "Look at Questionable or Illegal Payments by American Corporations to Foreign Government Officials." *Case Western Reserve Journal of International Law* 8 (Spring 1976), pp. 496–529.

Lowenfels, Lewis D. "Questionable Corporate Payments and the Federal Securities Laws." *New York University Law Review* 51 (1976), pp. 1–33.

Mann, B.A. "Watergate to Bananagate: What Lies Beyond?" *Business*

Law 31 (April 1976), pp. 1663–69.

McCloy, John J. "Corporations: The Problem of Political Contributions and Other Payments at Home and Overseas." *Record of the Association of the Bar of the City of New York* 31 (May–June 1976), pp. 306–14.

———. *The Great Gulf Oil Spill: The Inside Report; Gulf Oil's Bribery and Political Chicanery.* New York: Chelsea House Publishers, 1976.

———; Pearson, Nathan W.; and Matthews, Beverly. "The Boy Scouts at Gulf Oil." *Business and Society Review* (Fall 1976), pp. 58–60.

McLaughlin, G.T. "The Criminalization of Questionable Foreign Payments by Corporations: A Comparative Legal Systems Analysis." *Fordham Law Review* 46 (1978), pp. 1071–114.

McManis, Charles R. "Questionable Corporate Payments Abroad: An Antitrust Approach." *Yale Law Journal* 86 (Dec. 1976), pp. 215–57.

Melching, Thomas B. "The Mythical Ethics of Law, PR, and Accounting." *Business and Society Review* (Winter 1976–77), pp. 6–10.

Murphy, M.E. "Payoffs to Foreign Officials: Time for More National Responsibility." *ABA Journal* 62 (April 1976), pp. 480–82.

Murphy, R.A. "Problems with Questionable Corporate Payments at Home and Abroad." *Los Angeles Bar Journal* 53 (Aug. 1977), pp. 99–111.

Myrdal, Gunnar. *Asian Drama: An Inquiry into the Poverty of Nations,* vol. 2, pp. 937–58. New York: Pantheon Books, 1968.

Nehemkis, Peter. "Business Payoffs Abroad: Rhetoric and Reality." *California Management Review* 18 (Winter 1975), pp. 5–20.

Nye, J. "Corruption and Political Development: A Cost-Benefit Analysis." *American Political Science Review* 61 (1967), p. 419.

Ogren, Robert W. "The Ineffectiveness of the Criminal Sanction in Fraud and Corruption Cases: Losing the Battle against White Collar Crime." *American Criminal Law Review* 11 (1973), pp. 959–88.

Palmier, L. "Corruption in India." *New Society,* June 5, 1975, pp. 577–79.

———. "Indonesia's Agenda of Corruption." *New Society,* Sept. 16, 1976, pp. 594–96.

Parker, C. Wolcott II. "Bribery in Foreign Lands: The Difference

Between Expedite and Suborn." *Vital Speeches,* Feb. 15, 1976, pp. 281-84.

Pashigian, B.P. "On the Control of Crime and Bribery." *Journal of Legal Studies* 4 (June 1975), pp. 311-26.

Permanent Council, Organization for Economic Cooperation and Development. "Declaration on International Investment and Multinational Enterprises." OECD Press Release, June 21, 1976; reprinted in *Department of State Bulletin* 75 (1976), pp. 83-87.

Phelps, Thomas. "Can We Afford to Be Honest? Christ Was the Greatest Economist." *Vital Speeches,* Oct. 15, 1976, pp. 2-4.

"Prohibiting Foreign Bribes: Criminal Sanctions for Corporate Payments Abroad." *Cornell International Law Journal* 10 (1977), p. 231.

Rajkumar, R. "Political Corruption: A Review of the Literature." *West African Journal of Sociology and Political Science* (1976), pp. 177-85.

Redcliffe-Maud, J.P., chairman, Prime Minister's Committee on Local Government Rules of Conduct. *Conduct in Local Government.* Vol. 1, *Report of the Committee* (Cmnd 5636); vol. 2, *Written Evidence.* London: H.M.S.O., 1974.

Reed, Leon S. *Military Maneuvers: An Analysis of the Interchange of Personnel between Defense Contractors and the Department of Defense.* New York: Council on Economic Priorities, 1975.

Regulation of Questionable Foreign Payments." *Law and Policy in International Business* 8 (1976), pp. 1055-82.

Riemer, Svend H. "Embezzlement: Pathological Basis." *Journal of Criminal Law and Criminology* 32 (Nov.-Dec. 1941), pp. 411-23.

Rill, J.F.; and Frank, R.L. "Antitrust Consequences of United States Corporate Payments to Foreign Officials: Applicability of §2(c) of the Robinson Patman Act and §§1 and 2 of the Sherman Act." *Vanderbilt Law Review* 30 (March, 1977), pp. 131-65.

Rogow, Arnold A.; and Lasswell, Harold D. *Power, Corruption and Rectitude.* Englewood Cliffs, N.J.: Prentice-Hall, 1963.

Rose-Ackerman, Susan. "The Economics of Corruption." *Journal of Public Economics* 4 (1975), pp. 187-203.

———. *The Economics of Corruption: An Essay in Political Economy.* New York: Academic Press, 1978.

Rundquist, B.S.; Strom, G.S.; and Peters, J.G. "Corrupt Politicians and Their Electoral Support: Some Experimental Observations." *American Political Science Review* 71 (1977), p. 954.

Salmon, C., chairman, Royal Commission on Standards of Conduct in Public Life. *Report 1974–1976* (Cmnd 6524). London: H.M.S.O., 1976.

Santhanam Committee, Government of India, Ministry of Home Affairs. *Report of the Committee on Prevention of Corruption.* New Delhi, 1964.

Scanlon, James C. "Materiality as it Relates to Questionable and Illegal Foreign Payments to Officials." *Lincoln Law Review* 10 (1977), pp. 85–105.

Schmutz, A.W. "Payments to Foreign Consultants: Procedures and Remedies." *Institute on Securities Regulation* 7 (1976), pp. 49–69.

Schwartz, Joseph J. "Business Expenses Contrary to Public Policy: An Evaluation of the *Lilly* Case." *Tax Law Review* 8 (1953), pp. 241–49.

"Securities Regulation: Bribes to Foreign Officials by Multinational Corporations: Disclosure under the Federal Securities Laws." *Temple Law Quarterly* 49 (Winter 1976), pp. 428–43.

Severaid, R.H. "Regulation of Questionable Foreign Payments." *Law and Policy in International Business* 8 (1976), pp. 1055–82.

Shackleton, J.R. "Corruption: An Essay in Economic Analysis." *Political Quarterly* (1978), pp. 25–37.

Shamma, Samir; and Morrison, William D. "The Use of Local Representatives in Saudi Arabia." *International Lawyer* 11 (1977), p. 435.

Shapiro, Irving. "The Future Role of Business in Society, Personal Integrity and Accountability of the Individual." *Vital Speeches,* Oct. 15, 1976, pp. 16–19.

Shaplen, Robert. "Annals of Crime: The Lockheed Incident–1." *New Yorker,* Jan. 23, 1978, pp. 48–74.

———. "Annals of Crime: The Lockheed Incident–2." *New Yorker,* Jan. 30, 1978, pp. 78–91.

Sinkeldam, Michael S. "Payments to Foreign Officials by Multinational Corporations: Bribery or Business Expense and the Effects of United States Policy." *California Western International Law Journal* 6 (1976), pp. 360, 370–71.

Solomon, Lewis D.; and Linville, Leslie G. "Transnational Conduct of American Multinational Corporations: Questionable Payments Abroad." *Boston College Industrial and Commercial Law Review* 17 (March 1976), pp. 303-45.

Sommer, A.A. "The Disclosure of Management Fraud." *Business Lawyer* 31 (1976), p. 1283.

Sorensen, Theodore C. "Improper Payments Abroad: Perspectives and Proposals." *Foreign Affairs* 54 (July 1976), pp. 719-33.

Stevenson, Russell B. "The SEC and Foreign Bribery." *Business Law* 32 (Nov. 1976), pp. 53-73.

———. "The SEC and the New Disclosure." *Cornell Law Review* 62 (1976), pp. 50-93.

Stone, Christopher D. "Law and the Culture of the Corporation." *Business and Society Review* (Fall 1975), pp. 5-17.

———. *Where the Law Ends: The Social Control of Corporate Behavior.* New York: Harper & Row, 1975.

Taggart, John Y. "Fines, Penalties, Bribes, and Damage Payments and Recoveries." *Tax Law Review* 25 (1970), pp. 611-63.

"Tax Treatment of Bribes." *European Taxation* 16 (November 1976), pp. 382-86.

Tiedemann, K. "Droit fiscal international et la délinquance des entreprises multinationales." *Rivista delle società* 21 (Sept.-Oct. 1976), pp. 801-820.

United Nations, Commission on Transnational Corporations. "Formulation of a Code of Conduct: Elaboration of the Chairman's Annotated Outline on the Basis of Discussion in the Intergovernmental Working Group on a Code of Conduct." *A Note by the Secretariat* (Working Papers 1 and 2), March 24, 1978.

United Nations, Economic and Social Council. "Corrupt Practices, Particularly Illicit Payments in International Commercial Transactions: Concepts and Issues Related to the Formulation of an International Agreement." *Report of the Secretariat* (E/AC.64/3), Jan. 20, 1977.

———. "Transnational Corporations: Material Relevant to the Formulation of a Code of Conduct." *Report of the Secretariat* (E/C.10/18), Dec. 10, 1976.

———. "Transnational Corporations: Measures against Corrupt Practices of Transnational and Other Corporations, Their Intermediaries and Others Involved." *Report of the Secretary-General* (E/5838), June 11, 1976.

———. "Transnational Corporations: Texts Relevant to an Annotated Outline Suggested by the Chairman of the Intergovernmental Working Group on the Code of Conduct." *Report of the Secretariat* (E/C.10/AC.2/3), Jan. 26, 1978.

———. "Transnational Corporations: Views and Proposals of Nongovernmental Interests on a Code of Conduct." *Report of the Secretariat* (E/C.10/20), Dec. 30, 1976.

———. "Transnational Corporations: Views and Proposals of States on a Code of Conduct." *Report of the Secretariat* (E/C.10/19), Dec. 30, 1976.

———. "Transnational Corporations: Views and Proposals of States on a Code of Conduct." *Report of the Secretariat* (E/C.10/19/Add.), March 22, 1977.

United States, Congress. *Foreign Corrupt Practices Act of 1977,* 95th Cong., 1st sess., 1977, Public Law 95-213.

———. House, Committee of Conference, *Foreign Corrupt Practices: Conference Report to Accompany S. 305,* 95th Cong., 1st sess., 1977, H. Conf. Rept. No. 95-831.

———. House, Committee on International Relations, Subcommittee on International Economic Policy, *Hearings on Activities of American Multinational Corporations Abroad,* 94th Cong., 1st sess., 1975.

———. House, Committee on International Relations, Subcommittee on International Economic Policy, *Statement of Donald C. Alexander,* 94th Cong., 1st sess., July 17, 1975.

———. House, Committee on International Relations, Subcommittee on International Economic Policy, *Statement of Philip A. Loomis, Jr.,* 94th Cong., 1st sess., July 17, 1975.

———. House, Committee on Interstate and Foreign Commerce, *Foreign Payments Disclosure: Message from the President of the United States Urging Enactment of Proposed Legislation to Require the Disclosure of Payments to Foreign Officials,* 94th Cong., 2d sess., 1976, H. Doc. No. 94-572.

———. House, Committee on Interstate and Foreign Commerce, *Unlawful Corporate Payments Act of 1977: Report together with Minor-*

ity Views to Accompany H.R. 3815, 95th Cong., 1st sess., 1977, H. Rept. No. 95-640.

———. House, Committee on Interstate and Foreign Commerce, Subcommittee on Consumer Protection and Finance, *Statement of William F. Kennedy,* 94th Cong., 2d sess., Sept. 22, 1976.

———. House, Committee on the Judiciary, *Special Report on Commercial Bribery: Letter from the Chairman of the Federal Trade Commission Transmitting a Special Report Dealing with the Subject of Commercial Bribery,* 65th Cong., 2d sess., 1918, H. Doc. No. 1107.

———. Joint Economic Committee, Subcommittee on Priorities and Economy in Government, *Hearings on Abuses of Corporate Power,* 94th Cong., 2d sess., 1976.

———. Joint Economic Committee, Subcommittee on Priorities and Economy in Government, *Statement of Robert S. Ingersoll,* 94th Cong., 2d sess., March 5, 1976; reprinted in *Department of State Bulletin* 74 (1976), pp. 412-15.

———. Senate, Committee on Banking, Housing and Urban Affairs, *Foreign and Corporate Bribes: Hearings on S. 3133,* 94th Cong., 2d sess., 1976.

———. Senate, Committee on Banking, Housing, and Urban Affairs, *Foreign Corrupt Practices and Domestic and Foreign Investment Improved Disclosure Acts of 1977: Report to Accompany S. 305,* 95th Cong., 1st sess., 1977, S. Rept. No. 95-114.

———. Senate, Committee on Banking, Housing and Urban Affairs, *Prohibiting Bribes to Foreign Officials: Hearings on S. 3133, S. 3379 & S. 3418,* 94th Cong., 2d sess., 1976.

———. Senate, Committee on Foreign Relations, Subcommittee on Multinational Corporations, *Hearings on Multinational Corporations and United States Foreign Policy,* 94th Cong., 1st sess., 1975.

———. Senate, Committee on Foreign Relations, Subcommittee on Multinational Corporations, *Hearings on Political Contributions to Foreign Governments,* 94th Cong., 1st sess., 1975.

———. Senate, Committee on Interstate Commerce, *Commercial Bribery: Letter from the Federal Trade Commission, Transmitting, Pursuant to Law, a Special Report Dealing with the Subject of Commercial Bribery,* 66th Cong., 2d sess., 1920, S. Doc. No. 258.

United States, Department of State. *Statement by Mark B. Feldman before the United Nations Economic and Social Council's Intergovernmental Working Group on Corrupt Practices,* Nov. 15, 1976; reprinted in *Department of State Bulletin* 75 (1976), pp. 696, 698.

United States, Securities and Exchange Commission. *Report on Questionable and Illegal Corporate Payments and Practices,* CCH Federal Securities Law Reports. No. 642, May 19, 1976.

Volk, Klaus. "Strafrecht Gegen Insider?" *Zeitschrift für das Gesamte Handelsrecht und Wirtschaftsrecht* 1 (Feb. 1978), pp 1-18.

Wang, N.T. "Design of an International Code of Conduct for Transnational Corporations." *Journal of International Law and Economics* 10 (Aug.-Dec. 1975), pp. 319-36.

Waterbury, J. "Corruption, Political Stability and Development: Comparative Evidence from Egypt and Morocco." *Government and Opposition* (1976), pp. 426-45.

Whitney, Craig R. "In Soviet, Widespread Practice of Bribery Helps One Get a Car, Get an Apartment and Get Ahead." *New York Times,* May 7, 1978, p. 22.

Index